PRINCE PHILIP
An Informal Biography

PRINCE PHILIP

An Informal Biography

❈

BASIL BOOTHROYD

The McCall Publishing Company

NEW YORK

Library of Congress Catalog Card Number: *73-154246*

ISBN*0-8415-0116-5*

The McCall Publishing Company

230 Park Avenue

New York, N.Y. *10017*

Printed in the United States of America

Design by Tere LoPrete

To My Wife

I'd call her Phil, but don't want any misunderstanding

Contents

⚜

Contents

Author's Note

×C×

This isn't a blow-by-blow commentary. It doesn't begin at the beginning ("Born June 10, 1921, on the sun-drenched island of Corfu") and it doesn't end at the end, which is not yet. There are omissions. Pages xiii to xviii may explain that. Its subject is incompressible between covers only this far apart.

But I've tried to present most of the man, different in many ways from the one we thought we knew. Phil the Greek? The Gabby Dook? Master of Privilege? Prince of Arrogance? Ignorant bum? They've all been said (the last by him), and lots more. I'd like to think that this says other things, yet shows why other people said those.

We've had a running conflict of views—on whether he's something out of the ordinary (my view), or on the whole not (his).

I say on the whole, because his almost pathological honesty doesn't stop short at himself, so he knows what his qualities are, but sees no point in going on about them. He thought I should guard against it, and wrote, after seeing a draft, "So perhaps I do try to fill 'every unforgiving minute,' or whatever the line is, but if you pursue too breathlessly it looks as if I were doing something exceptional. I know a good many people, for instance, who get through a great deal more than I do." Possibly. But the chances are that they do it for cash, power or glory, none of which interests him at all.

My first thanks are owed to him, for the kindness no one had hinted at, and the patience I'd been warned he was so short on; for giving up time, tolerating tape recorders and returning typescripts with detailed corrections of fact and only one actual "Rubbish!" in the margin.

To name other helpers would be a hopeless exercise, and open to unintentional but possibly wounding omissions. The members of his Household, and in some cases of the Queen's, would be well up the list, also the girls in his office who foraged tirelessly for files, and never suggested by an eyelash that they'd be glad to see the back of me. That so many people offered help out of the blue I at first thought flattering as well as generous; then I realized that this was not for the author's sake, but the subject's. All the others, if they read this, will know who I mean.

Back at the palace, they also serve who only dust and clean. I didn't often see Eileen, who emptied my ashtrays for a year, but treasure her remark when the first one she got for me disappeared. "It came from down at the Privy Purse," she said, going off to find something more permanent. "They'll have taken it back. They get very snotty down there." I had intimations of fierce currents deep beneath the surface of those unruffled waters, but none of them ever trapped me in the undertow. I only met nice people, and with beautiful manners.

One morning I accosted the Queen's private secretary, Sir Michael Adeane, walking toward the front of the building. While he sympathetically heard out some problem that was teasing me I got the impression, faint as an echo, that he would like to be moving on. It was another minute or two before he said, "I do hope you'll forgive me, but I've just heard that my house is on fire. I wouldn't mind, but as it's a part of St. James's Palace . . ."

I hope this is a true book. That's been my only idea. If it isn't, it's more likely to be my fault than anyone else's, and Prince Philip's least of all.

BASIL BOOTHROYD

Cuckfield, Sussex

Spectrum[*]

Beyond a civil mention in the early pages, members of the Royal Family don't get an entry in *Who's Who*. If they did, Prince Philip's would look like this:

EDINBURGH, 1st Duke of, *cr.* 1947; His Royal Highness the Prince Philip (Mountbatten), KG 1947; KT 1952; OM 1968; GBE 1953 (Grand Master of the Order); PC 1951; *b.* Corfu, 10 June 1921; only *s.* of HRH Prince Andrew of Greece and Denmark, GCVO, and of HRH Princess (Victoria) Alice Elizabeth Julia Marie, elder *d.* of the 1st Marquess of Milford Haven, PC, GCB, GCVO, KCMG; *m.* 20 November 1947, Her Royal Highness the Princess Elizabeth, now Her Majesty Queen Elizabeth II, of Britain, elder *d.* of His late Majesty King George VI and of Her Majesty Queen Elizabeth the Queen Mother; three *s.* one *d.*

[*] "Image formed by rays of light or other radiant energy in which the parts are arranged in a progressive series according to their refrangibility." *Concise Oxford Dictionary*.

Educ: "The Elms," Paris; Cheam School, Berkshire; Salem, Baden; Gordonstoun School, Morayshire; and Royal Naval College, Dartmouth. Served in Royal Navy, since 1939; Midshipman, 1940; Sub-Lieutenant, 1942; Lieutenant, 1942; Lieutenant-Commander, 1950; Commander, 1952; Admiral of the Fleet since January 1953. Served in World War II, 1939–45, with the Mediterranean Fleet, in Home Waters, and with the British Pacific Fleet in South-East Asia and Pacific; mentioned in dispatches, Battle of Cape Matapan, 3 February 1942; Admiral, Sea Cadet Corps, since 1952; Captain General, Royal Marines, since 1953; Extra Master of the Merchant Navy, since 1954. Naturalized as a British subject on 28 February 1947, adopting the surname of Mountbatten. Granted the title, style and attribute of Royal Highness, 19 November 1947. *Cr.* Baron Greenwich of Greenwich in the County of London, Earl of Merioneth and Duke of Edinburgh (in the Peerage of the United Kingdom) 20 November 1947. Personal ADC to His Majesty King George VI, 1948–52; introduced and took his seat in the House of Lords, 1948; Privy Councillor of Canada since 1957. Croix de Guerre (France) with Palm, 1948; Greek War Cross, 1950. Granted Precedence next to Her Majesty, 1952. Granted the style and titular dignity of a Prince of the United Kingdom of Great Britain and Northern Ireland, 22 February 1957. Member of the Council of the Duchy of Cornwall, since 1952; Ranger of Windsor Great Park, since 1952; Lord High Steward of Plymouth, since 1960. Field Marshal, since 1953. Colonel-in-Chief, Army Cadet Force, since 1952; Colonel of the Welsh Guards, since 1953; Hon. Colonel, Edinburgh and Heriot-Watt Universities Officers' Training Corps, since 1953; Hon. Colonel, Leicestershire and Derbyshire Yeomanry, 1957–69; Colonel-in-Chief, The Queen's Royal Irish Hussars, since 1958; Colonel-in-Chief, The Duke of Edinburgh's Royal Regiment (Berkshire and Wiltshire), since 1959; Colonel-in-Chief, The Queen's Own Highlanders (Seaforth and Camerons), since 1961; Colonel-in-Chief, The Corps of Royal Electrical and Mechanical

Engineers, since 1969. Marshal of the Royal Air Force since 1953; Air Commodore-in-Chief, Air Training Corps, since 1952. Admiral of the Fleet, Royal Australian Navy, since 1954; Field-Marshal, Australian Military Forces, since 1954; Marshal, Royal Australian Air Force, since 1954; Colonel-in-Chief, Royal Corps of Australian Electrical and Mechanical Engineers, since 1959; Colonel-in-Chief, Australian Cadet Corps, since 1963. Admiral, Royal Canadian Sea Cadets, since 1953; Colonel-in-Chief, Royal Canadian Army Cadets, since 1953; Air Commander-in-Chief, Royal Canadian Air Cadets, since 1953; Colonel-in-Chief, Royal Canadian Regiment, since 1953; Colonel-in-Chief, Cameron Highlanders of Ottawa (Militia), since 1967; Colonel-in-Chief, Queen's Own Cameron Highlanders of Canada (Militia), since 1967; Colonel-in-Chief, Seaforth Highlanders of Canada (Militia), since 1967. Admiral of the Fleet, Royal New Zealand Navy, since 1958; Colonel-in-Chief, Royal New Zealand Infantry Regiment, since 1958. Hon. Colonel, Trinidad and Tobago Regiment, since 1964.

Patron: Amateur Boxing Association, since 1952; Army Boxing Association, since 1952; Australian Outward Bound Trust, since 1966 (Australian Outward Bound Memorial, 1960–66); Britain-Nigeria Association, since 1961; British Association for Commercial and Industrial Education, since 1952; British Council for Rehabilitation of the Disabled, since 1953; British Heart Foundation, since 1960; British Productivity Council, since 1964; British Travel Association, since 1952; Council for Nature, since 1958; Council of St. George's House, Windsor, since 1965; "Cutty Sark" Society, since 1952; English Schools' Football Association, since 1952; Gamekeepers' Association of the United Kingdom, since 1959; Highland Fund, since 1963; Industrial Society, since 1952; Institute of Marketing and Sales Management, since 1952; Institute of Navigation, since 1952; London Federation of Boys' Clubs, since 1947; Middlesex County Cricket Club, since 1966; Modern Pentathlon Association of Great Britain, since 1958; Muscular Dystrophy Group, since 1966; National Savings Committee, since 1952;

Norfolk Island Flora and Fauna Society, since 1968; Outward Bound Trust, since 1953; Outward Bound Trust in Canada, since 1969; Research and Development Society, since 1970; Royal National Institute for the Deaf, since 1958; Royal Tournament, since 1952; Sail Training Association, since 1955; Society of Independent Artists and Designers, since 1969; Society of Model Aeronautical Engineers, since 1955; Wildfowlers' Association of Great Britain and Ireland, since 1967. Patron and Twelfth Man of the Lord's Taverners, since 1950.

President: British Amateur Athletic Board, since 1952; British Commonwealth Games Federation, since 1955; Central Council of Physical Recreation, since 1951; Council for National Academic Awards, since 1964; Council of Engineering Institutions, 1965–70; English-Speaking Union of the Commonwealth, since 1952; Fédération Equestre Internationale, 1964–72; Guinea Pig Club, since 1960; Helicopter Club of Great Britain, 1968–71; Historic Churches Preservation Trust, since 1952; Medical Commission on Accident Prevention, 1968–71; National Book League, 1963–66; National Council of Social Service, 1970–73; National Maritime Trust, 1969–79; National Playing Fields Association, 1949–72; National Spastics Society, since 1957; Royal Aero Club, 1964–71; Royal Household Cricket Club, since 1953; Royal Mint Advisory Committee, since 1952; Royal Society of Arts, since 1952; Royal Yachting Association, 1956–70 (Hon. Member since 1948); Wildfowl Trust, 1960–65; Zoological Society of London, 1960–72 (Hon. Fellow since 1959). Former President, British Association for the Advancement of Science (1951), Marylebone Cricket Club (1949–50).

Chancellor: University of Wales, since 1948; University of Edinburgh, since 1952; University of Salford, 1967–71. Master of the Corporation of Trinity House (an Elder Brother since 1952). Chairman of Council of the British Red Cross Society, 1970–73. Royal Governor of Charterhouse, since 1953. Patron and Trustee of the Duke of Edinburgh's Award, since 1961. Grand Master of the Guild of Air Pilots and Air Navigators, since 1952. Admiral of the Honourable Company of Master Mariners, since 1957. Master of the Bench of Inner Temple, since 1954 (Treasurer for 1961). Visitor of the Institute of Science and Technology, Manchester, since 1957. Membre Permanent of the Jockey Club of France, since 1962. Life Governor of King's College, London. Trustee of the King William IV Naval Foundation, since 1969. Liveryman of the Worshipful Company of Mercers, since 1959 (Freeman since 1953). Member of the Court of Governors of the National Library of Wales, since 1949. Trustee of the National Maritime Museum, Greenwich, 1948–76. Chairman of the Duke of Edinburgh's Committee, Queen's Awards to Industry, for 1965 only. Member of Committee of Management of the Royal National Lifeboat Institution, since 1957. Honorary Academician of the Royal Scottish Academy, since 1963. Commodore of the Royal Sydney Yacht Squadron, 1961–68 (Patron since 1953). Commodore of the Royal Yacht Squadron, 1961–68 (Admiral since 1952). Visitor of St. Catherine's College, Oxford, since 1962. Permanent Master of the Worshipful Company of Shipwrights, since 1955. Trustee of the Tower Hill Trust, since 1969. Hon. Member, Honourable Artillery Company, since 1954. Visitor of Upper Canada College, since 1955. An International Trustee of the World Wildlife Fund, since 1961 (President of the British National Appeal). Liveryman of the Worshipful Company of Fishmongers (Freeman, since 1947). Also Patron, President, Hon. Member, etc., of some 540 other organizations, public bodies, and clubs, including: Hon. Member of the Anchorites Club, the Castaways Club, the Savage Club, the Goat Club, the Mudhook Yacht Club, St. Edmund Hall Teddy Bears' Club, the Grand Order of Water Rats, the "Punch" Table, the Concrete Society, Sydney University Tiddlywinks Society, the Danish Dragon Club, the Welsh Beekeepers Association; Member of the Bar Yacht Club (and Admiral), the Four Hundred Club, the British Dragon Association, the International Order of Characters (US); Life Member, "Le Bon Viveur," the Porcupine Rod and Gun Club (Timmins, Ontario); Patron, the Royal Naval Lay Readers Society, the Lucifer Golfing Society, the Society of Registered Male Nurses, the Cardiff Medical Students Club, the Egham and Thorpe Royal Agricultural Association, the Canadian Cutting Horse Association, the Windsor Forest Bowmen; Hon. Colonel of the Honourable Order of Kentucky Colonels; Deputy Sheriff of Harris County, Texas; Hon. Fellow of the Institute of Public Cleansing.

A Freeman of the Cities of: Acapulco; Belfast; Bridgetown, Barbados; Cardiff; Dar-es-Salaam, Tanzania; Edinburgh; Glasgow; Guadalajara; London; Los Angeles; Melbourne; Nairobi. Freeman of the Borough of Greenwich. Hon. Citizen of the Cities of Chicago and Montevideo. Holder of these principal Foreign Honours: Grand Cross of the Order of San Martin, Argentina; Grand Cross of Honour, Austria; Grand Cordon of the Order of Leopold, Belgium; Knight of the Order of the Elephant, Denmark; Chain of the Most Exalted Order of the Queen of Sheba, Ethiopia; Grand Cross of the Order of the White Rose, Finland; Grand Cross of the Order of George I, Greece; Grand Cross of the Order of St. Olaf, Norway; Member of the Order of the Seraphim, Sweden; 1st Class Order of the Brilliant Star, Zanzibar; etc. Degrees include: Hon. D.C.L. University of Durham, 1951; Hon. LL.D., Universities of Cambridge, Edinburgh, Karachi, London, Royal University of Malta, and Wales; Hon. D.Sc., Universities of Delhi, Reading; Salford, Lancashire; Southampton; Victoria, etc. Publications: *Selected Speeches*, 1957; *Prince Philip Speaks*, 1960; *Birds from 'Britannia,'* 1962; (with James Fisher) *Wildlife Crisis*, 1970; articles in learned journals. Recreations: Polo, travel, photography, shooting, fishing, sailing, painting, arguing, working. Addresses: Buckingham Palace, London, SW1; Windsor Castle, Berkshire; Palace of Holyroodhouse, Edinburgh; Balmoral Castle, Aberdeenshire; Sandringham House, Norfolk.

Table I

The British Royal Family

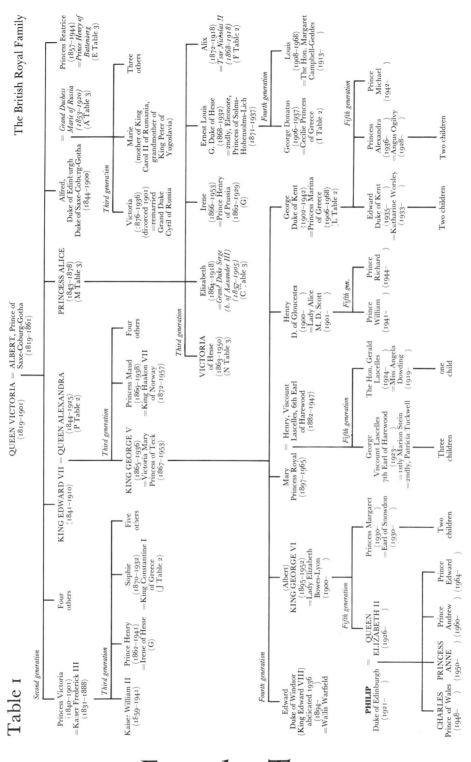

Family Tree

Table 2

The Greek and Danish Royal Families

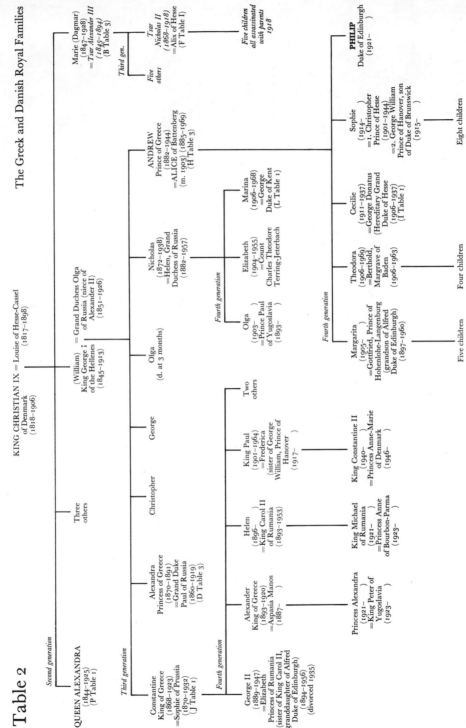

KING CHRISTIAN IX = Louise of Hesse-Cassel
of Denmark (1817–1898)
(1818–1906)

Second generation

QUEEN ALEXANDRA
(1844–1925)
(P Table 1)

Three
others

(William)
King George I
of the Hellenes
(1845–1913)

= Grand Duchess Olga
of Russia (niece of
Alexander II)
(1851–1926)

Marie (Dagmar)
(1847–1928)
= Tsar Alexander III
(1845–1894)
(B Table 3)

Third generation

Constantine
King of Greece
(1868–1891)
= Sophie of Prussia
(1870–1932)
(J Table 1)

Alexandra
Princess of Greece
(1870–1891)
= Grand Duke
Paul of Russia
(1860–1919)
(D Table 3)

George

Christopher

Olga
(d. at 3 months)

Nicholas
(1872–1938)
= Helen, Grand
Duchess of Russia
(1882–1957)

ANDREW
Prince of Greece
(1882–1944)
= ALICE of Battenberg
(m. 1903) (1885–1969)
(H Table 3)

Third gen.

Tsar
Nicholas II
(1868–1918)
= Alix of Hesse
(F Table I)

Five
others

Five children
all assassinated
with parents
1918

Fourth generation

George II
(1889–1947)
= Elizabeth
Princess of Rumania
(sister of King Carol II,
granddaughter of Alfred
Duke of Edinburgh)
(1894–1956)
(divorced 1935)

Alexander
King of Greece
(1893–1920)
= Aspasia Manos
(1887–)

Helen
(1896–)
= King Carol II
of Rumania
(1893–1953)

King Paul
(1901–1964)
= Frederica
(sister of George
William, Prince of
Hanover)
(1917–)

Two
others

Fourth generation

Olga
(1903–)
= Prince Paul
of Yugoslavia
(1893–)

Elizabeth
(1904–1955)
= Count
Charles Theodore
Terring-Jeterbach

Marina
(1906–1968)
= George
Duke of Kent
(L Table 1)

Margarita
(1905–)
= Gottfried, Prince of
Hohenlohe-Langenburg
(grandson of Alfred
Duke of Edinburgh)
(1897–1960)

Theodora
(1906–1969)
= Berthold,
Margrave of
Baden
(1906–1963)

Cecilie
(1911–1937)
= George Donatus
(Hereditary Grand
Duke of Hesse)
(1906–1937)
(I Table 1)

Sophie
(1914–)
= 1. Christopher
Prince of Hesse
(1901–1944)
= 2. George William
Prince of Hanover, son
of Duke of Brunswick
(1915–)

PHILIP
Duke of Edinburgh
(1921–)

Fourth generation

Princess Alexandra
(1921–)
= King Peter of
Yugoslavia
(1923–)

King Michael
of Rumania
(1921–)
= Princess Anne
of Bourbon-Parma
(1923–)

King Constantine II
(1940–)
= Princess Anne-Marie
of Denmark
(1946–)

Five children

Four children

Eight children

Table 3

The Mountbatts

The thick line indicates the male Battenberg line

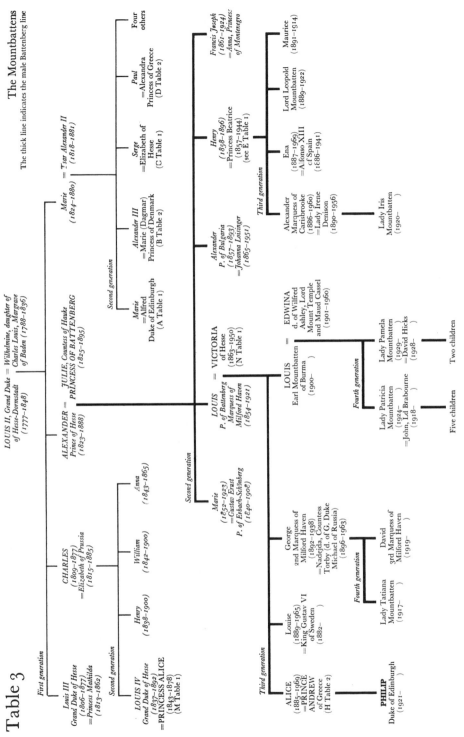

Engagements for week ending Sunday, 28th June, 1970.

Note: this card gives the actual times of engagements, not the times of departure
(which are given on daily card).
The Queen's engagements are underlined.
The Duke of Edinburgh's engagements and joint engagements are not

Birthdays

23rd:	The Duke of Windsor.
25th:	The Prince of Hohenlohe-Langenburg.
25th:	Lord Mountbatten.
26th:	Princess George of Hanover.
26th:	The Earl of St. Andrews.

Day	Date	Morning	Afternoon	Evening
Mon	22nd	1115 Guards Depot, Alexander Barracks, Pirbright. 1215 Marquess of Milford Haven Memorial Service, The Queen's Chapel.	1500 Young Volunteer Force Foundation, Wolverhampton.	2100 Anglo-Jewry Reception, Dorchester Hotel.
Tue	23rd	1045 Water Resources Board, Reading. 1150 Mr. H.G.M. Bass, H.M.A. Lesotho, and Mrs. Bass. 1210 Mr. R.G.A. Etherington-Smith, H.M.A. Khartoum, and Mrs. Etherington-Smith.	1250 Water Resources Board Luncheon. 1300 Governor-General of Canada & Mrs. Michener to luncheon. 1430 Warren Spring Laboratory, Stevenage.	2010 Talk of the Town Performance.
Wed	24th	1000 Sir Peter Runge & Sir Val Duncan. 1030 Lt. Col. Bidie & Lt. Col. Troughton. 1045 College of Art Representatives. 1100 Mr. P. Masefield & Commander Allan. 1240 Air Marshal W. D. Hodgkinson and Mrs. Hodgkinson.		1800 Hudson Bay Company Reception, Beaver House. 2030 High Commissioner for Canada and Mrs. Ritchie's Dinner.
Thu	25th	1015 Wildfowlers' Association of G.B. and N. Ireland Reserve, Sevenoaks. 1200 Mali Ambassador and Madame Diallo. 1220 Mr. H.F.T. Smith, H.M.A. Prague, and Mrs. Smith.	1255 Game Conservancy, Fordingbridge.	1755 David Davies Memorial Institute Lecture, S.W.1. 1905 Festival of Church Music, Royal Albert Hall.
Fri	26th	0915 Sir Ronald Bodley-Scott. 1028 25th Anniversary of the United Nations Ceremony, Westminster Hall.	1230 Royal Air Force Staff College Bracknell. 1645 Arrive Windsor Castle.	
Sat	27th	1025 Presentation of Freedom of Borough of Windsor to Prince of Wales.		
Sun	28th			Overnight train to Scotland.

PRINCE PHILIP
An Informal Biography

Man in Office

"It's almost like being self-employed, in the sense that you decide what to do."

Outside, martial music. Changing of the Guard. The inevitable sprinkling of loyal subjects will be braving the November chill to wedge their jaws through the gilt-topped railings. The thudding and blasting is around the front of the palace, and we're down the side, so it's remote enough not to worry the accustomed ear.

A helicopter cackles in low over the wall. Bags? Boxes? The Prince of Wales? No comment.

The music means it's eleven-thirty, so the meeting has run its first hour. Apart from its length, and it's going to last all day, it can't differ much from a thousand others now grinding through their agenda in other parts of London. The Head of Department presides at the desk, his staff gathered respectfully around. Three girls poised over files, papers, correspondence, colored tabs. Might be anywhere, from ICI to GEC. Granted, when your ICI or GEC brunette slips quietly in to the boss with another stack of folders she doesn't stop at the door to drop a curtsey. And she probably slips into a more spacious and elaborately appointed office. "Our trouble in this place," someone had said, leading the way along the kinked and carpeted corridor, "is that we're all working in bedrooms." They like to play down the grandeur.

Still, it's true that when John Nash made Buckingham House into Buckingham Palace for George IV he didn't see half its first and second floors flooded with secretaries, press officers, clerks, typists and all the attendant paraphernalia of a working monarchy, now further complicated by the addition of a working prince.

We're in the Admiral's[1] bedroom today. There's no actual bed. The only piece of reclinable furniture is a chintzy armchair, not in a sparkling state of maintenance. The Admiral has transferred himself to this, surrendering the desk chair to higher authority and capturing the main benefit of the two-bar electric fire. He rises with the rest when the boss sweeps in to be greeted by that sharp forward nod that passes for a bow in these circles, and must be hell for courtiers with bad necks.

The palace faithful tend to earn the Victorian Order in one or other of its degrees. It has a quaintly antique flavor for the entourage of a sharply modern prince. But it was founded back in 1896, as a means of marking "extraordinary, or important, or personal" services, and failing some jet-age foundation of equal intimacy, recipients must make do. And glad to. Other honors may now and again be hurled back where they came from by peevish subjects, but the chances are that the GCVO, KCVO, CVO and MVO stay put. James Orr,[2] the Duke's private secretary—and neither would care to define where their territories meet or over-

---

[1] Prince Philip's Treasurer, Rear-Admiral Sir Christopher Bonham-Carter, KCVO, CB (Retired, promoted to GCVO, November 1970).
[2] Retired, promoted to CVO, May 1970.

lap—is a member, and William Heseltine, the palace press secretary, a commander.

They're both present. His Royal Highness calls them Jim and Bill. He calls Major Randle Cooke, his principal equerry, Randle, perhaps because there's no suitable diminutive for mixed company. But equerries come and go, on short-term secondment from the Services, with less time to become old servants of the company. Randle is pink and brisk, with a look, behind his glasses, of a willing owl. There seems to be an amiable determination by the Admiral to take a rise out of him. When he goes out to get a letter and isn't back under the minute (the meeting is here, instead of in Prince Philip's office upstairs, because the administration and records are just across the corridor), the Admiral has a reverberating comment on what happens if you send the Cavalry to find anything. Cooke, returning in the middle of it, joins in the laugh.

Equerries used to look after the horses. Their aiguillettes were to tie them up with. Today the transport is different. The Major is much engaged with crackling and unmanageable large-scale maps, measuring distances as the plane flies. Or helicopter. "Couldn't I chopper?" It's a recurring murmur from the desk. Crackle-crackle goes the map. "A hundred miles by crow," muses Randle. The desk, impatient, reaches for an atlas. "Where's Ipswich? I don't seem to have anything here but southwest Russia." Orr, who doesn't say much, now says, "You couldn't drive. Four hours it took us to get to that wedding." He adds morosely that he's never been to Suffolk since.

Then there are the girls, one with a crippling cold. Colds aren't popular with Prince Philip. It isn't just that if he catches one it can mean a missed engagement; they signify an alarming lapse from full health, which for him is abominable. The girls are practiced interpreters of his verbal shorthand, half thoughts, groans, mutterings and sudden reflective silences.

HRH: Let's see, didn't we . . . ?

First Girl: Yes, Sir. In September.

HRH: What about the . . . you know . . . ?

First Girl: There's a list, Sir. (*Blows nose*)

HRH: I say, you have got a stinker, haven't you. But shan't we be . . . ?

Second Girl: No, Sir. Cumbernauld isn't until the twenty-ninth.

HRH: Good. All right, then.

There's a general rustling, and papers laid aside. Something's been settled. You have to be well on the inside track to know what.

This is the Duke of Edinburgh's Program Meeting. It happens twice a year, which is plenty. Everybody hates it, but that's understood. No point in going on about it. The purpose is to settle his personal engagements for the next six months. There are fixed points already. Joint jaunts with the Queen. Visits abroad. Causes close to the royal heart. MBTGs, which means Morally Bound to Go. What's left of the calendar, with some reasonable allowance for time off, goes to roughly a quarter of the EPs (Engagement Possible). Engagements impossible, for reasons other than the limited number of days in a week, have been combed out before the meeting. It is impossible, say, to visit a dye-works in Lanarkshire on the morning of the Garter Service at Windsor, or lunch with City bankers when you're already speaking in Sheridan, Wyoming.

So the meeting starts with the survivors of the first winnowing, a stack of crisp, white EP cards saying what, when, why, previous acceptances or refusals, and any backstage influences. "Who's pushing this?" is a frequent question from the desk. Often the resounding name that comes back only draws an "Oh, him," and the card clicks over into the legion of the lost. Engagements with fanciful titles are apt to be read out with inflections of secret amusement. "Institute of Public Cleansing? A paper will be read on the 'Purposeful Uses of *Solid Waste*'?" The laughter rolls around, then the long, long hush of rumination closes in.

Much is hushes. A rich smoker's cough from the Admiral. An ambulance brays its way along Constitution Hill. Impulses to chip in and help with a decision are diplomatically suppressed. From the desk, rapid mutterings of telescoped thoughts, sometimes a squeak of private mirth. A comment: "Afternoon on Sunday the eleventh. *Sunday* the eleventh? They must be out of their minds." (*Laughter*) Over goes the card. Somewhere in distant Scotland or Wales, if they only knew it, they can abandon their anxieties over new hats, red carpets, flowers for the platform, the strenuous plottings by executives to get their wives into the reception party.

"I've been trying to miss this thing since 1966. Start the round-Britain sailing race? But I've . . . oh no, that was power boats. . . . Well, we *could*. It's the day before Canada, though. Is this the same thing as the . . . ?"

The shorthand starts again.

"No, Sir. The Tall Ships is on the twenty-ninth. Torbay to Tenerife."

"But when's the . . . ?"

"Monday, the Royal International Horse Show."

"I thought that was the . . . oh, I see. I mean, if we do these World Cycling Championships, you see what I mean?"

"It's Goodwood, though," says the Admiral.

"Still," says HRH, "if they start the race later . . ."

There are advantages. With us, if we want to see the start of a sailing race we'd better be there when it starts. With him, it can start when he gets there. Wives of the round-Britain racing sailors, you can order your hats.

"I can chopper from Goodwood, should be quite easy. An hour? Start the thing, lunch, chop back." Major Cooke goes into an ecstasy of map-rattling. The ruler skims briskly. An hour and a half, he says. Hundred and twenty-five miles. Not as if you have to make a loop around London. Right. The girls, reading the unspoken affirmative, write in "EA." Engagement accepted. They'll write it some three hundred times this year, and the massive machinery of programing will be set in motion. Dusty answers, on James Orr's palace stationery, for about eight hundred.

For ordinary citizens, the first thought on being invited somewhere is probably how to get out of it. Here it's the other way around. Given a deserving occasion and a free date, the only bar is geography. (And, with foreign parts, money. Who's paying? It's the first question that has to be asked. State visits are taken care of, but if he goes alone to speak in New York, Karachi, Rome, the host organization has to come across with the cash. Funds at this end simply won't run.) But it's surprising how the geography can be bent. The cars, the planes, the overnight trains, the agile helicopter that puts Smith's Lawn at Windsor cheek by jowl with an army display at Aldershot. Groupings by location are constantly in mind.

"In a sense, I mean"—favorite phrases, diminishing overassertiveness—"we've got to do something for Scotland in Conservation Year, so why can't we fit in these lighthouses? What time do we finish at the whatever-it-is, Aberdeen Marine Laboratory?"

It's often the concern of the staff to curb excesses of energy. For one thing, it's probably their program too. When we read in the Court Circular, "Major Randle Cooke was in attendance," it could mean that Randle's been choppering around the country rather more than personal inclination might dictate. But to be fair, they're mostly thinking of the leading player.

"I could do this, on the seventeenth," he says, after a long mull, with pencil-tapping.

"Won't you want a day off, Sir, after Canada?" says the Admiral.

"Why?"

"It's right in the middle of Warwickshire," says Orr, as Randle's map utters a warning crackle.

"Well, where else can I go?"

The Admiral booms. "You can go straight home, that's where. You'll be tired. Have an ordinary normal weekend." The boom broadens into a laugh, to ease the plain speaking.

The desk picks up another card, changing course.

"How serious is this Prince Albert Foundation?"

Sometimes it goes the other way. He can put up a sudden resistance, for a not always apparent reason. Senior members of the meeting may even be emboldened to take issue. Today, as it happens, there's quite a skirmish with the Admiral over an agricultural invitation from Northamptonshire.

HRH: Who's pushing this?

Admiral: (*Unexpectedly*) I am, Sir. I'm worried that it's been announced you're president of the thing.

HRH: (*Somewhat moved*) I've been president of hundreds of things without *going* to them.
Silence

Admiral: (*On something between a laugh and a cough*) All right, Sir.
Silence

HRH: I mean, we *can* still go, but it means missing a garden party,[3] it's in the *middle* of the Commonwealth Games, which you knew was going to happen at the time, you've put it in the minute yourself!

Admiral: Yes. I didn't realize the FEI was—

HRH: The FEI's got nothing to do with it.
Silence
In fact, I mean, it does take two more days out of that week . . . and they're much more difficult to get out

---

[3] Official. At Holyrood.

of than this *show*, which goes on all the time (*on a rising note*), and it couldn't matter *less* whether I go to it, there are dozens of agricultural shows all over the blessed *country!*

Suddenly there seems to be a row on. Just as suddenly he goes off into laughter. At the absurdity of getting angry over this? At the Admiral's lost cause?

Presently he says, "You've got a bad conscience over it?"

"Yes, I have, Sir, very. Because I think it'll be a great disappointment if you don't do it. However, there it is. Can't be helped."

An interesting bit of naval strategy. The apparent surrender produces a show of magnanimity.

"Perhaps," says HRH, now almost affable, "we could agree to go next year, I mean?"

"Yes, Sir."

"I mean, was it an anniversary of some kind?"

"I don't know. Still, I did point out that if you accepted the presidency you'd have to go, I remember that."

"But I seem to remember, writing on the thing at the beginning, saying we'll accept the presidency, but the dates will be—you know—have to wait. We weren't obliged, anyway, to answer it before now, surely?"

"No, not the particular day, Sir. . . . Not that I want to jog back over it now, because if that's what you've decided, that's it."

Struck his colors, has he? Not quite. Just a hand to the halyard, and the battle not lost yet, because after more pencil-tapping and rifflings from the desk, mutterings of semi-exasperation, silent probings of possibilities, sudden outbursts of "crazy," "lunacy," and other expressions of reluctance, it seems that perhaps, after all, if we moved *this* to *there*, and that to somewhere else, even if it did mean flying down from Holyrood . . .

"Supposing," says the girl with the cold—and fires off a dizzying broadside of date permutations.

The craniums hum.

"Well . . . yes, we could do that," says HRH, now almost mildly. The rearrangements are debated in detail. It seems all right. Large erasers, bearing the arms and insignia of Her Majesty's Stationery Office, are brought smartly to the erasing position. The impression, when the smoke clears, is that the Admiral has triumphed over fearful odds. An honorable engagement, and could have gone either way. As it is, the loyal cattlemen of Northamptonshire have had their bacon saved, owe the Admiral a debt and will never know it.

So that's one more EA, and the birth of one more EA file. From this moment the machine takes over, and the paper work starts to build.

The Program Meeting has replaced an older system, scrapped some years back. Then, as the invitations came flooding in, to visit, to tour, to inspect, to open, to attend, to speak, to launch, to lunch, to dine, the book was filled up with the most deserving or desirable until the last cranny was gone. It meant that if anything came in later, even of overriding merit or desirability, nothing could be done. "Not a 'ope," as the Duke is apt to put it in his less fiery moments. Under the new scheme all heart-cries are acknowledged with a promise of a verdict later, and tucked in the deep freeze. Comes the agonizing biannual thaw, and the whole wild heterogeneous mass gets a start from scratch.

With only a one in four chance anyway, less if a block of dates has already been preempted for overseas, applicants need to deploy all their skills and wiles. To start negotiations well before the event is useful, if only to suggest a glimmering awareness of the congestion at the receiving end. ("I remember this chap," says

HRH, skimming a luckless EP card into the outer darkness. "He said, 'What about coming to lunch next week?'" [General laughter].)

An influential backer does no harm. Nor does at least a rough acquaintance with royal routine. "I believe it is His Royal Highness's practice to spend occasional weekends at Windsor in the month of November . . ." This is the director of studies at an accessibly placed Management Study Centre proposing a visit on a Monday morning. From such a source you'd naturally expect the strategy to be on a high level. In any case he's off to a good start. Industrial management is known to be a favored subject. The geography is right. The Dean of Windsor is a mutual friend, and can be put in to bat. And the director, it turns out, is married to a girl who did ten years in the Duke's office. All useful stuff.

That particular engagement was one of last year's, over and done with now, but to see how things went may be interesting. The director began in the previous November, with a formal letter of some length addressed to James Orr. Wisely. Some attempt the direct approach, which can mean heavy redrafting before the true gist breaks through the thicket of respectfully submitting and graciously requesting and obediently remaining: tortuous evasions of the presumptuous personal pronoun can land you with three Your Royal Highnesses to a sentence, and even when it's finally cut and polished you're not certain you'll escape being thrown into the Tower. (Prince Philip, while getting a certain amount of amusement out of these forms, wouldn't take too kindly to their abandonment.)

No, it's wiser to lower the sights, and write, with the director of studies, "Dear Mr. Orr: You may recall that I wrote to you in the spring of 1965 . . ."

So the start really had been early. But a false one. "In the event, he was unable to fit the visit into his program at that time . . ." And thus to the revived request, with cogent and detailed arguments, glossy promotional pamphlets a credit to the printer's trade, and the choice of two Monday mornings in April.

The letter is acknowledged. Grateful, noncommittal, crisp but not curt. But is it prudent to offer specific dates, unless they're locked inextricably to some unbudgeable occasion? Perhaps not. Enter the Dean. "Dear Jim, I have been made aware . . . May I commend . . . ?" But the timing has been poor. That half year's planning session was over. "I much regret that His Royal Highness did not find it possible to include . . ."

Ah, well. Until March the project hibernates. Then the director launches his spring offensive. "We were naturally disappointed to hear . . ." But the attractiveness of the proposition is now apparently greater than ever, what with new and fascinating courses, and other evidence of the Centre's onward and upward progress. Even a speech is boldly asked for.

Into File No. 5505 goes an EP card. Things look promising. But nothing is yet given away in Jim's reply. He has noted, it says, that the Duke of Edinburgh might be asked to visit the Centre. Brochures and acknowledgments come and go. Also another Program Meeting. And, late July, enter Major Randle Cooke, Equerry-in-Waiting. The very change of correspondent, did the Centre but know it, means the mystical change of an EP into an EA.

His Royal Highness has completed his plans for the Autumn, and would be able to visit you on Monday, 10th November, at approximately 1500 hours. May I now have an outline of the arrangements? I must ask that the matter remain confidential until His Royal Highness has approved the programme, and a date has been agreed for the Press release.

Director to Randle. Barely concealed rapture. "I have immediately prepared a draft program, a copy of which . . ." Earnest desire for a meeting with Major Cooke.

Randle to director, gently checking the excitement. He will be in touch "when the Duke of Edinburgh has had an opportunity to consider the arrangements you propose."

The arrangements, judging by the draft program, are elaborate. The visitor will see in action a Business Game, in which four teams of student-executives sit in sealed and separate rooms making decisions on business strategy. Below this select, white-collar level, a promised display of amateur dramatics, in which students present a scene straight from the shop floor, playing the parts of foreman, planner, progress chaser, setter, maintenance man, while machines "simulated by electro-mechanical devices" will break down, stop for lack of work and generally reflect industry as we know it in the great world outside. Moving on to the Lecture-Note Preparation Department, where a "special ring-binder will be made up as a presentation to His Royal Highness. . . ." It certainly promises to be a great day; and there are actual people to be presented yet. Some by name, others anonymous ("intelligence officers and librarians"). Fifty members of the Senior Executives Course "would be honoured if His Royal Highness would deliver an address."

Randle Cooke sends him the program with a brief note. "Will you speak?" Answer, in the royal hand, "No." Words aren't wasted.

The presentation ring-binder goes into the box-file, which is why the lid won't shut. Handsome blue leatherette, gold inscribed, a feast of colored charts and impeccable photocopy typewriting, estimated weight, three pounds. Not all presentations, incidentally, end up with the records. Here, in some other file, is a note begging the acceptance of "the enclosed dinner plate," with an office comment in anonymous pencil, "Pantry, or something?" Difficult, working this sort of odd item into a palace banquet.

But the preparations are still only halfway home. There are suggested amendments at the palace end, with requests for a revised draft: two copies arrive by return and are acknowledged. There are even minor amendments at the Centre end—and four revised copies are rushed in. And acknowledged. There are memos, telephone calls. The car. Transport timings. Minutes count. Arrival is now to be at 15.25. Prince Philip's pennant must fly, and there's a note: "Standards, 1, 6″ x 3″, sent to Mr. Kettlewell, 4.11.69." Police arrangements must be made. And it's only courteous to tell the lord lieutenant of the county what's going on. In this, as it happens, Randle Cooke's letter overdoes the courtesy, quite unintentionally. It adds, to the essential particulars, that "Prince Philip would not wish to put you to the trouble of meeting or attending him on this occasion, but perhaps you would let me know if you do intend to be present."

The reply, rightly or wrongly, is thought in the office to be capable of an umbrageous construction. "I note," writes the lord lieutenant, "that Prince Philip does not wish me either to meet or attend him, for which I am much obliged, and in that case I do not intend being present." Has an error of taste been committed inside the palace? Worrying. Internal memos are exchanged. Opinions differ. Randle Cooke says, defensively, "After all, he says he's obliged." Others feel that perhaps the form of letters to lords lieutenant could be softened; Prince Philip proposes that the form "do intend" should be changed to "would like" in future. There the matter seems to rest, but who knows where the repercussions may still be sounding? Meanwhile, the lord lieutenant is thanked for his decision not to be there. The director is notified of the intended absence, and replies with thanks and further drafts of the program, "so that you have some spares to hand round to any interested parties." Randle Cooke acknowledges, and warns of a slight timing adjustment, namely that "Prince Philip may leave at any time from 18.15 onwards, half an hour being about the right time for tea." It's also, in fact, about the right time for a visitor who has to get back from Buckinghamshire to draw breath, bathe, change, dine and be at the London Palladium at five minutes to eight for the Royal Command Variety Performance. But it isn't done to let any engagement know that another is sharing its thunder. The visit now bursting File No. 5505 at the seams, in fact, followed hard on the opening of a new probation hostel an hour and a quarter before. Correction, an hour and ten minutes—the timings are fine. And the opening had itself followed hard on an official lunch.

In his diary for January 21, 1941, Sir Henry Channon recorded his attendance at "an enjoyable Greek cocktail party. Philip of Greece was there. He is extraordinarily handsome, and I recalled my afternoon's conversation with Princess Nicholas. He is to be our Prince Consort, and that is why he is serving in our Navy."

Princess Nicholas was Philip's aunt by marriage, formerly the Grand Duchess Helen of Russia, mother of Princess Marina, Duchess of Kent. It seemed a powerful stroke of prevision. I asked about it.

Q: Could this possibly have been true, as long ago as that?

HRH: Well. This is precisely the sort of language that they used. It had been mentioned, presumably, that "he is eligible, he's the sort of person she might marry." I mean, after all, if you spend ten minutes thinking about it—and a lot of these people spent a great deal more time thinking about it—how many obviously eligible young men, other than people living in this country, were available? Inevitably I must have been on the list, so to speak. But people only had to say that, for somebody like Chips Channon to go one step further and say it's already decided, you see what I mean?

Some Greek Prince

*"Mr. Mountbatten left Greece in early childhood
and since then has known no home but England."*
—THE TIMES, July 10, 1947

※⚬※

A girl journalist—Olga Franklin, later of the *Daily Mail*—doing
court reporting (police, not royal) on the *Newcastle Journal*,
claimed a scoop in the spring of 1944. The first-ever interview
with Prince Philip of Greece. Not to hurt her feelings, it was a
scoop that nobody else was competing for just then, though this
was soon to change. In a year or two's time the palace press office,
which had begun to collect his cuttings, gave up. There wasn't
the storage space.

He was in Newcastle upon Tyne, sitting out one of those periods
of inactive service that occur even in a wartime navy, waiting for
the new destroyer *Whelp* to be commissioned. He would spend the
rest of the war in her, ending up in Tokyo Bay to see the Japanese
surrender. He was living in a small hotel, and the reporter re-

members being fascinated to learn that he was paying six guineas a week. It struck her as a huge sum.

She was even more fascinated by her subject once she found him, which wasn't easy. "There's some Greek prince in town," said her editor. So she took time off from the drunks-and-disorderlies and went hunting. It's hard to realize now that there were no photographs to go by. She was alert for her idea of a Greek. Flashing eyes and five o'clock shadow, broad gestures and broken English. The reality bowled her over, and she turned in a yard of panting admiration that brought tears to the editor's eyes, but only of despair. It was subbed into a ghost of its former self.

Shipyard Stranger Is a Royal Prince

Very few workers in a North-East shipyard are aware that the tall, ash-blond first lieutenant, RN, who travels by bus to work among them each day, is a Royal Prince.

Citizens have been equally unaware that this 23-year-old naval officer, Prince Philip of Greece, has been living quietly in an hotel while "standing by" on a British destroyer.

Prince Philip, who has the looks of a typical Prince of a Hans Andersen fairy tale, will certainly have been noticed by many a girl worker at the shipyard.

I found that his Scandinavian appearance is explained by the fact that his grandfather, King George I of the Hellenes, was the son of King Christian IX of Denmark, and was nominated for the Greek Throne by the British Government at the request of the Greek National Assembly in 1862.

Prince Philip, who has served with the British Mediterranean Fleet, and wears the 1939–43 Africa Star, is the only son of Prince Andrew (fourth[1] child of George I of Greece) and Princess Alice.

---

[1] Actually seventh child, fourth son.

The Prince was amused at my suggestion that he might find the northern dialect difficult to understand.

"I understand the local people perfectly," he said, "and am enjoying my stay."

This was confirmed by another naval officer.

The Prince said: "I last saw my home in Athens in February, 1941." He added that he had been in England twice before—to school.

This is the first time the Prince has been interviewed and reported in this country . . . and I thanked him for the good humoured and kindly way he had accepted "exposure."

It was still a nice long piece for a girl to get in about a naval nobody, and the facts, if sparse, were mostly right. They could have done with a bit of expansion, but these were the days of the four-page newspaper, one of the war's few blessings, and column inches were scarce. In any case, the ash-blond first lieutenant may have clammed up here and there, not only from a natural distaste for discussing himself, which reporters learned more about in the years to come, but because the interviews (it took five to raise the material) would get keen Admiralty scrutiny. Only official heroes were encouraged to sound off in the public prints. What's more, his commanding officer was there, alert for indiscretions, and he was the one, no doubt, to whip in the swift confirmation that his lieutenant was enjoying himself. He probably was. But lieutenants who weren't, and came right out with it, could cause Alarm and Despondency, a known drag on civilian morale, let alone a breach of the Defence Regulations. Whatever the reason, there were odd omissions, notably a gleaming uncle, Admiral Lord Louis Mountbatten. The full weight of rank and honors was yet to fall on him, but, even so, the name would have rung a sonorous bell

for the citizen-readers of Newcastle, if only as the hero of the
destroyer HMS *Kelly*—and, by transference, the Noel Coward
film *In Which We Serve*—or as Supreme Allied Commander,
Southeast Asia. He still had some dignities to pick up, whether
familiar and domestic, such as the Garter and the Bath, or the more
exotic White Elephant of Siam, or Special Grand Cordon of the
Cloud and Banner (China). He enjoyed them endearingly. A
member of the Greek Royal Household in the 1950s recalls that
Mountbatten would "travel" his decorations (if the theatrical jargon isn't out of place), several trays of them in a purpose-built
box, and produce them when visiting. "Did I show you my Star
of Nepal?" It was usually discovered after a tour of supervening
splendors. But he was born at Windsor Castle, notionally, at least,
in the line of succession, and was cousin and personal naval ADC
to George VI. Edward VIII, as Prince of Wales, had been a close
friend and best man at his wedding. And those handily placed for
a public reference library could have plotted his descent from the
Grand Dukes of Hesse on one side and Queen Victoria on the
other. And needn't have stopped there.

Early on in the quest they'd have come across this remarkable
uncle's remarkable father, Prince Louis of Battenberg. He was
born a German, in 1854. Just sixty years later, as Britain's First
Sea Lord, he was to send the signal, on August 4, 1914: "Admiralty
to All Ships. Commence hostilities against Germany. Louis Battenberg." It was his forty-sixth year of distinguished service in
the Royal Navy.

As a young boy he'd been fired with ambitions for a naval career,
partly because of visits to his home in Germany by an earlier Duke
of Edinburgh, RN[2] (Victoria's second son, Prince Alfred, an
uncle, or as near as makes no difference), who had tales of the sea

---

[2] The title lapsed on his death in 1900.

to tell. There were difficulties. Being born in a duchy with no coastline couldn't have helped—and that in a country where, as his elders kept insisting, soldiering was the only proper life. It didn't matter. In 1868, aged fourteen, he was at Gosport, swearing allegiance to the British Crown and about to become a cadet in the only navy worth having.

Less than three months after that memorable signal of 1914 he was writing to his political master, the First Lord:

Dear Mr. Churchill,

I have lately been driven to the painful conclusion that at this juncture my birth and parentage have the effect of impairing in some respects my usefulness on the Board of Admiralty. In these circumstances I feel it to be my duty, as a loyal subject of His Majesty, to resign the office of First Sea Lord, hoping thereby to facilitate the task of the administration of the great Service to which I have devoted my life, and to ease the burden laid on HM's Ministers.

I am,   Yours very truly,
                                  Louis Battenberg,
                                        Admiral.

Though there were other factors, none to the Prince's discredit— the war at sea wasn't going well—the name was the rock that sank him. The fury against all things German, making Beethoven a dirty word in that war, and causing blameless dachshunds to be booted on sight, had been boiling up for some time. Rumors of Battenberg's pro-German sympathies were everywhere, except among those who knew him. Jellicoe, Commander-in-Chief of the Grand Fleet, was grieved and appalled at his downfall. Later, even the papers that had carried the first open attacks came crawling back with praise for his past services. Churchill's letter of acceptance struck a note of genuine personal regret not always discernible in such documents. But he accepted all the same. Fighting a war, you need the people on your side, blindly emotional chumps though they be.

It was three years later, bowing to the same popular tantrums, that the King of England, under the highest advice, changed his own name from Wettin to Windsor (if it was Wettin in the first place—even high advisers didn't seem too sure; Wettin was Prince Albert's "family" name, as distinct from his "House" name of Saxe-Coburg-Gotha). He commanded that other royal connections, similarly afflicted, should also make prudent adjustments. Prince Louis lost the Battenberg and gained the Mountbatten. Lost, too, the princeship. In the England of 1917, serene highnesses hardly fitted in. But he gained the first Marquisate of Milford Haven, the Earldom of Medina and the Viscounty of Alderney. Medina had a frightfully Spanish ring, but it only turned out to be the English name of an English river near his English home on the Isle of Wight. They let it go. Barring, perhaps, Louis himself, everyone was happy. Louis, his son, lopped of the German handle, was already in the Royal Navy, and would eventually be First Sea Lord in his turn, trailing glory all the way. It was a pity to be overlooked like that in the *Newcastle Journal*, but even by 1944 he could afford to take it in his stride.

Besides, to include him would have wrecked the story. Give the readers a princely waif from nowhere, stumping up his twopence on the buses, straining his ear after the inscrutable cadences of an alien land, and you've got your drama. Trick it out with the English nobility, and the magic's gone.

The man in the library, scenting these whiffs of grandeur, could have groped back into bemusing genealogical thickets. The Greek Royal Family tree alone is a formidable monkey-puzzle, never mind its entanglements with trees adjoining. Having discovered that the lieutenant on the bus could claim a grandfather, an uncle and three cousins as kings of Greece; that, nearer home, George VI of England was a second cousin, and the Duchess of Kent a first, the researcher might have called it a day, and not chanced his neck on the spreading limbs of related royal houses—the Danes, the Swedes, the Germans, the Russians, the Spaniards, the Italians, the Yugoslavs, the Romanians, the French. But at least Lord Mountbatten of Burma's own proud probe into the past wasn't on hand at the time for further confusion. Those famous Relationship Tables, coming in an exclusively limited edition off the viceregal presses of New Delhi, weren't to appear until 1947, chiming neatly with the engagement of the future Queen Elizabeth II to Lieutenant Philip Mountbatten. For what it's worth, he has more blue blood than the Queen, whose ancestors include the admirable but nonpatrician Mary Browne, Joseph Grimstead and George Smith. Though he's not greatly absorbed by such things, his study at Windsor has his own family tree written in his own hand, done in concentric circles and not dropping much below grand dukes at the outer perimeter. But it's neither framed nor hung, just propped against the wall.

At the time of his engagement, his only title was Lieutenant. The achievement of British nationality in February 1947 had reduced him to common clay. No Prince, no Highness, no longer any place in the succession to the troubled throne of Greece. Granted, he rose to Royal Highness again on November 19, 1947, the eve of the wedding; and to Duke of Edinburgh, Earl of Merioneth and Baron Greenwich. But it was another ten years before the royal wand waved him back to Prince, this time "with the style and dignity of a Prince of the United Kingdom." Meanwhile, there had been other promotions. From Lieutenant, RN, to Lieutenant-Commander, to Commander. More spectacularly, in 1953, he zoomed up the seniorities and became, at a blow, Admiral of the Fleet, Field Marshal and Marshal of the Royal Air Force. It was good going, but less fulfilling than those dogged old rewards on merit.

Earl Mountbatten's Tables, as might be expected from the author of a revolutionary book on naval signaling, used a coding system. Without it, the ramifications would have been worse than those Old Testament begattings. He leaned heavily on the family history remembered by his mother. As one of Victoria's proliferous grandchildren she was a rich source. She had been Princess Victoria, daughter of Princess Alice, herself Queen Victoria's daughter and eventually the wife of Louis IV, Grand Duke of Hesse, two of whose other daughters married well into Russia, one to the brother, the other to the son, of Tsar Alexander III. Princess Victoria had married the hapless victim of British xenophobia, Prince Louis of Battenberg, and at the time of the Tables was Dowager Marchioness of Milford Haven. So there's trouble already, as the branches begin to tangle.

She nominated, as a starting point, fifteen heads of families, born in the early part of the last century. Ten of them were kings, queens and emperors. Grand dukes and princes made up the rest. Their geography covered Spain, Belgium, Denmark, Sweden, Russia, Prussia, the Netherlands, Greece, Great Britain. Prince Philip's grandfather, George I of the Hellenes, was there, and his great-great-grandmother, Queen Victoria. Their descendants were coded in letters and numerals (if Prince Charles had arrived in time, he would have come out as G-7-E-1).

The Tables in the main burrowed back for only a century or so, to 1851, when Grand Duke Louis III of Hesse-Darmstadt and by the Rhine received appalling news—that his younger brother, Prince Alexander, had eloped with Julie Hauke, a mere maid of honor to their sister, Princess Marie, wife of the Russian Tsarevitch, who was to become Tsar Alexander II. "Blödsinnige Gefühlsduselei!"

said the Grand Duke, according to one astonishingly well-informed chronicler; he had his troubles already, including the gout.

Julie was sweet but tough, and had disengaged the Prince from a wilderness of admirers. She needs a book on her own. Up to her unacceptable marriage ("You expect us to have a 'Fraulein Hauke' in the family?" fumed Louis) it would be a tale of wars and horrors. She had seen her father, serving Tsar Nicholas I as a general in the Imperial Army—though at the time, by the tortuosities of European politics, Polish Minister of War—dragged into the streets of Warsaw and sabered to death by nihilists, who were later to assassinate Alexander II. She was not, in fact, a "Fraulein Hauke." Though her father was of common parentage, he had been made a Polish count. But this was chicken feed. In the view of Grand Duke Louis, his brother Alexander had run off with an orphaned serving wench; and one who now, to save the family face, must be made respectable. Her marriage was ruled morganatic, she was forbidden to style herself a Princess of Hesse and her children would have to rub along as counts and countesses, but a long-extinct title was revived, and in November of the elopement year she found herself Countess of Battenberg.

Her husband, shamed out of the Russian Army by his marriage into the lower orders, became a general in the Austrian, and in the course of his varied postings Julie bore him five children: at Geneva, Graz, Verona, Milan and Padua. The boy born at Graz was to be Prince Louis of Battenberg. Seven years after Julie's marriage there had been a relenting—she became a princess after all, and her children royal.

They took to it, all but one making royal marriages. This was the second son, another Alexander, and it was a near miss even with him; his romantic attachment to Princess Victoria of

Prussia was voided by the politicking of Bismarck, and he settled for an opera singer from the Darmstadt Court Theater. He had put in seven tumultuous years, 1879 to 1886, as ruler of Bulgaria in the meantime, so was hardly a disgrace. Of the rest, Prince Henry of Battenberg married Queen Victoria's daughter Beatrice; Prince Francis Joseph a Princess of Montenegro; Princess Marie a Prince of Erbach-Schonberg; and Prince Louis, as we have seen, Queen Victoria's granddaughter, Victoria (his first cousin, in case that isn't entirely clear)—and the Royal Navy.

A son of this last marriage was to be Lord Louis Mountbatten, and a daughter Princess Alice, later Princess Andrew of Greece and Philip's mother.

Julie's elopement was in 1851. For the most part, Mountbatten followed things only back to there. But he made exceptions. For Lieutenant Philip Mountbatten a not undistinguished lineage was traced, from Charlemagne (742–814), demolishing the pagan Saxons, routing the robber kings of Hungary, larruping the Lombards and topping off by founding the Holy Roman Empire, to such local late-comers as Henry Percy, the legendary Hotspur (1364–1403), without whom the Wars of the Roses wouldn't have been the same. It was a tricky exercise. Those Percys alone must have taken some unraveling. They were lords of Northumbria. Not surprising, perhaps, that the shipyard stranger had no trouble with the Newcastle accent?

But the harassed British citizen of 1944 knew little of all this. And not much more in July 1947 when the engagement was announced. It was hardly a bolt from the blue. "Long-awaited" crept into most editorials. The Lieutenant had already been seen at social occasions where the Princess was also present, and really forward-looking cameramen had even got them into the same shot.

Hadn't he appeared in a newsreel actually helping her off with her coat? Infallible indications.

All the same, information on the forthcoming bridegroom was still sketchy. Asked a columnist of the time:

"What is he like, this young, fresh-faced sailor, a naturalised Englishman, who once was sixth in line of succession to the Greek throne, but who, since his childhood, has grown up in the ways and customs of these very isles in which he is now to marry?"

It was a good question, if hard on the lungs, and one much put, with variations, in the papers of that July. It was also enough to send a young fresh-faced sailor ducking for cover down the nearest hatch. With his arrival on the royal scene, vocabularies were hard pushed for epithets of beauty and grace. "The Prince from the Sea," they called him, those craggy old hard-nosed pressmen. "This genial giant with corn-colored hair." The hair exercised them most. "Gold," "golden," "flaxen"—even curly, if the picture editor came up with a shot that lent itself. Then there was the figure ("tall and slim"), the mouth ("strong"), the chin ("firm"), the eyes ("blue and wide apart") and the profile ("reminiscent of the god-like statues of antiquity"). Somebody got that one off even two months before the match was official.

But the hair was the thing. It made a comforting ethnic point.

"The only outward sign of his mixed blood is perhaps in his extreme fairness, for his hair is so blond, with reddish tints in the sunlight to give it almost the colour of new minted gold, that in the days of his Danish Viking ancestors he would undoubtedly have been known as Philip the Fair."

Though one doubts that "undoubtedly"—wouldn't you have to be dark, in a blond community, to be named after your hair shade? —the blondness certainly made it easier to forget the mixed blood. The Anglo-Saxon look was fine.

While the romantics went to town with the theme of the Princess and the commoner—though, even so, 40 percent of polled *Sunday Pictorial* readers were at one time against the marriage, mostly deploring an alliance with a "foreigner"—more sober opinion doubted the wisdom of getting mixed up with the Greeks. What was the domestic political feeling? George VI, after doubts and delays, had given his consent under the Royal Marriage Act of 1772 (it laid down that "no descendants of George II shall be capable of contracting matrimony without the previous consent of His Majesty, his heirs and successors")—also after examining a purely parental heart. And no one could fault Philip as an individual. But he was popping up as an awkward political question mark. "The King," said the *Manchester Guardian* sternly, "would not assert his personal judgment on such a matter against that of the Government." The Government, which was Clement Attlee's in 1946, pondered the whole delicate business of attaching a Greek prince to the British monarchy without upsetting the international as well as the domestic applecart. When the marriage prospects loomed, the Greek civil war was already well fired (and had another three years to burn). Russia was arming the Communists. British troops were propping up the reascended but uncertain throne of George II, this itself a policy on which Cabinet and parliamentary opinion were divided.

In short, though it was nothing new, Greece was a mess, and seemed to many a shady source of royal husbands, however blond and genial. There was even a suspicion that political opportunism in Athens was at the root of it all, and that early leaks into the world's press starting with *Hellicon Aema*, an "official" Greek paper, were tries for a self-fulfilling prophecy. The link could stabilize Greece's international reputation. Certainly King George of Greece, before his return, had sounded out King George of England, who at the time was cool about it.

There were the Dominions, as they were still called, to think of, particularly South Africa, where the ties of allegiance were fraying a bit even then, though it wasn't until 1961 that they finally parted. The royal tour there, from February to May 1947, an elaborate exercise that diplomatically took in Princess Elizabeth's twenty-first birthday, was chiefly designed to nourish those loyalties: for the Family to board HMS *Vanguard* in a cloud of bickerings over a Greek husband would have been less diplomatic, and it was all damped down. The tour served a secondary purpose, no novelty when loving parents are in doubt; it removed Elizabeth, testing whether absence would make the heart grow fonder. It did. And when the engagement was announced, on July 9, the *Daily Telegraph*'s ecstatic round-up of world comment ended with a dispatch headed "South African Enthusiasm."

Lieutenant Mountbatten—while they were away he had become a British citizen—was in the still eye of the storm, conscientiously instructing petty officers at Corsham in Wiltshire. He may well have wondered what he was getting into. He'd thought things out, and foreseen much. But political, constitutional and ceremonial fuss on the grand scale can defeat the liveliest imagination. You pick a wife, and half the world, as of right, joins in.

No one should think, as some chose to think at the time, that he saw marriage to the most eligible of heiresses as a stroke of high gamesmanship. There was no quiet hand-rubbing at being on to a good thing. From all the thinking, which had been long, deep and lonely, what came out on top was a clear concern for Elizabeth's future rather than his own. If his was to be a hard assignment, hers would be harder. Besides, he wasn't the only one with rare graces. He'd seen more of Elizabeth's show-stopping smile, the outer mark of an inner gaiety, than most of the photographers and artists—especially Signor Annigoni in his middle period—ever manage to capture.[3] Perhaps all the crooning about a love match, which rose from a thousand pages in the summer of 1947, went overboard a bit. But a marriage either of convenience or ambition it certainly was not.

---

[3] "She's lovely, she's a pet," said Winston Churchill, five years later. He went on, "I fear they may ask her to do too much." It's something that also worries her husband.

Q: There must have been a time when you decided you were
        going to marry Princess Elizabeth?
HRH: Well, certainly not at Dartmouth. [A royal visit in July
        1939 to Dartmouth, where he was a cadet, had been pin-
        pointed by many commentators of July 1947 as the oc-
        casion when romance first struck. She was fourteen.]
Q: So you weren't thinking about this until . . . ?
HRH: Well, we'd met at Dartmouth, and as far as I was con-
        cerned it was a very amusing experience, going on board
        the yacht and meeting them, and that sort of thing, and
        that was that. Then I went to—did I go to Windsor? I
        think I came here [Buckingham Palace]. Or I went to
        the theater with them once, something like that. And
        then, during the war, if I was here I'd call in and have a
        meal. I once or twice spent Christmas at Windsor, be-
        cause I'd nowhere particular to go. . . .

        [Natural enough. You're home on leave, cut off from
        your immediate family, you breeze in on the nearest
        available branch. They're always glad to see you. The
        cooking's all right.]

        I thought not all that much about it, I think. We
        used to correspond occasionally. You see, it's difficult to
        visualize. I suppose if I'd just been a casual acquaintance
        it would all have been frightfully significant. But if
        you're related—I mean, I knew half the people here, they
        were all relations—it isn't so extraordinary to be on kind

of family relationship terms with somebody. You don't necessarily have to think about marriage.

Q: No. [If you can call that a Q.]

HRH: I suppose one thing led to another. I suppose I began to think about it seriously, oh, let me think now, when I got back in '46 and went to Balmoral. It was probably then that we, that it became, you know, that we began to think about it seriously, and even talk about it. And then there was their excursion to South Africa, and it was sort of fixed up when they came back. That's really what happened.

3

Member of the Wedding

"Constitutionally, I don't exist."

❧❦❧

November 20, 1947, was a Thursday, fine but gloomy. "His Majesty the King," said the Lord Chamberlain's final draft of the day's arrangements, "with Her Royal Highness, the Bride, will leave Buckingham Palace at 11.16 A.M., and will be received at the West Door at 11.28 A.M. by the Dean and Chapter." The typescript was large and clear, and had that ring of cast-iron inevitability that goes with all royal programs. Her Majesty the Queen was to drive forth at 11.03 A.M., and did. Her Majesty Queen Mary would have left Marlborough House on the same inexorable dot.

The bridegroom, later in the list but earlier in the countdown, was at the Abbey already, having incurred a pleasing typing slip: on arrival at the Poets' Corner door he would go to his seat at the

(*34*)

south side of the steps "leading to the Scararium." Read Sacrar-ium. But bridegrooms the world over, however much they loved the girl, would sympathize with the scare bit. Did this one, more than most, feel the primitive urge to cut and run? It had been fun in the Navy. Even with sluggish peacetime promotions you wouldn't be a lieutenant all your life, and might well be First Sea Lord in the end—it ran in the family. But it wouldn't be a simple matter of leaving, reluctantly enough, the bride at the altar. The mighty engine of State was in motion. And there'd be a terrible lot of presents to send back, some with special difficulties, like the 32,000 food parcels from CARE. (One of the first, and long-for-gotten acronyms: "Cooperative for American Remittances to Europe." They eventually went to poor British widows, selected by ballot.)

If the impulse was there, and it isn't an admission you'd get out of him, it passed, as they mostly do. It was too late, anyway. The carriages were already rolling, buffed to a high gloss; the Life Guards and Household Cavalry, plumed and burnished, were strategically deployed. Inside the Abbey the Lords of the Church were assembled, visiting royalties robed and fidgeting and two thousand less distinguished worshipers congratulating themselves on being invited. (Some who weren't and thought they should have been later wrote injured letters, including a few peers whose names had failed to come out of the hat, or coronet, in the House of Lords ballot.)

Besides, there were the people, the legions of loyal and romantic citizens who, after huddling on the cold stones all night, were now stacked in the vertical under the flags and banners, solid from the palace to the Abbey. Soldiers barred them from the sanded streets, but they seethed on the pavements all down Whitehall and the Mall; Trafalgar Square was full to the fountains, Landseer's lions at the bottom of the scrum.

To such a Crown all broken spirits turn:
And we, who see this young face passing by,
See her as Symbol of a Power Etern,
And pray that Heaven may bless her till she die.

There was no quarrel, of course, with the sentiments. But if the pressures of occasion could bring great old Masefield down to this, it's likely that the bridegroom felt a comparable tremor. He didn't appear in the verses, perhaps because neither Edinburgh nor Mountbatten falls easily into a line, and raises problems of rhyme at the end of it—though a poet capable of a purpose-minted "Etern" might well have solved that one. No, it's more probable that he just got left out—a minor, if in some respects indispensable, character. The impression from other documents of the time is that he didn't make the scene very much. He'd be there when he was wanted, and wouldn't keep dropping his hat, but until then, let's get our priorities right.

For the people, a touch of the ceremonial was timely. The isles in which the Prince from the Sea was now to marry were much battered. The islanders were digesting the doubtful fruits of victory. Their ways and customs included queueing for rationed bread in rationed clothes, then home to a fire of rationed coal and a rinse with rationed soap. Seamy times. Moreover, the new peace was beginning to feel brittle, even so soon. Our laughing Russian friends, after a brief period as human beings like the rest of us, were turning back into bears, and Truman and Uncle Joe—we'd really called him that in the jolly old days?—warned each other regularly in the front-page headlines. That photogenic mushroom that had seemed so hideously gratifying at its first appearance was losing its charm with bigger and better blasts over Bikini. And if Stalin hadn't got it yet, you could bet he was working on it. Present and future both looked rough, and an escape into Hans Christian Andersen was just right. Or, as an American reporter put it,

"The glamour of it all, in the midst of Britain's drab existence nowadays, has jerked millions out of their one-candlepower lives and tossed them into dreamland."

This was from an oddly backhanded article entitled "The Amazing Success Story of Young Philip Mountbatten," in a leftish organ called *P.M.* It continued:

> After being the wallflower in these royal nuptials Philip at last got a break. It took Napoleon many years to rise from corporal to emperor. But in a twinkling young Mountbatten has added to the hum-drum rank of Lieutenant the titles of Sir Philip, Your Lordship, and Your Grace.

Well, near enough. And a cartoon showed the bride, very tall, flourishing an attempt at a scepter more like a field marshal's baton and saying, "To love, cherish and *obey*. . . ." And the bridegroom, very small, looking apprehensively upwards. The likenesses were not good. It was the sort of comment to prompt his later disrelish for the press, though what would probably have annoyed him most was the way they'd got it all wrong.

The approach wasn't representative of American comment, which was mostly warm, if lacking the full ecstasy of the home and Commonwealth papers. *The New York Times* applauded "this welcome occasion for gaiety in grim England, beset in peace with troubles almost as burdensome as those of the war." And *The Herald-Tribune* wrote of "the way, which no egalitarian American can understand, that the British Crown binds together the British people." That was a point. The yelling throng on the sidewalks, though short on bread, joyously acclaimed the circus. God bless the happy couple. Let them eat cake.

There were a few dissenting voices, among them that of the Camden Town First Branch of the Amalgamated Society of Woodworkers. Buoyant on the tide of the first Labour administration since 1929, they cut out all the intermediate rubbish and wrote to the King direct. The CTFB of the ASW had passed a resolution:

> It wishes to remind you that any banqueting and display of wealth at your daughter's wedding will be an insult to the British people at the present time, and we consider that you would be well advised to order a very quiet wedding in keeping with the times. . . . May we also remind you that should you declare the wedding day a public holiday you will have a word beforehand with the London Master Builders' Association to ensure that we are paid for it.

The letter ended, properly enough, "I am Your Obedient Servant. . . ."

There were other letters, from individuals and bodies. They criticized the choice of processional route, deplored the expenditure on "food and fuel"—it's hard to see where the fuel came in, on a largely equestrian occasion, but petrol was an emotive commodity, and some correspondents, going off in the other direction, asked for a commemorative extra gallon or two to boost the nation's joy. There were those who warned sternly against the use of a checkrein on the Royal Greys. Somebody wanted an "amphibious bridge" (*sic*) erected to take overflow spectators. A gift of wedding cake was requested by "The Girls of Brompton Sanatorium." A widow from Chigwell would be pleased to have "a small seat (I only weigh eight stone) inside the Abbey," and the less ambitious Mr. Thomas Jackson, seventy-three, says he is too old to stand and would like special arrangements made for him on the route. Others write for "a few of Your Majesty's cigarettes" for celebration purposes. A lady composer submits a minuet for piano, violin, cello and harp (parts enclosed) to be played at the post-wedding ball, and would wish to know how it is received. Somebody offers to sell the King one of His Majesty's own wedding photographs, also one of great-grandmother Victoria in a broken frame, or would swap for a portrait of the present royal couple. (All get courteous replies, returning the proffered merchandise: "His Majesty would not wish to deprive . . .") A philatelist from Wakefield, Massachusetts, sends the King three self-addressed envelopes, to be mailed back on the wedding day with the specially designed franking—an intertwined E and P, with lovers' knots.

The engaged pair narrowly avoided a tribute from the London Passenger Transport Board—their photographs on billboards outside every tube station. The King and Queen were grateful, said the palace, "but would prefer that this scheme should not be proceeded with."

From a lady in Wales, to the bride:

> Dear Madam, I am getting married on the 28th November and if you have a dress to fit me I would be very grateful as I take W size 36 Bust and again thanking you from the Bottom of my heart . . .

There were many outraged letters on the announcement that the wedding ceremony would not be filmed. This was the King's personal decision. It's surprising how many things were, though whether as monarch or father of the bride it's sometimes not easy to see. When the matter of acceptable communications media was put to him, he wrote, on a tiny sheet of ruled scratch-pad, in hard-lead pencil and the round, unaffected hand familiar from the signature, "Photography and broadcast commentary, yes. No Filming or Television. G.R." (A BBC man, pressing the claims of the still infant TV service, had reminded the palace, with a puny foretaste of the omnipotence to come, that "we sent a man and a camera to South Africa to cover the royal tour.") However, the decision against filming was later reversed, which made the film people happy, or those of them who were found perches among the Gothic traceries; but the representatives of the printed word felt in the main hard done by, owing to the limited allocation of press seats, particularly for Commonwealth papers. Colonel the Hon. J. J. Astor, owner of *The Times* and president of the Commonwealth Press Union, wrote spiritedly to Sir Alan Lascelles, the King's private secretary. The Commonwealth countries, "to sustain the sense of the bonds that link them to the Throne, require abundant intelligence of all royal doings, conveyed to them by their own writers in an idiom to which they are accustomed. Many such writers have traveled thousands of miles for this express purpose . . ." (and then didn't get in, and were pardonably piqued). There had been no precedent since 1129 for "the wedding of an immediate heiress to the Throne," and none at all for the celebration of such an event on British soil. (He seems to have been going back to Matilda, daughter of Henry I.) Sir Alan's reply was sympathetic but regretful. The Abbey just wouldn't run to it.

No one, as far as the records show, tried to touch the Lieutenant. In any case, they knew from the papers that he was on only about £11 a week, and not even a wife's allowance yet.

It was no joke being an executive member of the Royal Household at this time. They hadn't only to stave off the seekers of boons—there were the generous hearts to be dealt with too. Loyal and lamentable poems poured in. The Long Island Broadcasting Association sent a purpose-made disc entitled "Salute to Romance," to help wile away the honeymoon. Offers to provide the honeymoon itself, mostly from America, were frequent arrivals on the heaped palace desks, calling for tactful rejection. (The Americans, commendably anxious to get their forms right, sometimes got a bit mixed with the adjectival-respectful, as when a Florida hotel, try-ing to hasten a decision, wrote, "Can Your Majesty advise whether acceptance will be made of our gracious offer?") And what do you say to the Llandaff and Monmouth Diocesan Association of Change Ringers, when they report "a complete peal of 5,040 changes of grandsire triples"? Some things, trivial on the face of it, had to be gone into with care. A Mr. Whigham, representing the Manors of Wormshill Bobbing Ayington and Bedmonton, sent a gold sovereign, with the information that it was the custom of the monarch to "levy an Aid," on the marriage of the eldest daughter. This set off a rare old scuttering through the constitutional ar-chives, with Home Office experts eventually called in for a ruling; it was possible only then to tell Mr. Whigham that the practice had ceased with the abolition of all feudal dues in 1662, and here was his gold sovereign back.

There were decisions where precedent was no help. The Lord Chamberlain reported to Sir Alan Lascelles a message from the office of Mr. Aneurin Bevan, Minister of Health: in support of his socialist principles he would "under no circumstances wear evening dress" at the Buckingham Palace wedding party to which he had been invited. (Deciding on those guest lists alone had been a Solomon-size problem.) Service dress, or evening dress with decorations, had been a royal command: would the King wish the Lord Chamberlain to communicate with Mr. Bevan on the subject, or to take no further action? Earlier monarchs might have paraded the Minister's head on a pike, but in this case Sir Alan replied, "His Majesty approves that no further action be taken in the matter."

Another member of the Government, whose view of these falderals might have been even cooler, was lifelong Socialist Eman-uel Shinwell, then Minister of War. He went the other way. But for him, the escorting soldiers on November 20 would have been in battledress, the drabbest costume known to the history of military uniform. "Manny" had read the papers and felt the common pulse. Ten days before the event he wrote to Lascelles:

> As you are aware, there is considerable agitation in the Press that, for the occasion of the wedding of Her Royal Highness the Princess Elizabeth, the Household Cavalry should be in full dress. I personally have some sympathy with this. I do not think it would be inconsistent with any of our principles, and I believe it would have public support. Until recently it was thought that there would be insufficient time for the Regiments to fit their clothing and rehearse for full dress. I understand now, however, that the Commanding Officer thinks he can get the Escorts ready in time. . . . Little or no extra expense will be involved, as clothing required by other ranks already exists in store, and those officers not in possession of their own full dress are able to borrow from ex-Household Cavalry Officers. . . ."

(The other ranks' clothing had been in store for eight years. So, no doubt, had the full dress of those ex-officers who were now so obligingly to shake the moths out. It all points up with some poignancy the plight of a victorious nation down on its uppers.) Shinwell went on:

> I would therefore be grateful if you would take His Majesty's pleasure. [Delicious phrase.] It is of course of the greatest importance that nothing should be said in public regarding the dress which will in fact be worn. The trials may be a failure.

But they weren't. In the end, there they were, the plumes, the breastplates, the blinding boots. It was inconceivable that they shouldn't be.

To be fair to Clement Attlee, whose sense of austerity was keen, and reinforced with skinflint zest by Stafford Cripps at the Treasury, he had heard and approved the Shinwell scheme for a brighter wedding. But he torpedoed a lobby to make the day a public holiday. "Present economic difficulties . . . these hard times . . . stoppage of work unwise . . . open to misconstruction . . ." He also seems to have been alert for any royal infringement of continuing wartime legislation. Clothes rationing was still on, and should apply as rigidly to a princess's bridal gown as to a prime minister's socks. At a purely social encounter, he mentioned to Lascelles a shocking rumor. Norman Hartnell, it was said, had used Lyons silk in the wedding dress; the buzz was that he didn't hold the required permit. Even if he did, would the people tolerate such a thing on this fiercely British occasion?

A top-level investigation was set afoot, and a report rushed to Downing Street. It cleared Hartnell and all concerned: the wedding dress indeed contained silk, which "originally emanated from Chinese silkworms, but was woven in Scotland and Kent." The train contained silk, but it was "produced by Kentish silkworms, and woven in London." The going-away dress contained four or five yards of Lyons silk (Ha!). But Mr. Hartnell just happened to have it in stock, from "a consignment held under permit."

While he was at it, Lascelles added a paragraph saying that he and his advisers were fully alive to the dangers of the whole bridal-gown position. The Keeper of the Privy Purse had just spotted a frightful blunder by the Board of Trade, which had recommended the purchase of accessories from a firm whose proprietor "only very recently became a British national." (Even more recently than the bridegroom? Not quite the same thing, perhaps.)

But these were minor skirmishes. The nuts and cranks broke over the in-trays in a steady tide, and included a lady who wrote in the first instance to the mayor of Winchester—he dutifully sends it on, a prolonged tirade against the entire Royal Family ending with a sudden twist: "Best wishes to you from the lawful Queen of England, commonly known as Mrs. E. M. Ottewell." On the main battlefront there were heavier engagements. Ecclesiastical troubles, for example. Leaving aside the Romford correspondent who wrote bluntly to "The King, Buckingham Palace," to say that "Fisher, the Archbishop of Canterbury, like his erstwhile predecessor Lang was, is a fraud and a humbug," and the protests against the possible use of the 1928 Prayer Book, the chief religious to-do was over the bar on Roman Catholic bishops, under the Ecclesiastical Titles Act of 1871, from marking the occasion by presenting loyal addresses to the King.

Everyone else seems to be presenting them, amid plenty of constitutional confusion on who should and who shouldn't, with elaborate consultings of precedent. Those officially entitled to do so are richly varied, from the Lords and the Commons to the Royal Academy and the Bank of England—and, naturally, the two primates of the Established Church. But then the thing mysteriously snowballs until official and unofficial bodies overlap indistinguishably, with addresses humbly submitted by the International Language Club, the Borough of Hove, the Chief Constables (Scotland) Association and—particularly wounding—the Methodist Church of Australasia, it was hardly surprising that the *Catholic Herald* burst out with its furious front-page story: CATHOLICS ALONE DEBARRED FROM PRESENTING LOYAL ADDRESS TO THE KING. There followed much energetic to-ing and fro-ing between the Home Secretary and Cardinal Griffin (then the Archbishop of Westminster), with the palace caught in the crossfire. Our man in Rome, at the British Legation to the Holy See, comes in on the sidelines to complain that the Pope's personal representative in England, the apostolic delegate, Archbishop Godfrey, is not to be invited to any of the wedding parties; the Pope is going to be "a little hurt," especially since His Holiness has given Her Royal Highness a present of twelve Meissen chocolate cups with saucers and covers "which the King has approved." (If the impression is that Lieutenant Mountbatten didn't get much of a look-in over all this, Princess Elizabeth also seemed to have a lot of things taken out of her hands.) This somewhat unsporting stratagem at least got the Archbishop an invitation. And eventually the 1871 Act was found to have a convenient flexibility: the Cardinal could present an address after all, on the understanding that his bishops didn't claim to be bishops *of* anywhere. The Lord Chamberlain and associates breathed again.

An earlier religious difficulty, and with a more personal bearing, had been put to the King by Dr. Geoffrey Fisher, Archbishop of Canterbury:

Sir,

There is a matter upon which I think I should consult Your Majesty. There was a paragraph in *The Times* which said that while Lieutenant Mountbatten was baptised into the Greek Orthodox Church he appears "always to have regarded himself as an Anglican." The same paragraph also misrepresented the relations between the Church of England and the Orthodox Church, but I need not trouble Your Majesty with that.

In the Church of England we are always ready to minister to members of the Orthodox Church and to admit to the Sacrament. No difficulty therefore arises of any sort on our side from the fact that Lieutenant Mountbatten was baptised into the Orthodox Church. At the same time, unless he is officially received into the Church of England he remains formally a member of the Greek Orthodox

Church, which, though on the closest and most friendly terms with us, is not able to enter into full communion with us. If it be true that Lieutenant Mountbatten has always regarded himself as an Anglican I suggest for Your Majesty's consideration that there would be an advantage if he were officially received into the Church of England. It can be done privately and very simply. It may be that you and the Princess Elizabeth would feel it more fitting and happy that he should thus have his position regularised as a member of the Church of England.

If Your Majesty agrees that the matter deserves consideration I will most willingly discuss it further with you, or, if Your Majesty thinks fit, with Lieutenant Mountbatten.

I am, Sir,

Your faithful servant,

Geoffrey Cantuar.

The Lieutenant might have been pleased to know that he was getting a mention, and four right off was certainly good going for a mere walk-on in the national spectacular. Most of those loyal addresses skipped him altogether, though the King's replies, helpfully drafted by the Home Office, would decently get him in as a secondary responder. It's true that King Frederick X of Denmark, a relation of the groom, proposed to make him an honorary lieutenant in the Danish Navy, seeking and receiving King George VI's approval, but it's not clear whether the recipient was consulted. King Frederick later came through with another nice gesture, offering to confer the Order of the Elephant on both bride and groom. Sir Alan Lascelles replied, to the Danish ambassador who had sprung this surprise, that "His Majesty was much touched by the proposal . . . and cordially approves it." (One of the myriad minor complications at the palace was the question of whether royal guests, in London for the wedding, should be permitted to confer awards and dignities on people looking after them during their stay. It was decided against, for some reason—possibly to reduce any air of outdated royal splash. But you have to watch the open-hearted Scandinavians. The King of Norway got in under everyone's guard and slapped a Knighthood of the Royal Order of St. Olav on his British ADC for the visit, Commander Colin Buist, RN. The first intimation of this was when the Norwegian Embassy, via the Foreign Office, sent the Commander's medal and diploma to Buckingham Palace for onward transmission, with a form of receipt for completion and return. Sir Alan's letter to the FO opened pleasingly: "By conferring a Knighthood of the Royal Order of St. Olav on Colin Buist, King Haakon has put us all in the kareol, which, if I recollect aright, is the Norwegian for cart. . . ." It's an agreeable example of the unstarched Lascelles style. When the music for the Abbey service was under discussion—much of it was largely governed, incidentally, by its suitable length for processions—he had written to the Dean of Westminster saying that Princess Elizabeth would like the Scottish metrical psalm *The Lord Is My Shepherd* sung to the tune "McRimmon." The Dean naturally enough replied that there was no such tune, "and I assume that she means 'Crimond.'" Sir Alan wrote back that he had no doubt that Her Royal Highness had got it right. "The responsibility for the *lectio varia* must rest with me, whose mind was probably running on bagpipes." Though Prince Philip, once initiated into the formalities of palace life, found a lot of them clogging and oppressive, he wasn't the first to liven exchanges with a lighter touch.)

After a fortnight the Archbishop got an answer. Even with the wedding only a few months off, you don't rush about. The King had arranged with Lieutenant Mountbatten to "have his position regularised." But it was early October before the news was slipped out by the Press Secretary, and then as an "intimation" rather than an announcement. There are subtleties. *The Times*

(47)

dutifully soft-sold it: "It is understood that Lieutenant Philip Mountbatten has recently been formally received into membership of the Church of England."

British citizenship, achieved on the last day of February 1947, had been more elusive than entry into the Anglican communion. The diviners of a royal romance saw the naturalization announcement as their vindication. Though the palace was still denying it, what else, asked the gossips, could it mean? He hadn't simply become British, he'd cleared the way for the marriage by renouncing his Greek rights of succession.

The truth was that the decision to become British had been taken long before, not with an eye to matrimony at the top but to a career in the Royal Navy. In his early days as a midshipman on the battleship *Ramillies,* Greece still being neutral in the first part of 1940, the Foreign Office could see awkwardnesses if a member of the Greek Royal House got himself blown up in British naval uniform. *Ramillies* was in safe waters, convoying Australian and New Zealand troops to Alexandria. Nor did later postings to the *Kent* and *Shropshire—Ramillies* having got inconveniently near to gunfire in the Mediterranean—provide the sort of war he wanted to be fighting: they, too, were convoying in the more serene latitudes (he left *Shropshire* at Durban). Even as far back as that he was making moves to become British. But he posed a bureaucratic puzzle. Ordinary aliens in the British forces could change allegiance with comparative ease. Princes were different. The Home Office, like the Foreign Office, had its hands full already, without untangling tiresome knots of this kind.

With the Italian invasion of Greece in October 1940, however, he was a legitimate combatant, and allowed to get nearer the action. Six months later he was mentioned in dispatches by Admiral Cunningham for his services at the searchlight controls in HMS *Valiant* during the Battle of Matapan, the Greek mainland's most southerly cape. It was a famous victory. It cost the Italians three cruisers, two destroyers and all hope of commanding that sea. He was nineteen, and not displeased by the recognition. King George of Greece hastened in with an award of his own, the Greek War Cross of Valor. Many people think he was unlucky not to bring a British gallantry decoration out of the war. He wasn't alone, of course, in that. But when it comes to decorating princes, those responsible may be sensitive to suspicions of favoritism.

Perhaps he felt English enough after all this not to worry, for the time being, about getting it in writing. It was three years later, after his appointment as first lieutenant on the *Whelp*, that he returned to the attack with another try. Again it was hung up, either in the confusion of wartime paper, or more deliberately. His influential uncle wrote from Southeast Asia to George VI in the hope of getting things moving, but was told that another king's pleasure should be taken. And George II of Greece, in retreat from his kingdom but still its king (his ministers were with him in London, and Greece's gold reserves in the Bank of England), wasn't too keen to lose his promising young cousin[1] from the roll of the Royal House. During the wartime wanderings to Crete, to Egypt, to South Africa, to London, George planned continuously, with Crown Prince Paul, to return to Athens. If it came off he would need all the family support he could get. By 1944, when he gave his consent, *Whelp* and her new first lieutenant were busy in Asian waters, and matters again lapsed.

So it was only in early 1947 that the ties of birth were at last cut, and the *London Gazette*'s list of more than eight hundred freshly adopted citizens, many of them German–Jewish refugees, others Poles who had fought the war in British uniform, included

---

[1] Because of Philip's late arrival in his parents' marriage there was an age difference of thirty-two years. King George was only seven years younger than Philip's father, Prince Andrew, and must practically have ranked as an uncle.

the name of Prince Philip—not to be seen again, in that style, until February 1957; from the marriage until then he'd been the Duke of Edinburgh, a form to which his office at Buckingham Palace still clings.

To take the name Mountbatten seemed to most people an obvious move, but it was never so for him. A surname had to be found. He'd never had one. Once when he hired a car, on leave in Australia, and the garage objected that he'd signed for it with a plain "Philip," he hardly put their minds at rest by adding "Prince of Greece." But they rented him the car.

(An autograph hunter at Gordonstoun, during Philip's schooldays there, got a signature even less convincing: "Baldwin of Bewdley." His disinclination to sign his name as a collector's piece, except in a formal visitor's book, was there long before he qualified for the convention that British royalty doesn't give autographs. It comes from an abhorrence of being regarded as a "celebrity," most hollow of twentieth-century accolades. Lunching one day at St. George's House, Windsor, he allowed the menu cards, circulated in the usual fashion for the company's commemorative signatures, to pile up beside his coffee cup. The warden, an admirable man, but new, assumed that the guest of honor was too deep in conversation to notice, and leaned across asking him to sign and pass on. "I'm not a pop star," was all he got. Bad luck. Know better next time. Or there was the occasion of an official day with a RAF station in Germany. It had been a success throughout. Clockwork organization, impeccable displays, lots of laughs in the mess and the CO warmly conscious of a great show and golden opinions—until at the last moment, on the departure tarmac, he confidently presented a copy of the day's program for a signature. Ice formed. "This is not usual," said the visiting marshal. There was a hushed count of ten before he got a pen out, signed and boarded without another word.)

Somewhere back up that knotted family tree there had been

German Dukes of Oldenburg. The College of Heralds, putting their best men on the job, plucked out this possibility, and suggested its anglicization into Oldcastle. Lieutenant Oldcastle? Well, we might have accepted it in time. But suddenly sprung on a starry-eyed public it could have lacked the looked-for ring. Mr. Chuter Ede, Home Secretary, told the bride's father that he felt "something grander and more glittering" could be found. Interesting, from a Socialist minister. Besides, it wouldn't have taken the papers long to worry it back to its German origins. With the Luftwaffe's scars still visible, and the trials at Nuremberg barely over, it wasn't going to match too harmoniously with Windsor.

What about Mountbatten? Its origin as Battenberg was old history, so that should be all right. The most illustrious present bearer was the King's cousin and a blinding popular hero. Though this was perhaps why Philip, as he now says, "wasn't madly in favor." He was always a jealous guardian of his own self-sufficiency; the famous uncle and the promising nephew, as an easy image, was already getting plenty of play, and this could clinch things uncomfortably. "But in the end I was persuaded, and anyway I couldn't think of a reasonable alternative." Official records show that the choice of name was approved by the King on the advice of Chuter Ede. Where Chuter Ede got his advice from needn't puzzle anyone much. One commentator wrote that "when Philip of Greece became Philip Mountbatten, Uncle Dickie was delighted." No doubt. But the suggestion of gratified surprise was overdoing it a bit.

For a few weeks after Elizabeth became Queen she kept the surname of Mountbatten. But in April 1952 it was declared in Council that she, her children and descendants, except for females who married, should be called Windsor. It was a change that the King had set afoot before he died, in discussion with Sir Winston Churchill through Sir Alan Lascelles. Prince Philip had his own ideas, that the change of patrimony could be met by the title "Family of Windsor of the House of Edinburgh." They didn't appeal. But he didn't fight to keep the Mountbatten.

Eight years later there was another twist, with the announcement, just before Prince Andrew's birth, that certain descendants of the Queen, notably the grandchildren of her younger sons, should be Mountbatten–Windsors. Prince Philip again was not the originator, and the ins and outs of it all are better left to the constitutional historians. Whatever the source, a Declaration in Council made it official on February 8, 1960, producing the usual onslaught on the palace press office, which said that the Queen had for some time wanted her husband's name to enjoy perpetuation. Of course. It's hard not to think, all the same, that when the first Mountbatten–Windsors appear—two generations hence, at the earliest—the Mountbatten part will somehow conjure up Louis rather than Philip. Said the *Daily Express:* "One spectre has always confronted Earl Mountbatten of Burma: that his family name should not die out." (It won't, in fact. By what's known to genealogists as Special Remainder it will descend through the female line.)

But even the *Express* didn't dig up, as the *Mail* did, the Earl's father: "Prince Louis of Battenberg, whose name did not then ring sweetly in British ears . . ." The "then" was 1917. It was certainly going back a bit.

However, little of this fuss and fury was around to put a damper on the wedding day. November 20, 1947, went off with our usual flawless instinct for pageantry. The sun didn't shine, but the rain didn't actually fall. The happy pair clearly qualified for the cliché. Elizabeth's smile had an added ingredient, as with all new wives who have their husbands firmly by the arm. Philip's was proud, delighted and perhaps slightly relieved. It wasn't just that he'd come unscathed through the Scararium, but after all those huge doings in high places that had left him on the outside looking in, he was finally on the inside looking out. Not counting instant additions by marriage, about twenty-five of his relations got seats at the wedding breakfast, largely majesties and highnesses.

There were ten thousand telegrams of congratulation from, among others, Admiral Halsey, Charles de Gaulle, the mayor of Sutton Coldfield and the Chinese Navy. And enough letters and messages from ordinary people, movingly warm, to sink the Royal Barge. Nothing from the Camden Town Woodworkers.

We flew to Greenland, six takeoffs and landings. Mostly in snow. Early February, no time to be skirting the ice cap, and I thought of the arctic survival kit they'd shown me at the Queen's Flight. I could manage the quilted parka, knee boots, white stockings, snow goggles and mitts, perhaps even the self-igniting fire pellets. I wasn't so sure about the animal snare and hunting knife (with whetstone in case of blunting on too many bears), and I'd already decided to stick close to HRH if we skidded to an unscheduled halt. I could see him snaring animals right and left, ending up with enough skins to start a trading post. From what I'd heard, he would also take care of the cooking.

He did most of the flying, with time off to come aft and eat, or get through another chapter of *The Optimum Population for Britain* (Institute of Biology Symposium No. 19). At Storneway, first refueling, he strolled with his co-pilot, tut-tutting at the place where an earlier arrival's nose wheel had strayed over the frost-stiff grass. It wouldn't have done for the Duke. Then they began the usual fliers' reminiscences of engine failures and radar breakdowns, and I moved away, checking that the fuel was going in all right.

Three hours later, Keflavik, with snowplows on the next runway just about holding their own against the blizzard. Cheerful greetings for the Icelandic chef de protocol (even for a half-hour stop, royalty has to make a courtesy contact with the representative of a foreign country), the British ambassador and the US admiral in command, who drives us off to meet his wife and family. The central heating is stupefying. Lots of hospitable coffee, as always.

"More coffee?" murmurs HRH, but privately. "My stomach's washing about like a snipe-bog." On parting, the admiral presents an emblazoned cigarette lighter, which his nonsmoking guest accepts with convincing delight.

It was gusty and −25°C. when he put us down at Sondrestrom, Greenland ("You have to come in here with one wing scraping the rock face"), and the exhausts of the waiting cars belched white clouds over the smiles, handshakes and introductions. The base commander showed us to our overnight quarters at five o'clock, their time, with directions where to join him in the bar as soon as we'd had a wash. "Should we make it about six?" said HRH. Fourteen hours since Heathrow, it seemed a good idea to put the feet up. I was getting my shoes off when he looked in to report with some glee that his NO SMOKING IN BED notice next door had a rider saying "Violators Will Be Prosecuted." So had mine, but I'd missed it, being past putting funny interpretations on USAF fire warnings.

In the bar, at six, it turned out that instead of putting his feet up he'd written an article on pollution, promised three days earlier when he'd flown to Strasbourg for the European Conservation Conference. He saw nothing out of the way in this, except for a mild amusement that it would be printed in eighteen languages. The commander, a merciless man, broke the news that the American and Danish communities who share that glacial outpost (they tend the Distant Early Warning system) had organized a slap-up dinner for about eighty in the Duke's honor, and we should soon be thinking about moving.

It was certainly a great night, for those who didn't feel like nodding off in the soup. The toasts were many, and mostly frivolous. It's the Scandinavian way to bounce up, shout "Skol!" and get off the latest one about the Swede, the Dane and the Norwegian. Though I was glad to see none of my pilot's wine-glasses went down much below the level of first pouring—we were due out at nine in the morning for Ottawa, and I like a steady hand at the controls—he eventually got up and told the best story of the evening all the same.

We retired at two, by a London-based metabolism, and at breakfast he was well to the front of the cafeteria queue, collecting his pancakes, beef hash and the toast that burped from its mechanized dispenser with an inconsiderately loud twang. He rocked the table with an account of ceremonial feasts in Fiji, demonstrating a native delicacy that expanded to fill the mouth and then proved indestructible. It was courageous even to try for a laugh among all those tender heads from the night before. To get it was a triumph.

4

The Name of the Game

"I look at it as a job, and I imagine I do it at much the same pressure that I would do any other job."

William Blake had a word: "Energy is eternal delight." So it is for those endowed, but even to see it in full fizz can be exhausting, like watching acrobats; and those who rush around with Prince Philip learn to live briskly, eat fast and have the answers ready. His engagement cards are annotated (S), (T) or (E), meaning that his secretary, treasurer or equerry will be present. They split the commitments, but he does all of them. His two detectives and two valets are turn-by-turn.

His foibles sometimes madden, more often amuse, seldom alienate affection, never reduce respect. He is always "Sir" to his face, and to third parties "Prince Philip" or "P.P." at a pinch. He has no nickname among his staff, or familiar reference, but is the pervading topic, and their whole preoccupation is to smooth his path. If they mess up the arrangements, and say so before the event, he's likely to laugh first, and then see how things can be put right. To leave it until it happens doesn't go so well. If he's sharp for no reason, he'll find a way of saying something at the next encounter that has the flavor of an apology if not the form. Among the staff's few complaints is his general taking for granted, the calm assumption that the cars will be there, the airways cleared for takeoff, the bags packed, the uniforms laid out. They usually are, but he isn't pleased if they aren't. He knows perfectly well what goes into all this. "The trouble is that I'm spoilt—everything's nearly always right, so the odd occasion when they go wrong is more noticeable. . . . I get just as angry with myself if I make a mistake or do something silly."

Perhaps because there are so many practical things to be done, he hasn't a lot of use for the half-thought or floating reflection, and tends to seize the substance of it and worry it into a debate. There's a pragmatism, in the Greek sense. He wrote in 1970:

> I think on the whole it is better to start by taking a factual and realistic view of any given problem, because it is worse than useless to apply moral principles from a position of ignorance, or with a complete disregard for the practical consequences.

It says a lot about his general approach, though here he was in fact discussing ecological matters.[1] Sloppy thinking and infirm arguments come in for prompt demolition, often with the dry laugh

---

[1] It was in his long contribution to the book *Wildlife Crisis*, where he combined a lot of hard thinking with entertaining personal stuff about photographing birds and animals. (Anyone who thinks that the conservation problem looked like everybody's bandwagon that year might remember that he'd been worrying about it since 1961, as an international trustee of the World Wildlife Fund and president of the British National Appeal. And those who can't reconcile these interests with his shooting might read what he says about it in the book.)

quite different from the outbursts of true mirth and soon identified as a danger signal. "No, hold on a minute"—and the accusing forefinger stabs out. He's tenacious and often perverse in argument, but faced with supporting facts can yield gracefully. He said one day to Jumbo Thorning, his number one policeman, and often his companion (Leaving the plane at Mexico City, I was interested to see that they both kissed the waiting Merle Oberon.) that he'd been seriously thinking of taking a royal bicycle, instead of the royal Rolls, from Buckingham Palace to Windsor, to beat the traffic snarls. He dislikes having roads cleared for him, unless ceremonial demands it; thinks you can work strenuously for an acceptable public image, then ruin it by mewing up innocent motorists while you roll past in privilege.

"You could do London to Windsor in an hour and a half on a bicycle."

"Two hours," said Thorning.

"Two hours? Nonsense."

"No, Sir."

"Why do you say that?"

"I've done it, Sir."

"When?"

"Last year."

"Why?"

"You'd mentioned at the time the idea of cycling. I got a bike and tried it. Twenty-six miles, Sir. Two hours."

A roar of laughter. Pleased. "Oh, all right, then."

Beyond the call of duty. If it hadn't come up it wouldn't have been mentioned.

You have to be sure of your case to hold out like that. He's sometimes oversure of his. "Spanish is the easiest language, it's pronounced just as it's written." (Fine, if you're English, but supposing you're Chinese?) "If it hadn't been for all that so-called security, Jack Kennedy wouldn't have been assassinated." (But,

Sir . . . ?) Still, that one was born of his distaste for police protection—his detectives are the Home Office's idea—and of the not
too practicable wish to be treated like anyone else when he goes
about his business.

He says that he's a fund of useless information. (The European
buffalo is *not* extinct, it's conserved in Poland; the only genuine
Liebfraumilch is really Liebfrauenmilch, and without the *en* it's a
fake.) None of it is really useless for the sort of life he lives. He's
expected to know something about everything. If he knows less
than he appears to, he's the first to say so. He claims it's a trick.
Produce a bit of their own jargon and they think you know the lot.

If it's a trick, it's a neater one than that. Confronted with the
top space eggheads at Cape Kennedy he was firmly on their wavelength. Lecturers inviting questions got them in abundance. "Is
it a passive dish?" "How do you retransmit all this?" "Supposing there's a telemetry failure?" "When do you lock on to the
S-Band?" "So the attitude control system gives you a slight Delta
B?" "But aren't these frequencies preselected?" "I take it the
solid fuel burns faster at the bottom than the top?"

But he'd toured Houston on an earlier trip, and picked up useful
hints for this one. Even earlier, astronauts Armstrong, Aldrin
and Collins had splashed down at Buckingham Palace for a chat.
He'd have used them for Houston. Granted it's more specialized
than the knowledgeable chat at cattle shows or management training centers, but the pattern is the same. You ride halfway with
the lord lieutenant, the next half with the lord mayor and by the
time you come to inaugurate the docks, or present the cup, you
can amaze the platform party by knowing all about the local row
over bus-shelter design.

Or you carry the gleanings from one engagement and display
them at the next. Shortly after that management center visit he
was with British Army units in Germany, confounding them with
advanced notions for re-jigging the administration. There was no

point in saying he'd pinched it all from somewhere else. "No, hold on a minute, there's a better way of doing this." When he finally moved up to the flight deck of the aircraft (shedding his field marshal's regalia on the way, while his valet put him into a tweed jacket and scooped up the discards), the saluting brass would be reflecting anew on his remarkable talent for getting to the nub of things. Whether they did any re-jigging is another matter, but they would feel, with the director of studies at the management center, that they had "greatly enjoyed having His Royal Highness, and found his visit a tonic to the organisation and a boost to staff morale."

If you can keep doing even that for a quarter of a century, averaging three hundred engagements a year in all corners of life, you're earning your pay, whatever republican-minded members may say when the Civil List comes up for parliamentary scrutiny.

He also has to be socially agreeable, whether he feels like it or not, remembering that what, for him, may be just another hat factory, refinery, bankers' luncheon, British Week in Helsinki or display by the Girl Nautical Cadets of Kingston, Ontario, may be a once in a lifetime glimpse at the receiving end. He's good in crowds, remembers to smile up at the top windows, and excellent with children. "How did you cut your knee?" (There's always a cut knee.) Besides, there are the ever-present cameras to record a moment of sagging interest, and directional microphones to pick up what wasn't meant to be picked up. He could play it safe and not go. "There's no reason," said one of his staff, looking out over a Florida beach, "why he shouldn't spend most of his time lying around in places like this." Why exhaust yourself, stumping the country and the world? A year's mileage comes out at about 75,000. Say 1500 by sea, 2500 by train, 6000 by road and 65,000 by air. Not a lot on foot, though his 1969 New York program had an item: "His Royal Highness walks to the dining room of the Waldorf Astoria Towers." He doesn't like walking, and time

(*61*)

won't allow it, but as he was in the hotel already, apart from a sedan chair it was the only way.

He could cut most of it out. Accompany the Queen on essential fixtures, otherwise get lumbered with as little as possible. Drop those speeches, which so often annoy by actually saying something, or at least let somebody else write them, then all you have to do is recite the neutered clichés and avoid the scandalized headlines: "Duke Angers Drainage Men." "Philip in Tinned Fruit Uproar." Better say nothing at all, in fact. When a lady in New Zealand told him on the 1970 visit that she hadn't been back home to England for thirty years, he said, cheerfully, "You're missing very little." (What would you have said, apart from nothing, as you pressed on through the mob?) On the Sunday it made the front page of *The People*. "What DID Philip Mean?"

Prince Philip was in the centre of a new storm last night after making a remark which apparently knocked Britain.

Angry Labour MPs wanted to know just what he meant when he told a woman . . .

The MPs, telephoned for their views on something they hadn't even heard about, were hand-picked for predictable quotes. "If he doesn't like it here he doesn't have to stay." "If Prince Philip decided to settle in New Zealand we'd miss him very little." Even the single Tory, brought in for a show of fair play, bungled his defense by agreeing that this wasn't a happy country, and the harder people worked the more they were taxed. (The Socialists were still in office at the time.)

It's a bit difficult. To become a royal cipher, in a new sense, might seem tempting. He's obsessed instead with making what he calls "a sensible contribution." It's greater than it need be, but that's his own fault. Those around him are fondly resigned by now, including the Queen. "I gave up trying to stop him years ago."

After all, there's no productivity norm laid down. He invented the game, and made his own rules. Its prize is the satisfaction of his own standards.

Creating the job in the first place wasn't easy. He had to prepare the ground, with some care, in which the sensible contribution could seed and flourish. The crusted old operators at Court, tending the constitutional juggernaut, closed their ranks around it, hoping to rumble on without a lot of tinkering from a newcomer for whom there was literally no place.[2] It was less distressing for them at first, when they only had the husband of the Princess to contend with. When she became Queen they could see real trouble. It was their duty and privilege to advise her, as they had advised the King, and the sudden arrival of an energetic assistant, with plentiful ideas of his own, was alarming.

It should be said that he was as sensitive to their situation as he was to his own, and, contrary to what is sometimes suggested, took his first steps into their territory with care and consideration. He knew that the death of the King had been a brutal blow, and that they were feeling badly shaken. He leaned over backward not to come the new broom. His suggestions and innovations weren't designed to establish himself as a new force to be reckoned with, but to help the Queen with some commonsense streamlining. Inevitably it meant hollowing out a place of his own big enough to swing the ideas in. (You can imagine the diplomacy needed in National Productivity Year 1962, persuading the old guard to let a team of business efficiency experts go through the palace. Heads of departments had to be assembled and talked around, with assurances that no one would be sacked. In fact the opposite happened, which he recalls with huge amusement—pay went up, and about six more people came on the strength. Cartoonists had a ball with

---

[2] After the Accession there was a minor skirmish over the question of a second throne in the House of Lords for the ceremonial openings of Parliament. It was eventually conceded. Until then he'd had to stand.

the whole exercise, and the *News of the World* comment still hangs in one of the palace washrooms.)

It was all part of the adjustment that began on November 20, 1947. Adjustment from the single to the married state is delicate in all circles, and in this one, with a bride long palisaded by protocol, it called for special skills, and not only from him. His knack of breezing headfirst into any company and taking it over wasn't at first easy to catch on to, and though the Queen even now retains something of her natural reserve, his self-sufficiency has rubbed off liberally, and her latent sense of the comic, not given much chance in the sheltered days, has been brought much nearer the surface. (She has a lively gift of anecdote, especially of observed behavior, and enjoys, with Charles and Anne, embroideries of dialect.) Even so, those Australian walking tours in 1970 weren't as effortless as they looked, and Prince Philip was behind her not only in terms of precedence, but was devotedly bolstering.

Adjustment to the marriage was nothing compared with adjustment to the Accession. His elder sister, Margarita, remembers being at Clarence House, still his home then, during the two days after George VI's funeral. He was in a black depression, and could hardly be got to stir from his room. "You can imagine what's going to happen now," he said. After Clarence House, which was truly a home, and the scene of much laughter despite the inevitable "office" tucked away at the back, the move to Buckingham Palace was a depressing prospect.[3] It had been bound to come sooner or later. This was too soon. The death of the King at fifty-seven, even despite the ominous pointer of his illnesses, was a depth charge.

---

[3] They'd wanted to keep Clarence House as a domestic refuge, after Elizabeth became Queen, using the palace as a work place (which it is). Winston Churchill was immovably against it.

What was going to happen now? For himself there could be near-extinction as an individual under the grinding constitutional millstone. He had been head of the family, in the ordinary, comfortable sense. "Within the house, and whatever we did, it was together. I suppose I naturally filled the principal position. People used to come to me and ask me what to do. In 1952 the whole thing changed, very, very considerably."

It was only partly as head of the family that he wanted to handle things. He simply felt that he was the one who should bear the weight of the decisions. From the Accession, private matters apart, there was the dismal certainty that all would fall on the Queen. Desperately anxious to ease the load, he had no entitlement to do so, and the courtiers were far from keen that he should. It was natural enough. It was their pride and joy to deal directly with the new monarch, as they had with the old. But the King had had a Queen to help him. The new Queen was out on her own, at least in matters of State. Her husband, rational and practical, found it absurd that the system wasn't equipped to adjust from a male to a female monarch:

> Because she's the Sovereign, everybody turns to her. If you have a King and a Queen, there are certain things people automatically go to the Queen about. But if the Queen is also the *Queen,* they go to her about everything. She's asked to do much more than she would normally do, and it's frightfully difficult to persuade . . ." [he hesitates, wanting to put it fairly]. Many of the Household . . . the fact that they report to the Queen is important to them, and it's frightfully difficult to persuade them not to go to the Queen, but to come to me.

He persuaded them where he could, and it took time, caution and a curb on natural impatience to make a few inroads (at least he managed to take over the management of the estates). But exclusion from the inner shrines of procedure meant that he also had to carve out a personal subkingdom if he didn't want all that energy running to waste.

Would he like to participate in the mysteries? It doesn't arise. One of those hypothetical questions that exasperate him. He can't, so there it is. Privately, he's probably not too sorry to be excluded from some of them. Though appointed to the Privy Council, for instance, just before the King's death, he doesn't attend. As its business is purely formal, with no discussion, there are more useful things to do. He's against the continuance of any system beyond its practical usefulness, unless, that is, it can adapt to the new times. An example is the monarchy itself, and his own part in nudging it toward flexibility can't be denied, least of all by those who want it to stay muscle-bound. Adapt and preserve. "Most of the monarchies in Europe," he told a TV audience in America, "were really destroyed by their greatest and most ardent supporters. It was the most reactionary people who tried to hold on to something without letting it develop and change."

An old unknown quantity is bound to creep into the equation between the Prince and the Queen: x is for Albert. Prince Philip, before his marriage, and looking, as he then thought, far ahead, read all he could find on the husband of great-great-grandmother Victoria, but perhaps without discovering any very useful parallels. Prince Albert was Consort, Prince Philip is not—at least in any officially proclaimed sense. It isn't too clear, in any case, what Consort means. It's often assumed that it entitled Albert to put his spoke in the wheel of State, see the "boxes," advise on policy, draft documents for the Queen's signature. When King Louis Philippe of France stayed at Windsor in 1844, he by no means treated Albert as a mere matrimonial appendage (though public and political opinion at the time could have wished that he was). "Le Prince Albert," he told his hostess, "*c'est pour moi le roi.*"

Victoria, confident of her preeminence next to God, might by expectation have had him thrown the length of the Grand Corridor. Instead, she was delighted. "How lively, how sagacious!" she said later of the departing guest.

But Albert's constant presence at her elbow had little to do with his being Consort. She hadn't anyone else to help her. No private secretary, with assistants, and office, and clerical staff. Her ministers, in a limited way, were her secretaries, but only for their own departments. Who more deliciously acceptable as managing director than an adored husband and lover? Long before he revealed his executive gifts, she had noted, in her diary, his "exquisite nose," "delicate moustachios," "beautiful figure." It was business with pleasure.

In Philip's case, as far as we know, such rapturous moonings were left to the papers (at least before they switched to panic speculations on whether his hair was getting thin, or what right he had to speak his mind when he felt like it). He himself has certainly no delusions of majesty. Though letters from people who should know their forms better sometimes open with the thundering superscription "Sire," he probably doesn't even notice. Anyway, the margin doesn't carry one of those pencil scribbles— "Clot!" "Chump!" "Rot!"—that so often garnish his incoming correspondence.

"Your grandfather was a king," said an American interviewer, "your great-great-grandmother was a queen, your wife is a queen. Have you ever thought, maybe it would be nice to be king? Or have you thought, I'm glad I'm not king?"

Pause. Then, amused, "Oh, I'm glad I'm not."

"Why wouldn't you like to be king?"

"Well, I'm not. It's a hypothetical question."

"You mean you're making the best of your present lot?"

"Oh, yes. But I would anyway."

It's a dead-end job, and you'd think him the last man to be

happy in that, but he's made it a job in its own right, and at fifty he's happy in it on the whole. The adjustment is as much of an achievement as any of its subordinate parts.

His overriding concern, despite the necessary and carefully constructed personal world, is for the Queen. He is always anxious for her, and never more touchy with press, police or public than when he thinks she may be harassed or embarrassed. His bossy moments during the walking tours down-under weren't on his own behalf but hers. This isn't to say he doesn't shoot off private rockets—the pressures behind them are seldom allowed for—but he's much more likely to be on edge for her sake than his own. It was something that surprised the makers of the film *Royal Family*. Though he'd had a large hand in the planning, was vigorously in favor of the project and sparking with intelligent suggestions, he had periods of pronounced sulkiness during the shooting (it went on for a year, by fits and starts, which couldn't have helped in a busy life). The unit had expected the Queen to be stiff and difficult, which she wasn't; she'd get in and out of uniforms and on and off horses with inexhaustible patience and cheerfulness. But HRH, whom they'd expected to be relaxed and easy, was neither, at any rate in the early stages, before he'd seen that the Queen had taken to it, and was going to do the part proud.

He also hated, as always, having to "perform." To sit at his desk making imitation telephone calls with no one at the other end isn't his idea of getting on with life as he understands it.

His watchfulness for the Queen has been there ever since the wedding. If he didn't feel sorry for her, and to put it as high as that is to distort the whole relationship, he felt deeply that an accident of birth had let her in for a tough life. Even as Princess, already launched on the taxing round of public engagements, she would need help and encouragement, someone to lean on. As Queen, though the time then seemed comfortably distant, she'd need the infusions of confidence and admiration even more.

These he felt from the first that he could, and passionately wanted to, provide. He felt it with vocational conviction, and has provided them, when the dragon of protocol hasn't barred the way, ever since. Much of his wretchedness on the King's death was because he knew there would now be other helpers by the drove, and a shattering separation of activities.

He had a choice between just tagging along, the second handshake in the receiving line, or finding other outlets for his bursting energies. In the event, he's brought off an astonishing compromise. He goes where the Queen can't go, meets people she can't meet, does things she can't do, hears things she can't hear—and brings it all back—not only to particularize, with all the up-to-date data on fruit imports, afforestation, the armed forces, drug addiction, fishing rights, Finland, the state of the Church, or what you will, but as a fountain of general knowledge about the country and the world that a king and queen between them couldn't acquire. He can act, in the words of Michael Parker,[4] "as a kind of super Chief of Staff who can give her the complete lowdown on absolutely anything."

Comparatively, the Queen's own life is narrow. Apart from the occasional escape, if that's the word, into heavily programed overseas visits, it's governed by the oppressive limitations of a monarch's cans and can'ts. People complain, and even her husband teases, because her only publicized personal interests seem to be dogs and horses. It can't be helped. Their world is harmlessly nonsectarian. Good works apart, she can't be openly associated with other single elements in the nation's life without seeming to lend them the invidious patronage of the Crown. But he can prod the working parts of the whole system, and offend only the captious few. Not all of it's fun. Quite a bit is. What of it? If

---

[4] Lieutenant-Commander Michael Parker, CVO, RN (Retd), their joint equerry from 1947 to 1952, and Prince Philip's private secretary from then until early 1957.

we can't get a laugh out of the daily bread, it's a pretty poor out-look.

There's a well-worried old bone. Does he discuss with the Queen those things which constitutionally he shouldn't discuss at all? No one will ever know, without asking the only two people who wouldn't say. It's a question that his innumerable interviewers put somewhere near the top of the list, and if the list's submitted in advance a member of his staff will helpfully remove it, thus saving breath all around. Still, it's no crime to guess. Anything can come up, after all, when you get a couple of Privy Councilors together over the breakfast table.

"I suppose they know I was born a Prince of Greece, but one impression that I think needs to be corrected is that the whole of my life has been spent here, and that I was brought up by Lord Mountbatten, neither of which is true. This impression that I've lived here all my life, and that I'm a Mountbatten, which of course I'm not. I mean, I'm a Mountbatten in exactly the same way that everybody else is half mother and half father, but normally speaking you're concerned with the father's family. I don't think anybody thinks I had a father. Most people think that Dickie's my father anyway."

I said, "Well, everyone tends to suggest that your father was always busy fighting wars, and that you hardly ever saw him."

"That's not true. He never fought a single war after I was born. He was in exile for the rest of his life. I grew up very much more with my father's family than I did with my mother's. And I think they're quite interesting people. They're the sort of people that haven't been heard of much."

CHAPTER

5

Uneasy Heads

"Where is the human being who ever conferred a
benefit on Greek or Greeks?"
—Byron, in a note to
CHILDE HAROLD'S PILGRIMAGE (1812)

If, at the time of his marriage, he was still wondering just what he was getting into, he probably had a fair idea, as between British royalty and Greek, what he was getting out of. This isn't to say that he didn't feel his roots strongly. Pulling them up was painful. But he was putting them down again in a new stability. Despite the currently fashionable auguries of change and decay, the British monarchy displays a defiant durability. Somebody once shot at Victoria—and missed, which seemed only natural. There was a nasty hiccup over Edward VIII. (And the Family, George VI most of all, found the episode deeply painful, particularly its rather jubilant handling by the papers.) But on the whole the successions

(72)

succeed, the crown passes and palace and people are content to get through history in each other's company. The occupants of the Greek throne have had a rockier ride, from Philip's grandfather, George I, to his latest successor, and Philip's cousin once removed, Constantine II—or XIII, as some dedicated delvers name him, perhaps attracted by the unlucky number—dislodged by the colonels in 1967.[1]

Exile is a Latin word, but if vocabularies had more recently been in the making it might suitably have been a Greek one. It sounded a recurring knell in Athens, though George I himself never heard it. ("No one who has not trodden that *Via Dolorosa*," wrote his son Nicholas—like all the other sons, daughters and families, he was to go in and out of banishment like a shuttle—"can understand the bitterness of being deprived of one's home and, above all, one's native land.") George stuck it out grittily from 1863 to 1913, through wars, attempts on his life, party feudings, pressure from the powers and the queasy heavings of Balkan politics,[2] always with a deep and even fanatical devotion to his people.

They weren't, in any ethnic sense, his people at all. A Dane, born Prince William of Denmark, he was nominated King of the Hellenes by the greater nations of Europe. The Greeks, although they'd just dethroned a previous outside nominee, Otto of Bavaria, during his ill-advised absence on a sea voyage, still relished their new taste for kingship after four centuries under the Turks, and had at first mysteriously set their sights on Prince Alfred, Duke of Edinburgh, Victoria's second son. She wasn't having any. She didn't fancy the idea of a Prince of the Royal House going the same way as Otto. The Russians had candidates. So had France. The compromise on the eighteen-year-old Willy of Denmark suited her

---

[1] The earlier Constantines, one to eleven, ended in 1453, when the Greeks entered into their four hundred years of Turkish domination. The twelfth, had he so chosen, would have been Philip's uncle, crowned as Constantine I.

[2] Those Balkans! Their names today, for most people, mean football teams.

better. There would be British influence there. His sister Alexandra was newly married to the Prince of Wales, much, much later to be Edward VII.

Nor did Russia mind Willy. He was a remote Romanov connection. The French had hopes of the lad's malleability. The Greeks themselves, though not seriously consulted, see-sawed for a time; but at least there was the English link, and Byron's memory was still green. The scale was finally tipped by a free gift, taped to the royal package: with Prince William, once he became King George (a nod to the patron saint of Greece), would go the return, by Britain, of the seven Ionian Islands. So the new Greek Royal House was founded by a boy who had had no immediate thoughts of crowns and scepters, and had never seen a Greek. He made the obedient round of his sponsors—in London a briefing from Gladstone, at Fontainebleau a cautionary word from Napoleon III—and was led, as it seemed, to the slaughter. Horace Rumbold, the British chargé d'affaires in Athens, was present as Willy took the oath in the Athenian Assembly:

> The sight of this slight, delicate stripling, standing alone amidst a crowd of callous, unscrupulous politicians, many of whom had been steeped to the lips in treason, and swearing to observe the most unworkable of charters, was indeed painful and saddening. . . .

But he learned Greek, loved the Greeks and stayed for nearly half a century, until one of them shot him in the back in Salonika, in March 1913, at the end of a victorious war. A man of character. Grandfather, though he never lived to know it, of Prince Philip, born eight years later, in 1921, on the island of Corfu, greenest of the package-deal Ionians.

George's son, Constantine I, was twice exiled, first in 1917, when the Allied powers bundled him out and installed his old po-

His father was Prince Andrew Greece, fourth son of King Geor I. A professional soldier. His moth was Princess Alice of Battenber great-granddaughter of Queen Vi toria. "I think they're quite inte esting people."
(*Radio Times Hulton Pictu Library*)

Above: Mon Repos, Corfu. Born here, with no public acclamation, June 10, 1921.
Below: A year later, his first visit to London, when his mother attended the wedding of her younger brother, Lord Louis Mountbatten.
(Radio Times Hulton Picture Library)

His parents in London, December 1922, after Andrew had been tried for his life by the Greek rebel government and brought to safety by the intervention of his cousin, King George V.
(*Radio Times Hulton Picture Library*)

His father's father, George I of Greece.
(*Radio Times Hulton Picture Library*)

His mother's father, Prince Louis of Batt
(*Radio Times Hulton Picture Library*)

Above left: With his mother, Princess Andrew (her favorite photograph). And with his cousin Michael. King of Rumania, beside the Black Sea near Constanza, *below left.*
(The Press Association)

Schoolboy at Gordonstoun. (*Miles, Black Star*) "Once a boy is made aware of his own possibilities his confidence increases, and his sense of uncertainty in a rather bewildering world is correspondingly reduced." (*Topix*)

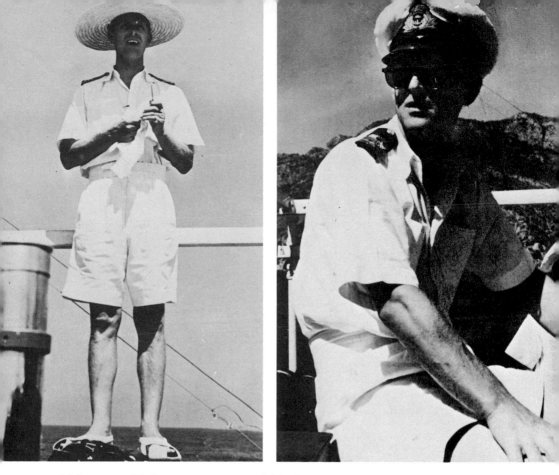

Malta, 1951, his last year at sea, and his first and last command, HMS *Magpie*. "I make no secret of the fact that I enjoyed my time in the Royal Navy."
(*Camera Press*)

Above: Rowing in a whaler race. Sometimes *(below)* others were allowed to do the work: Venetian volunteers ferry him from the island of St. Francisca, near Venice.
(Camera Press)

litical adversary, Venizelos, in full charge. The threads of the
episode were hopelessly knotted, but at their center was Constantine's refusal to commit his people to the Allied side in the war.
And the British and French press, loud with his "treachery," didn't
forget that his wife was Sophie of Prussia, the Kaiser's sister.
There were hysterical allegations. His country house at Tatoi
harbored secret radio transmitters, tapping out information to the
Germans and Bulgarians. (At the height of the fuss the house
was set fire to, probably by Allied agents. Nearby Athens was
full of foreign secret police.) He was conniving, it was said, at
the refueling of German submarines. The point wasn't made that
the Kaiser had intimated, in July 1914, that he expected Greece
to fight on the German side, and that Constantine had telegraphed
a blunt affirmation of neutrality. That telegram was later found
in the German archives, with a note in the All Highest's personal
hand: "To be communicated to Athens that I have concluded an
alliance with Turkey and Bulgaria in case of war with Russia, and
that I will treat Greece as an enemy if she does not join us immediately."

Hoping to stem the tide of calumny, the King sent two of his
brothers, Prince Nicholas and Prince Andrew (Philip's father),
on the rounds of the Allied statesmen, to present the truth. They
didn't want to know. Greece should do as she was told, and not
come badgering with excuses. The emissaries weren't made to
feel exactly welcome, certainly not in London, where Andrew was
bagged by a *Daily Mail* photographer, and the accompanying text
explained that he had been "scheming with Colonel Metaxas, formerly of the Greek general staff and a prominent member of the
Germanophile group, who had smuggled out information from
Greece to Berlin, disclosing Allied troop movements." While
Nicholas was earnestly making his royal brother's case to the Russian Prime Minister, that statesman undisguisedly dozed off. Even
relations weren't much use. The days when the royal tribe could

help each other by pulling political strings were beginning to pass. Tsar Nicholas II, Constantine's much-loved, and loving, cousin, was kind. But he had his own troubles. The rumblings of the Revolution that was to end, in just two years, with the slaughterings at Ekaterinburg, were already under his feet. In London, at Marlborough House, the widowed and increasingly vague Alexandra, who had so often prodded her husband, Bertie (Edward VII), to do something for her Greek brother, the Danish William who became George, could now only sympathize, and ask for the family gossip. Bertie's successor, George V, was friendly. He gave Nicholas lunch at Buckingham Palace, and it was at least implicit—but kings must choose their words—that he no more believed what his ministers were saying of Constantine than his mother, Alexandra, did. Nor was he any better placed to do anything about it.

Defeated, the princes went back home, and soon, with Constantine, his Queen, their brothers and sisters, wives and children, were in exile in Switzerland. It wasn't the people, but the politicians, at home and abroad, who had wanted them to go.

One prince, Alexander, stayed behind. No longer a prince, but King. His elder brother, George, was really the next in line, but the Allies had lumped him with his father as a Kaiser's man. The new reign was short and shabby. Alexander was nothing but a crowned Venizelos puppet. His family had gone and he was forbidden to communicate with them. His mother, Sophie, never saw him again. Once in 1918, when their visits to Paris coincided, she tried to call him, and was told by one of his servants, who in effect were more like warders, that His Majesty was unable to come to the telephone. He had no friends; the prisons on the islands were soon filled with holders of "undesirable" political opinions, an eerie pre-echo of another Constantine's banishment in 1967. And there was that tragi-comic death to come, in 1920, by blood poisoning from a monkey bite.

So now who? Through the Greek minister in Berne, Venizelos approached Constantine's third son, Paul, who turned him down flat—constitutionally, his father was still King; he'd signed no instrument of abdication. But a king must be found. Not only the people, strangely hooked on the monarchic idea, wanted it, but even some of the political elements. Venizelos, in a show of amenability, blundered. He offered a general election, with a choice between Constantine's supporters—if they won it could mean a restoration—and his own. Shrewd bird though he was, it seems never to have occurred to him that things wouldn't go his way. He lost by a landslide, and when a plebiscite was later held, for or against Constantine's return, Venizelos polled only ten thousand votes out of more than a million. It's hard to say whether he or the Allies were more shaken. A stiff note from Whitehall began with a nice touch: they "had no wish to interfere with the internal affairs of Greece," but Constantine's conduct during the war had caused them "great embarrassment and loss," and they would interpret his return "as a ratification by Greece of his hostile acts." Let them gripe. He returned, to a frenzy of welcome, together with his banished relations.

Two of them actually preceded him, Andrew and his younger brother, Christopher. On landing, and battling their way to the car, they were yanked out of it again and carried the four miles from Phaleron Bay to Athens on the shoulders of the roaring citizens. It was painful, alarming and marvelous. Prince Andrew at least came through in good enough shape to make a speech from the palace balcony.

By September 1922 Constantine had at last been forced to abdicate, a scapegoat for the Army's defeat in Asia Minor. It was more than unjust. The latest slash at the Turks wasn't his idea, but a hangover commitment from Venizelos. He was simply landed with it, and knew from the start that he was on to a loser. (Lloyd George, no doubt pursuing the policy of noninterference,

insisted that he should hang on at all costs against Mustapha Kemal
—Ataturk to be—despite the miserable condition of his under-
equipped forces, bemused in the treeless Anatolian wastes.)

It was like Constantine to bend his full powers on the assignment all the same, both as King and booster of morale in the field.
He was a fighter of old—probably, as Professor Brogan has said,
"the only good soldier any dynasty has produced in modern
times." As Crown Prince he had first fought the Turks in 1897
and was Commander-in-Chief in 1912, recovering Salonika, Epirus,
South Macedonia and all the islands of the Aegean. This was the
first Balkan War, with George I assassinated at the end of it. With
the second, Constantine was now King as well as Commander-in-
Chief, this time against the Bulgarians, his allies of the year before.
He clawed back Bulgar-occupied Thrace, whose people were nine-
tenths Greek, and again returned in triumph, to scenes of fierce
Athenian rejoicing.

But Asia Minor was different. He was lucky, if the word could
come his way at all, to get out of it with his life, though Greek,
not Turkish, bullets were the threat. The war was lost, five of his
ministers and his commander-in-chief were shot for losing it, and
Lieutenant-General Prince Andrew, a commander in the field when
the collapse set in, nearly went the same way.

Constantine's second and last exile was short. He died in Sicily
three months later. Of a broken heart, wrote his brother Nicholas,
and for once it's tempting to accept that faintly embarrassing di-
agnosis.

His son, now George II, who himself called his situation "impossible and ridiculous," survived a year before the familiar political machinations bundled him out, and from 1924 to 1935 was a
decorative member of London society, monocled, tailored in Savile

Row and among the most English-looking residents of the universally respected Brown's Hotel. His brother, Crown Prince Paul, was soon in London too, on the staff of an eminent British car manufacturer. (When both were haled back to Athens in November 1935, the Greeks being king-hungry again after eleven years as an unsteady republic, he called it "the best job I ever had.") Though almost anything, one might think, must have compared favorably with the profession of royalty, whether on the throne or off, or merely seeing, like Paul, that it was bound to get you in the end.

Not too eagerly, George returned, to the statutory acclaim of the transported Greeks. Flags, banners, bands, salutes of guns, escorts of planes, sirens of ships, a cavalcade of royal carriages newly bedizened from dusty retirement, and thirty-two bishops to attend him for the Cathedral's joyous *Te Deum*. Crown Prince Paul, doubtless in a lower standard of vehicle than he'd been used to, shared the plaudits.

Despite a decree, the following year, damaging to his personal popularity and defiant of the democratic ethic—under political pressure he appointed Metaxas to absolute dictatorship—it was neither the powers nor his own people who next got rid of the King, but Hitler's invading armies. The Italians were the first to overrun the country. They were kicked out spectacularly. It took just twenty-one days, and by March 1941 they'd been shoved back half across Albania. But in April the Germans rolled in from Yugoslavia. The King, the Crown Prince, their families and the Cabinet, if the government was to be preserved, had to get out; first to Crete, until the Stukas came screaming, with General Kurt Student's parachutists hard behind. Then by British destroyer *Decoy* to Alexandria.

It was a dramatic departure. General Freyberg, whose thankless job of saving the island was further complicated by his royal responsibilities, would have packed them off before the twelve-day battle began. Crown Princess Frederica,[3] with her children (including the infant Constantine II to be) and other assorted princesses, had already left by flying boat from Suda Bay. But it was the wish of the War Cabinet in London that the King should keep a toehold on the last bit of free Greece (the Germans were already in Athens) as a rallying point, at least morally, for his people. He stayed, with the Crown Prince and others, ten in all, until Crete was clearly lost. He was no embarrassment as a man, only as a king. His courage and dignity wrung tributes from those whose problems were redoubled by his presence; he joined the Allied generals in their desperate tactical conferences, and Freyberg wrote afterward of his "unfailing help." The official War Office account, *The Campaign in Greece and Crete*, was later almost sentimental: "Though of all the party he had the most reason for sorrow, and the greatest burden of years, he won their unstinted admiration for his cheerfulness and endurance."

But there were too many near misses around the royal villa, and parachutes were floating down six hundred yards away. The north of the island was a battlefield, from Canea east as far as Heraklion. They went to the south, with a Cretan guide, an escort of New Zealanders and one donkey for transport, baking in the daytime, freezing at night, over the awesome White Mountains and through the dank gorge of Samara (which today's tourists are warned to think twice about tackling), until they finally stumbled down into the coastal hamlet of Aghia Roumeli. The King, who'd started on the donkey, had surrendered it to one of the party who was ill, and finished up on foot. They'd been taken for Germans,

---

[3] Crown Prince Paul had married her in 1938, daughter of Ernest, Grand Duke of Brunswick. Her full title was Princess of Hanover, Great Britain and Ireland —remotely in succession to the British throne. She, too, was to have her troubles. Her personal gaiety and charm, which so captivated the Greeks when she was Crown Princess, failed to hold off political antipathies once Paul became King.

and fired on, by a Cretan patrol. Their food had been scrounged en route.

The next day, after sleeping the night on the beach, they were ferried out to the British destroyer *Decoy*, and so to Alexandria, amid bombings and submarine alerts. The Battle of Crete has been well chronicled, but the escape of the King was a drama within a drama, a small epic on its own. All very different from Brown's Hotel.

The Mediterranean Fleet couldn't spare much by way of protection on the crossing to Africa. It was heavily engaged between Greece and Crete, staving off German seaborne landings. One of the ships involved, and sunk, was the *Kelly*, her commander a distant connection of the retreating King, Captain Lord Louis Mountbatten. Among others present, in the battleship *Valiant*, was a closer relation, the King's nineteen-year-old cousin, Midshipman Prince Philip of Greece.

It was another five years, in 1946, before George II was back on his throne, in a country not only crippled by Hitler's war but trying to finish the job off with a civil war of its own. Ah! The Greeks. Within a year he died at his desk of a heart attack, and Paul, resigned but dutiful, was crowned.

Telegrams to the Foreign Office from the British Legation in Athens:[4]

Private and Secret.   November 28 1922, 8.30 P.M.

There is no doubt that Prince Andrew's position has become much more dangerous since execution of Ministers and I hear his trial is to begin on November 30th.   Mr. G. Talbot, who arrived this morning after executions, is concentrating on saving Prince Andrew and I think he will have a better chance of succeeding than legation now that rupture of diplomatic relations has taken place.

We both agree that a show of force such as presence of man-of-war would do more harm than good.   On my suggestion he is considering possibility of bribery. . . .

Another:

Private and most secret.   November 30 1922, 1.0 A.M. Most urgent.

. . . Mr. Talbot has obtained this evening promise from Minister of War and also from Colonel Plastiras, the two leaders of government, that Prince Andrew will not be executed but allowed to leave the country in charge of Mr. Talbot.

---

[4] *Public Record Office Documents.*

Following is arrangement agreed upon:

Prince will be tried on Saturday and sentenced to penal servitude or possibly to death. Plastiras will then grant pardon and hand him over to Mr. Talbot for immediate removal with Princess by British warship to Brindisi or to any other port en route to England. British warship must be at Phaleron by midday December 3rd and captain should report immediately to legation for orders, but in view of necessity for utmost secrecy, captain should be given no indication of reason for voyage.

This promise has been obtained with greatest difficulty and Talbot is convinced that above arrangement be strictly adhered to so as to save Prince's life. As success of plan depends on absolute secrecy of existence of this arrangement, even Prince and Princess cannot be given hint of coming. Talbot is convinced that he can rely on word given him and I see no other possibility of saving Prince's life.

I should be glad of early intimation that ship will arrive at appointed hour.

6

Andrew of Greece

"I regret that you considered it necessary to give me your assurance that the accusation of abandoning your position before the enemy is not true. You might have known my opinion of you by now, that I consider you an honourable, conscientious and able soldier."—Letter from King Constantine I to his brother, Prince Andrew, December 1922.

In October 1903 in Darmstadt, capital of Hesse and the Battenberg family home, an earlier wedding was to affect the London one of November 1947 to some purpose. Prince Andrew of Greece married Princess Alice of Battenberg; they had become engaged at King Edward VII's Coronation the year before; Prince Philip would be their fifth child and only son.

The marriage was in triplicate: a Protestant ceremony, another to satisfy German civil requirements and the grand spectacular of the Greek Orthodox Church, with a cast of hundreds. If Edward VII, doting great-uncle of the bride, had had his way it would have been in quadruplicate. He had once said that no throne in Europe would be too good for her, and though he was now settling for a Greek prince of less than sparkling prospects, with three older brothers in the line of succession, he wanted things to be done right, with a clincher at the British Legation. But in the end he let that go.

Darmstadt overflowed with rejoicing throngs, heavily swelled by the relatives and attendants of the bridal pair. Kings, queens, princes, princesses, archdukes and grand duchesses rolled up in force, their carriages and escorts jangling in the narrow streets.

King George and Queen Olga of Greece, parents of the groom, brought sons and daughters with their wives and husbands. Edward VII's blessing was signified by the presence of Queen Alexandra, with princesses Victoria and Beatrice. Tsar Nicholas II steamed magnificently in with the Tsarina Alexandra and four young Tsarevnas. Grand Duke Paul of Russia was there; also, on the Tsar's command, but no doubt traveling separately, eighty members of the Imperial Russian Choir. There were the Kaiser's brother, Prince Henry of Prussia, and the bride's parents, Prince and Princess Louis of Battenberg, with their three-year-old son and brother of the bride (the future Lord Louis Mountbatten's first formal appearance). Prince Louis, taking time off from the British Admiralty, where he was busy trying to promote his policy of arming the merchant navy,[1] housed countless cousins in the nearby castle of Heiligenberg, left him by his father, Prince Alexander of Hesse; even with the spacious accommodations in Grand Duke Ernest's own local establishment, it looked as if hospitality might be a bit pushed. (This was at Wolfsgarten, later the stately home of Prince Philip's third sister, Cecile, after her marriage to George, Hereditary Prince of Hesse and by the Rhine. Philip as a boy, sometimes with his father, spent holidays there.)

---

[1] He had vision. Even in early 1914 Winston Churchill still wouldn't believe that any "civilized power" would attack merchant ships.

It was a great Battenberg occasion, and the last to see so many of them happily together in the secure old world before crowns began to roll. Some of the relationships are worth a moment's study.

To begin with the Greeks . . . and yet with the Russians: Queen Olga of Greece, the bridegroom's mother, was of the Russian Imperial House, daughter of Nicholas I's son, Grand Duke Constantine. Her husband, King George of Greece, was the Danish "Willy," but with German blood from his mother, Princess Louise of Hesse-Cassel. Four nations already. As for the English, Willy's sister was now Queen Alexandra, after nearly forty years in the wings as Princess of Wales, and since her marriage to Edward the ties had again been tightened in 1874, when his younger brother, Prince Alfred, whose father was Albert of the "delicate moustachios," and German, married the Grand Duchess Marie, daughter of Tsar Alexander II and sister-in-law to, among others, Princess Dagmar of Denmark—so here come the Danes again by another door. (Dagmar married Tsar Alexander III and was known as Marie Feodorovna, just to snarl things up for the genealogists. Her eldest son was Nicholas II, the last of the tsars, also among those present. So the Romanovs curve back in, among them the Grand Duke Paul, who had married Princess Alexandra of Greece, sister of today's bridegroom. Re-enter the Greeks.)

And we're only beginning.

Willy and Olga's first son, Crown Prince Constantine—with another brother, Nicholas, he held the jeweled crowns over the heads of Andrew and Alice during the Greek Orthodox rites—was husband to the Kaiser's sister Sophie. Constantine's daughter Helen was to marry Carol II of Romania; it was the Romanians' first showing, but Constantine's son, later George II of Greece, would double the thread when he married King Carol's sister Elisabeth. She, for the record, and again not to forget the English, was Prince Alfred's granddaughter.

Andrew's brother Nicholas had married the year before the Grand Duchess Helen, granddaughter of Tsar Alexander II. Of their three daughters, Princess Olga would marry Prince Paul of Yugoslavia, Princess Elisabeth a mere Count Toerring-Jettenbach (but never mind, his aunt married Albert of the Belgians) and the third, Princess Marina, was to be Britain's admired and cherished Duchess of Kent, friend and confidante, as well as older cousin (there were fifteen years between them), of Prince Philip. He was often at Coppins, her home in Buckinghamshire, during school and navy leaves.

But these are just names, as flat as a telephone book. They were a huge family of real people. The royal tribe overflows purely national boundaries, however busily the statesmen try to keep them above water. It is a race on its own. The blue blood, as Andrew's brother Nicholas once wrote, "is just as red as anybody else's, the tears just as bitter." It sounds inanely obvious, but the cultivation of that enameled, unassailable public exterior makes it something often forgotten. The prismatic pile-up of repeated Alexanders, Nicholases, Constantines, Olgas, Helens and Sophies may have driven Mountbatten to the impersonality of coding—his own fourth name was Nicholas, but the glut of Nickies when he visited his Russian relations turned him into Dickie for simplicity's sake, and it stuck—but it was the bonds of affection that changed them through the generations to Sacha, Tino, Alicky, Ducky, Palo, Drino, Sandro, Liko, Vicky and (for Marie Feodorovna, Empress of all the Russias), Auntie Minny. Her sister, Queen Olga of Greece, had an amusing nephew she called "Sunbeam," later Britain's King George V.

Andrew had been to Darmstadt before, and met Alice there. He was on training attachment to the Hessian 23rd Dragoon Guards, Germany being the only place to make soldiers. His army career, planned from the first, got under way pretty early. At fourteen he was a cadet at the Athens military school (drilled by German officers), and at seventeen was being crammed through his commissioning course by a private tutor, this time a Greek. He was a Major Panayotis Danglis, familiar to ballistics fanciers of those days as the inventor of a highly versatile mountain gun which could be carried on muleback and assembled in ninety seconds flat, a handy bit of weaponry for the Greeks at a time when obsolescent old field pieces were being dragged over formidable terrain by men and bullocks. One of Major-General Prince Andrew's many grievances, facing the Turks in the weary summer of 1921, was that his command was given none of these guns; also that he had no wireless, a heliograph of outdated design and nothing at all that would signal by night.

It offers a dismal glimpse of the Greek military-political pattern that Danglis in 1916, by then a general, was one of the anti-Royalist triumvirate who, while King Constantine was grimly hanging on to neutrality, slipped off by destroyer and opened up Salonika for the landing of Allied troops. The other two were Venizelos and an Admiral Condouriotis, once a trusted ADC to Constantine's father, George I. And Danglis had himself been on Constantine's military staff. Points of macabre interest. Prince Christopher, Andrew's younger brother, was in Athens at the time, heard whispers of the plot and got Prime Minister Kalogoropoulos out of bed in the small hours. He wasn't pleased, and pooh-poohed the whole story, but eventually agreed to telephone the Navy Minister, who pooh-poohed even louder. Betrayal by an admiral, and particularly by the Honorable Condouriotis, defied contemplation. Two days later, when the treacherous threesome stole off exactly as foretold, it turned out that the Navy Minister was in on the deal anyway. Condouriotis, thus a prime mover in getting rid of the King, became President of the Greek Republic. It was all a fair slice of the times.

But in 1899 Danglis was an industrious enough tutor to the seventeen-year-old Prince, whom he noted privately to be tall, quick, intelligent and handsome. The description could have gone for all five of George's sons: army photographs taken during the Balkan wars of 1912 and 1913 show Constantine and Andrew towering above the group, or very straight and hollow-backed on horses. Something else they shared was an irreverent addiction to practical jokes. "Anything could happen when you got a few of them together," his son Philip now says. "It was like the Marx brothers." (But Nicholas was the more serious, with a fair talent for painting, and in exile when times were hard could sell pictures for real money, even signed in an assumed name.) Danglis also found Andrew "short-sighted and wearing spectacles." They don't appear in the photographs: only a monocle in later years.[2]

Danglis' pupil, certainly at first, was less industrious than his master, whose tests on the previous day's lessons tended to become recaps of what had been taught already. The subjects were Artillery, Fortifications, Military Technology, Military History, Military Geography and Military Topography (nothing on treachery). Topography drew the readiest response, perhaps because its interest wasn't exclusively strategic. There are hills, woods and valleys, after all, that aren't provided by nature as mere fire cover, or perches for mountain guns.

But the curriculum was crowded, as Danglis would plead in answer to the King's frequent demands for progress reports. Artillery and Fortifications had to compete for time with other tutors and more formal branches of education. Anyone with the fairy-

---

[2] There was a heredity of short-sightedness. Andrew's mother, Olga, suffered badly, and used to go to Paris to see specialists. Prince Philip is short-sighted to some degree, but doesn't proclaim it. Those driving out of Buckingham Palace through the inevitable crowds, with him at the wheel, learn to brace themselves slightly for the disquieting wobble as he clears close inspection and puts his glasses on. (*Daily Mail*, January 1958: "Prince Philip piloted his Heron aircraft from London Airport to Norfolk yesterday . . . and he was wearing *SPECTACLES*.") He also has contact lenses, often lost on the polo field.

tale notion that princes lay around in silks, reaching languidly for the occasional sweetmeat, would have been jolted by the regimen at the court of George I. It was up at six, cold bath, lessons at seven and a day's work fit to have a modern trade unionist in tears. (Prince Philip is no natural early riser. Perhaps there's such a thing as a heredity of resentment.)

It went on for eighteen months, and Danglis was constantly urged by the King to increase the hours of tuition. When the Royal Household went to Corfu in the spring of 1900, Danglis went too, and Andrew was mostly debarred, in the interests of his studies, from the picnics and excursions. That summer he had a month in Crete with his brother, Prince George, thirteen years older, and then High Commissioner of the island. Danglis and his military textbooks were there. Even when a squadron of the British Mediterranean Fleet steamed into Suda Bay, twelve ships to support Admiral Sir John Fisher in his mission to invest George with the KCB, Andrew didn't see much of the action. (The powers had nominated Prince George for the job, and this was a present for a good boy. Later they went off him, and he was removed. But he wore the insignia, decades afterward, at both the wedding and the Coronation of Elizabeth II. At the Coronation he was eighty-four.) There were high jinks, including a full-dress banquet in the flagship *Renown*. He missed the lot—though it wasn't only school hours that kept him away. He'd been pre-surfeited with military history and geography, no doubt, and was in bed with a temperature.

But to suggest a tyrannous parent is misleading. Danglis noted down that the Prince was "in some awe" of his father, but this was only proper, and not incompatible with love. The King was no poker-back, with either family or subjects. He had the easy habit of strolling unescorted through the streets of Athens, often stopping to talk to passers-by. It was one that eventually got him assassinated, when he unwisely tried it in Salonika.

No, he simply wanted the lad to excel, and drove him hard to that end. It came off. The examinations began on May 14, 1901, and lasted three days. The board was forbidding—the King, Crown Prince Constantine, Prince Nicholas, the Archbishop, the Prime Minister, the Minister of War, the Commandant of the Athens Military Academy, the King's Military ADC and all the tutors. They were unanimously satisfied. At the formal lunch on the last day, the King proposed Andrew's health and commissioned him a subaltern in the cavalry.

He then decorated Danglis with the Gold Cross of the Order of the Redeemer. It's not known whether he continued to sport it after the events of 1916.

Prince Andrew, launched at nineteen on the soldiering life, pursued it with the family single-mindedness, one of several characteristics later to appear in Philip, among them the sense of fun. He was more likely to be laughing than not, partly from natural buoyancy but also from a quick recognition of the ridiculous, which has descended through Philip to Charles; they both have a struggle sometimes with starchy occasions. One of Philip's best exercises in the straight face was during a solemn naval ceremonial in Trafalgar Square. Inspecting the ranks of impeccable ratings, he came to a man with a pigeon on his head, inspected both and passed on.

When Alice first met Andrew, a young cavalry lieutenant fresh off the parental leash, he had a doggishness that was new and exciting for a girl brought up between Victorian tight-lacing and Darmstadt's prim provincialism. It suffered an eclipse in the middle years before his final exile, but his great-niece, Alexandra,[3] who

---

[3] Princess of Greece, daughter of Andrew's nephew, later Alexander I. She married King Peter of Yugoslavia after his exile in 1944. George VI of England was best man; George II of Greece gave the bride away.

as a child knew him in Paris when the emotional bruises of Asia Minor were beginning to fade, remembers him as a great laugher. Later, in Monte Carlo, he easily made new friends, not exclusively masculine; out of uniform, out of Greece, out of his marriage, he seemed to take almost with relief to the unbuttoned life, but privately he never forgot the somber circumstances of his emancipation. In 1930 he published a book, doomfully titled *Towards Disaster*, a detailed raking-over of his military downfall. It contained absolutely no jokes.

He wrote it in Greek, though he'd grown up in a family of many languages. His father, George, was Danish, and Olga, his mother, Russian, but they spoke German to each other and English to the children. (The King was always surrounded by English magazines, *Punch, The Tatler, Illustrated London News.*) When Danish or Russian relations stayed, they naturally used the visitors' languages. The children were made to speak Greek among themselves, though according to Christopher they all had "five or six languages fairly fluently." He remembered being told that his mother, arriving in Athens as a Queen of sixteen (she brought her dolls in her baggage), with neither English nor Greek, was speaking both within a year. Royalty might complain that we take this sort of thing for granted, expecting nothing less. If Prince Charles hasn't quite mastered Welsh to bardic standards, he doesn't make the fool of himself in it that most of us would. In Iceland once, his father politely made a speech in Icelandic, and as president of the Fédération Equestre Internationale chairs most of their meetings in French.

Andrew, devoted to the country of his birth despite what it did to him, insisted on sticking to Greek as his first language. Alice translated his book into English, and supplied a belligerently loyal preface. It must have been a product of their last period of close association. Expelled from Greece, their possessions impounded, they had at first managed a fairly modest joint existence in Paris with the children. Philip's schooling began there. But in 1929 he went off to start his British education, and in 1930 and 1931 all four daughters married within a year of each other. The place was suddenly emptied. Alice's eccentric religiosity and Andrew's uncomfortable memories didn't get along.

Andrew had another streak in common with Philip which must have heightened the vexations over Asia Minor: he had no time for ignorance, stupidity, inefficiency or deviousness. For the informed, intelligent, capable and forthright such lacks in others are hard to take, though some rare spirits can make allowances. Andrew couldn't, and didn't try, to make allowances for the blunderings and worse of the politicians and general staff. And his undisguised contempt for the lot of them couldn't have sweetened his name at their end.

The month when Philip was born, June 1921, brought his long-awaited command at the front, as Major-General, 2nd Army Corps. From the day of his commissioning in May 1901 he had been a career officer like any other. Well, there had been two breaks ("spent in idleness, to his great grief," wrote Alice). In 1909 elaborate jealousies of the princes, too involved to sift in detail here, caused Andrew, Nicholas and Christopher all to resign from the Army, and Prince George from the Navy. With war in 1912, Andrew hastened to be reinstated, as a cavalry colonel. The old feuds looked dead—deceptively, as it proved. After Constantine's departure in 1917, Venizelos, short on military vision, sacked three thousand officers of Royalist sympathies, Andrew among them. But he was exiled anyway, a double bar to professional continuity, until, with the King's return in 1920, and another war against the Turks already mounted ("the first act of which," notes Andrew, in characteristic style, "will always be notable for the imbecility of its conception"), he could again get into the fighting. Even so, it was six months before they'd have him. The feuds were back. The appointments to those three thousand vacancies, and the promotions that followed, were mostly rewards for political rather than military usefulness, and there was small welcome for a banished prince coming back with the rank of major-general.

Three months later, appalled at the opportunist intrigues, smarting under personal slights, impatient with the inept direction of the campaign from above and the incompetence of both officers and men, he asked to be relieved of his command. He had already expressed his views from time to time. In a long letter to the C-in-C, General Papulas, on July 22, 1921, he had something to say about a brigade of mountain artillery sent to him after many requests: "Its personnel was so ignorant that for days it was unable even to find the Division, in spite of all my instructions. It was so untrained that in yesterday's action at Alpanos, in which the Division fought for six hours against a strongly entrenched force of 8000 men, only four guns of one battery supported the attack. The brigade, during the whole of the action, was engaged in making endless reconnaissances, and when it did fire once, it fired at our own troops."

Though he wasn't out of the Army, and the war lost, until the next year—he was told by the rebel government that he could live undisturbed in Corfu if he resigned his commission, a promise soon broken. *Towards Disaster* deals only with those three months. Meant as an almost academic statement of the true facts of the campaign, it somehow has the overall flavor of a desperate tirade, which makes him seem to come pettishly out of it all. Heaven knows he was misused, but by sad tradition the commander in war has to fight his own top brass as well as the enemy. He may have lacked this double mettle, but not the qualities of courage, patriotism or, perhaps not too desirable in a soldier, sensibility. . . . His book ends:

> For the first time after many centuries, since the time of the Byzantine rulers, a Greek King and a Greek Army trod

the immense plains of Asia Minor. Full of eagerness, faith
and self-sacrifice, the Greek soldier threw himself into the
age-old struggle of his race—the struggle of civilisation
against Asiatic barbarism.

The glitter of Greek bayonets was seen once more on the
fields of Kiutahia and Eski-Shehr, on the Twin Mountains,
on the shores of the Sakharia and in the Axylos desert.
Gordium, Justianopolis, once more heard the shouts of
Greek victory, the echoes reaching as far as Angora. . . .

Alas! the Greek soldier, who had strewn his bones during
an entire decade in Macedonia and Epirus, in Thrace and in
Russia, did not know that all his sacrifices were in vain;
he did not know that there was a traitor in his ranks, who,
jealous of the fame of his predecessor at Thermopylae, sur-
passed him in his efforts, and brought the Greek Army to
the catastrophe of 1922. . . .

Meanwhile our glorious dead lie by the side of their ancestors, the Hoplites of Alexander the Great and the
Stratiotes of Heracles and Nicephorus Phocas, and the murmur of the waves of the Aegean bears to the Greek shores
the re-echoing sounds of their message:

"O stranger, go, tell the Lacedemonians that here we lie,
faithful to their orders."

It's the voice of a man deeply moved, and deeply disillusioned.
Not a bad bit of writing, either.

Andrew lived to learn of the D-Day landings in Normandy. He
died at the end of the year, on December 3, 1944. Touchingly,
the pocket Principality of Monaco rose to the occasion for his
funeral, and a French Army escort accompanied the exile to the
Russian Orthodox Church in Nice. It wasn't his last journey. In

1946 he went by Greek cruiser, the *Averoff,* to his home port of Piraeus, and from there to the Gardens of Tatoi. ANDREA VASILO-PAIS, says his gravestone: "Prince of Greece, Prince of Denmark. 1882–1944."

Vasilopais: Son of a King.

If it hadn't been for Alice, and George V, he might have been dead twenty-two years before. It was a close shave.

From his villa of Mon Repos, on Corfu, he was bidden to Athens in October 1922 to attend the court of the Revolutionary Committee. Ostensibly he was needed as a witness in the proceedings against Constantine's ministers made whipping-boys for the Greek defeat. On arrival he was arrested, held prisoner for seven weeks, and then put in the dock on a charge of treason. It was preposterous. Prince Christopher went to see the King. He was literally powerless. Alice, who had meanwhile learned the horrifying truth, made frenzied appeals for intervention in all quarters that came to mind: to the Pope, to Alfonso of Spain, to Poincaré of France, to George V of England. All sympathized, all deplored, most made representations, but it was England that did something. A talk with the King by Alice's young brother, Louis Mountbatten, may have moved things along. He also saw the British Prime Minister, Bonar Law. Curzon, then Foreign Secretary, was brought in. Strange indeed that Britain, who only a few years before had been heaping abuse on "the German Greeks," was now reaching out to snatch one of them from a firing squad.[4] But then, the English . . . besides, George V was Andrew's cousin.

---

[4] The six men executed included the vanquished Commander-in-Chief (General Hadjianesti) and five former ministers. There was a piece of gruesome sub-drama when the bullets hit M. Protopapakadis. One of the young soldiers himself died of a heart attack as he pulled the trigger. Protopapakadis had been deputy for the island of Naxos. The boy was a Naxos boy, who had revered and respected the old man.

One of those Foreign Office telegrams of November 1922 read: "The King is most anxious concerning Prince Andrew. Please report on His Royal Highness's present position, and continue to keep us informed by telegraph of any developments." He was always rather proud of the part he played. Philip, aged thirteen, and in London for Princess Marina's wedding in 1934, remembers standing aside in a Buckingham Palace doorway as the King came stumping through. He gave the lad a thoughtful stare. "You're Andrew's boy!"

The rescue was near-melodrama. Commander Gerald Talbot, once Naval Attaché in Athens, was sent back there by Curzon from Geneva, his posting at the time, to see what could be done. He traveled in full spy-fiction rig with disguise and false papers, and somehow managed to get to General Pangalos, leader of the revolutionaries and a member of the trial court. Also to Colonel Plastiras, another eminent rebel. (Plastiras served under Andrew in the fateful campaign, and Pangalos was a fellow cadet with Andrew at the Athens Military Academy all those years before.) What considerations weighed, or what pressures were brought, isn't clear. Talbot was later knighted.

Though he had apparently been prepared to "abduct" the prisoner, whether or not with rebel connivance, it didn't come to that. Things were smooth, and embroidered by an oddity: Pangalos himself took Andrew from the prison during the night after the trial, and drove both him and Talbot down to the quay. Aboard HMS *Calypso,* there under secret orders, Alice was waiting, in tears and thanksgiving.

The terms of the so-called pardon were brutal. Andrew was found guilty of disobedience to orders and of abandoning his post in the face of the enemy. "But consideration being given to extenuating circumstances of lack of experience in commanding a large unit, he has been degraded and condemned to perpetual banishment."

In 1970, when documents on British foreign policy, 1919–39, were being prepared for publication, copies of the two dramatic telegrams were sent to Sir Michael Adeane, the Queen's private secretary, in case "there would be any objection to their being printed." They reached Prince Philip. His only objection was to an editor's footnote on one of them, setting out the terms of the verdict. He hoped, as he said in his jotted comment, that this needn't appear: "People might think it was true."

"Princess Andrew of Greece, the mother of the Duke of Edinburgh and sister of Lord Mountbatten, died yesterday at the age of 84 at Buckingham Palace.

"Of the many tragedies that afflicted members of European Royalty in this century, hers were perhaps among the most poignant and harrowing. She bore her vicissitudes with courage and fortitude. A lonely figure in her late age, she was noticed at her rare public appearances for the grey monastic full-flowing robe and coif she always donned, the uniform of the Christian Sisterhood of Martha and Mary which she herself had founded in 1949. . . .

"During the 1914–18 War, which brought the Greek royal family at loggerheads with the politicians, she had her share of the trials and tribulations that followed. In 1917 she followed her husband and the Greek royal family into exile in Switzerland and, after three years, when her brother-in-law was restored to the Greek throne, they returned to Greece and took up residence at Mon Repos palace in Corfu, where Prince Philip was born in 1921.

"This turned out to be one of the most tragic periods of her life. Prince Andrew, who had commanded an army corps during the Greek Military debacle in Asia Minor in 1922, was arrested by the politicians who . . ."[5]

---

[5] *The Times,* December 6, 1969.

7

Alice of Battenberg

"The prettiest princess in Europe is said to be Princess Alice of Greece, the elder daughter of that popular naval officer, Prince Louis of Battenberg."
—HOME NOTES, September 1908

Those who saw her obituaries in December 1969, if their particular paper found space for one, were surprised to find that she'd died in Buckingham Palace, and even that she'd been living there. Or was still living at all. "My mother's life is her own business," Prince Philip had once told a reporter. So it was. And a long and tumultuous one. The odd thing was that the reporter should have wanted to report on her. She had never really become known to the British—a gauze-gray background figure, mysterious in nunnish clothes, an old Greek lady, some sort of religious crank. Hard to tie her in at all with the dashing, dominating and gratifyingly English Duke. But she'd been born at Windsor sixteen years before her great-grandmother Victoria died, and lived to play with her youngest English grandchild, Prince Edward. It was some span. During her last two years at Buckingham Palace, if she didn't actually give the Queen any mother-in-law trouble in the music-hall sense, she was a force to be reckoned with, and domestic or family decisions that she had her own ideas about could get badly hung up. Royalty isn't much different from the rest of us in this sort of thing. (Prince Philip has plans to re-landscape the approach to Sandringham House, but the Queen Mother likes it as it is, and that's the way it stays.)

On her wedding day at Darmstadt, October 9, 1903, Alice was eighteen, as pretty as a peach, but with a serious look and a hint of vulnerability. Also an air of remoteness, which may have been from a congenital deafness that wasn't serious at this stage, but worsened with the years until it became crippling. She then taught herself to lip-read, not just in her own language, which of course was English (her father, Prince Louis, had been in the British Navy for seventeen years by the time she was born), but in Greek, French and German. If her son got the looks, humor and impatience from his father, a lot of the drive and application came from her. And a dose of stubbornness from both sides.

The appearance of vulnerability was deceptive. Without a hard center she could never have stuck out her eighty-four pulverizing years. She came in for the ricochets of all the misfortunes that hit the Greek Royal House, sustained Andrew through his personal tragedy, in World War I suffered for her father, Prince Louis, in his victimization for being a Battenberg, and was on the receiving end of the general mud-slinging at what Allied propaganda called the "German Greeks," even though she was by birth an English princess, with both her brothers fighting in the English Navy. In World War II there were other poignant stresses. Her brother Dickie and son Philip were in the Royal Navy, while three of her daughters, Margarita, Theodora and Sophie, were married to German officers.[1] (Cecile had died, with her children, in 1937, when the aircraft bringing them to London for the wedding of her brother-in-law, Prince Louis of Hesse, crashed in fog near Ostend.)

But the day at Darmstadt had been a good day, even as good days went when royal extravaganzas seemed the natural order, as immune to change as the planets. Bells rang, crowds cheered and the imperial choristers let fly. Liturgical splendors were followed by secular rompings—under the jewels, stars and sashes, the time-honored family larks that properly attend these affairs in all brackets of society.

At the wedding feast Grand Duke Ernest and the four Greek princes waited table. There was the ever-amusing joke of exchanged headgear, in this case mostly tiaras. Everyone pulled the leg of the dumpy Grand Duchess of Württemberg, who always anchored her coronet and other accessories with elastic—though that day, as blizzards of rice hit the departing couple, someone managed to knock her glasses off and she blindly boxed the wrong prince's ears for it. While the distraught Darmstadt policemen tried to deploy themselves for the safety of the hilarious kings, queens and lesser nobility, the Tsar of Russia butted head-down through the mob as the honeymoon carriage came in sight and hurled a white satin slipper at the bride, who made an adroit catch and hit him over his imperial head with it, leaving him behind laughing helplessly. High old times. Happy, innocent, absurd.

Not only Alice and Andrew were in for more sobering days. George I was to be murdered. So, in even more piteous circumstances, were the Tsar, the Tsarina, the Tsarevnas, and the ailing and adored son, Alexis, not yet born at the time of that Darmstadt wedding. There were to be grinding agonies over the Rasputin

---

[1] In another set of wrenched allegiances in the same war, Princess Frederica of Hanover, who sustained the Allied cause vigorously and saw Greece—her husband's country—overrun by the Germans, had four brothers in Hitler's armies.

affair. Andrew's brother Nicholas' wife, Helen of Russia, was to lose eighteen of her close family at the hands of the Bolsheviks, and King George's wife, Queen Olga, in Russia when the Revolution began, narrowly got out with her life after an odyssey of privations to join her son, Constantine, ill and exiled. She was to have griefs afresh over Constantine's second exile, his narrow escape from the burning of Tatoi, and over Andrew's trial and banishment. Wars apart, and they were to touch everyone, the English guests that day were among the few to glide serenely on.

Not that the newlyweds were marked down for instant tribulation. It would have been too much even for Greek destinies. They lived at first with the King, Andrew's father, in the Old Palace in Athens. It was barnlike and cold, keeping out the sun and letting in the wind. Heating was by the occasional stove of ornamental china. The plumbing was volatile. Family high spirits warmed things up by roller-skating and bicycling (the new thing) through its corridors and galleries, when the King could often be persuaded to lead the procession. He afterward gave them a small house in the grounds of Tatoi, fifteen miles north of the city, one of several he provided for his immediate relatives. The first two girls were born, Margarita and Theodora, and played around the estate with Prince Nicholas' daughters, Olga, Elisabeth and Marina, who were sternly overseen by their English Nanny Fox.[2]

The Prince Andrews traveled. They found, as their children found later, that a handsome spread of family connections with

---

[2] Does Britain still lead the world in nanny and governess exports? Constantine's daughters had Miss Nichols, Andrew's Miss Roose, who stayed on for Philip. Philip's once-removed cousin, Alexandra, had Nanny Foster. Constantine II had Miss Macnair. And this was only Greece. Sociological historians short of a subject might consider the influence of these ladies on young minds in high places all over the world. It could have swayed the course of things significantly.

large, well-sited homes and a sufficiency of means eased the problem of what to do for a holiday. (Even as a child, and long before the British acclaimed him as an agreeably ordinary young naval officer, Philip was no stranger to palaces.) At home, Andrew was beginning his active military career, and Alice, even so early, was interesting herself in good works. She spent a lot of time at the School of Greek Embroidery, at first learning, later teaching. She was still beautiful.

Then the clouds began to gather. Distant at first, as far as Alice's personal happiness went, with the Balkan wars of 1912 and 1913, though no wife likes her husband away on the battle-field. In 1916 Allied pique at Constantine's defiant neutrality brought British and French warships to Piraeus. It was only a token show of support for the pro-Allied Venizelos, but the exuberant French opened fire on Athens, and Alice, rushing home from her embroidery through the bombardment, found a shell had burst outside the children's nursery windows. In 1917 Constantine had to go. With him, into their first exile, went the rest of the family, for three years of reduced circumstances in Switzerland, under intimate surveillance from Allied agents. There was a bright interval with the jubilant restoration in 1920, but next year the clouds really rolled up, and in 1922 came the crash of Andrew's trial, and the last exile.

The commander of the British light cruiser *Calypso*, Captain H. A. Buchanan-Wollaston, RN, wrote to an aunt on December 6, 1922, to wish her a happy birthday. He went on:

> Little of interest has occurred to me since my last. The one thing interesting is our little voyage from which we are now returning. We were hurried off secretly to Phaleron Bay without an idea of the reason. We found on

arrival we were to quietly slip off with Prince and Princess Andrew of Greece. He was possibly to be condemned to death as you will know, anyhow in danger of life. Well, we slipped off all right and picked up their 4 daughters and baby son from Corfu next day . . . and disembarked them yesterday at Brindisi.

. . . Princess A. has two brothers in our Navy (she was a Battenberg). The Prince is delightful, and so English, and I am quite in love with the youngest daughter aged 8. They were rather amusing about being exiled, for they so frequently are. . . .

Nearly forty-seven years later, in November 1969, the letter was sent to Prince Philip by a descendant of the aunt. He had found it among some family papers, and thought that the "baby son" must be His Royal Highness. (He mentioned, in passing, that the Captain, now a retired Vice-Admiral, was still alive at ninety-one. Against this paragraph of the covering letter Prince Philip wrote "Cor!" His secretary, replying, interpreted this: "His Royal Highness was glad to hear that the Admiral was still alive.")

It says something for the fugitives that they managed to be so delightful and amusing. To be so English, in the circumstances, was perhaps less difficult. They went on to Paris this time, after a pilgrimage of thanks to those who had helped, which took in London and an audience with the Pope. Life there was chiefly made manageable by the kindness of Andrew's second eldest brother, Prince George, now a Parisian of long adoption, and his wife. After eight years as High Commissioner of Crete, installed and then humiliatingly removed by the powers, who disapproved of his tactics in quelling the disruptive activities of Venizelos, George had renounced his rights of succession and withdrawn, disenchanted, to France.[3] In 1908 he married Princess Marie Bonaparte, and it was her money, deriving from a maternal grandfather who had owned the Monte Carlo casino, that enabled him to patch up Andrew's and Alice's threadbare finances. He first found them an apartment in Paris itself, and later a cottage on his estate at nearby St. Cloud. Was it on these slender grounds that Andrew developed his later attachment for Monte Carlo? After he and Alice had parted—it was more of a drift than a rift—he went there to spend his last separate days. Alice was back in Athens. She had scorned to take flight in 1941 with her nephew George II and the rest. She stayed through the occupation, to watch, nurse and pray. At Philip's wedding in 1947 she made a concession to the occasion by discarding her nun's habit for the day. And went in to the wedding breakfast on the arm of His Majesty, King George VI. Proudly enough, no doubt.

She had once had even prouder hopes. From the villa of Mon Repos on Corfu, waiting for her fifth child to be born, she wrote to her brother Dickie, early in 1921:

> If the child will be a boy, he will be sixth in succession
> to the Greek throne. As things are today, with Alex dead,

---

[3] Eleutherios Venizelos, though he is bound to appear in these pages as the villain, at least to the extent that he bedeviled so many members of the Greek Royal House, was as strong for Greece as they were. But perhaps too much so, and by different approaches. It was his ambition for Greek expansion that caused the debacle in Anatolia, and its magnitude would have been reduced, and public feeling against Constantine less inflamed if Greece's eventual involvement in the First World War—by Venizelos' earlier manipulations—hadn't brought the prize of Smyrna in the reparations settlement. The fresh loss of that city in 1922, charged as it was with high emotion for the Greek people (who regarded it as theirs though it had belonged to the hated Turks for nearly a thousand years) inspired their support for the rebel government of Pangalos, and for the second expulsion of Constantine. Venizelos, a Cretan lawyer of great political gifts and personal charm who at one time even hypnotized the King into embracing his policies, was four times Prime Minister. But he, too, in the end, died an exile. There are books in which he is the hero.

Tino threatened by Venizelos, and George and Andrew
unacceptable, my son if God wills could become one day
the King, if Monarchy prevails.

But God didn't will, and her son only married a Queen.

Alex was Alexander, King from 1917 to 1920 after the removal
of Tino (Constantine) by the enraged powers. Tino was indeed
threatened by Venizelos when he came back to the throne after
Alex's death, to preside over a military and political shambles,
though Venizelos himself had got out from under for the time
being—long enough for Constantine to come in for the backfire
of his half-baked plan to demolish the Turks. It was the rest of
the anti-monarchist Venizelos faction who were there to engineer,
as Alice foresaw, the King's next and final downfall. George was
also out of things in Paris with Princess Marie. And Andrew's
eligibility was badly holed by the attacks on Constantine; like the
rest of them, he'd been liberally sprayed in those broadsides.

After France was overrun in June 1940 Philip didn't see his
father again. A sprinkling of occupation troops had been found
to keep even Monaco in line. It wasn't until 1946 that he could
get to Monte Carlo and wind up the estate. It wasn't a big job,
and showed a debit balance at the end.

But as soon as it was possible he met his mother again, and they
saw each other regularly from then on.

If she didn't spoil the children, as their other grandmother tended
to do, a great affection developed, and for Charles and Anne, old
enough to recognize real-life drama, she had stirring tales to tell.
The last ten years or so were less troubled than any she'd known
for half a century. But she was often ill. In August 1966, hearing that she was in a bad way in Munich and wanted to be home,

At noon two torpedo bombers attacked us, but a quick alteration of course foiled their attempt and their fish passed down the port side. Shortly after this sixteen German dive-bombers (Ju. 87B.) attacked the Illustrious. She was hit aft and amidships and fires broke out. Then the bombers concentrated on us and five bombs dropped fairly close. A number of splinters fell on the ship but there were no casualties. A terrific barrage was put up by the fleet, but it did not seem to have any effect on the artifficially courageous men. The Illustrious remained out of control for about thirty minutes and then managed to regain control and made off towards Malta. All her aircraft seeing her trouble all arrived safely in Malta. Later in the afternoon the Illustrious and the convoy were subjected to high level bombing but no damage was done. Shortly after this we received another dose from the dive-bombers. Fourteen, this time concentrated on us. All their bombs fell very close and most of their attacks were delivered from right astern. Bomb splinters and machine-gun

Midshipman's Journal, an entry early in 1941. He was nineteen. The handwriting hasn't changed much in thirty years.

Philip flew out and took her there. It was a typical Philip exercise. He was at Balmoral. He flew from Aberdeen to Munich, supervised the loading of her stretcher into the plane, on to Athens, leaving the flight deck at intervals to come aft and shout comfort above her deafness, and back at Balmoral the next day. Sixteen and a half hours in the air.

8

Seascapes

"The colour of the sea can vary enormously. The North Sea, for instance, has a peculiar greyish-green colour even in fine weather. The sea off the west of Scotland has a special black look about it, although in the sun it produces the most glorious aquamarines and amethysts. The wine-dark seas of Homer's Mediterranean are again different from the inky black of the Antarctic and the much greener blue of the Indian Ocean. The long spume-streaked rollers of the North Atlantic and the generally grey climate that goes with them are quite different from the gigantic swell of the South Pacific, with its very clear atmosphere and garishly streaked sky of brilliant ochres and purples."—HRH the Duke of Edinburgh, in Birds from 'Britannia'

On the brilliant afternoon of June 15, 1953, the Queen, crowned less than a fortnight, reviewed her Fleet at Spithead from HMS *Surprise,* the acting royal yacht. Old *Victoria and Albert* had gone. *Britannia* wasn't yet ready. More than two hundred ships tugged at their anchors in a strong southwesterly wind.

Also on *Surprise* was Admiral of the Fleet, the Duke of Edinburgh, KG. Less than six months ago he'd only been a commander. It had taken thirteen years' hard sailing to work up to that and a ship of his own. He probably gave his old command, the frigate *Magpie,* a specially critical look as he steamed past today, though it would be dangerous to assume any sentimental twinges. His promotion to Commander was in June 1952, and the upward leap to the top in the following January, when the Queen had approved his "appointment" as Field Marshal, and Marshal of the Royal Air Force, but his "promotion" to Admiral of the Fleet—even he, self-contained to a fault (it makes people think he's colder than he is) hasn't quite forgotten the Coronation Review. "All those admirals," he says. In *Vanguard,* when the thing was over, he dined with forty of them, and seventy-five captains, from the Royal and Commonwealth navies. Not to mention a few of your commanders, and similar low life, into the bargain. If some of the brass were tempted to look down their weathered noses, as they respectfully made way for him to get a better look at the fireworks that closed the show, it didn't last. The new Admiral of the Fleet would judge the situation exactly, slipping easily into the skin of the part, yet somehow staying the same chap.

Twelve years or so before, he'd written in his midshipman's log (Admiralty form S.519, Journal for Use of Junior Officers Afloat):

A few minutes after nine o'clock, on Sunday, October 1st 1940, I walked aboard His Majesty's Ship 'Shropshire,' the third ship in eight months to receive this singular honour.

(*111*)

Private joke, though true, as it turned out. The entry, like most of the early ones, was cheerful schoolboy in style. He was less than a year out of Dartmouth.

Admiralty form S.519 isn't a form at all, but a ruggedly bound volume with marbled end papers and a hundred and fifty foolscap pages, ruled feint, as the stationers say. If you had to dispose of it at sea, to keep it out of the enemy's hands, it wouldn't need weighting to sink. It is "to be kept during the whole of a Midshipman's sea time," and must be produced periodically for inspection by the Captain or other superiors, also "at the examination in Seamanship for the rank of Lieutenant."

> Midshipmen are to record in their own language all matters of interest or importance in the work that is carried out, on their Stations, in their Fleet, or in their Ship. The objects of keeping the Journal are to train Midshipmen in (a) the power of observation, (b) the power of expression, (c) the habit of orderliness.

Maps and plans of anchorages and coastlines are also required; charts of courses steered; sketches of ports, fittings of ships. This midshipman is pretty forthcoming on the artistic and draftsmanship side. We get the Suez Canal in three colors, diagrams of electro-hydraulic steering gear, the Weymouth Cooke Sextant Range-finder, elaborately shaded maps, earnest depictions of the rigging of awnings. There's a relish about the technical annotations. Cringles, thimbles, shackles, rams, yokes, thrust-blocks and cable-holders crowd enjoyably in, sounding like C. S. Forester at his most raptly researched. An elevation of an earring stanchion, which looks fine to the land-locked eye, gets a chilling pencil note by the Captain or other superior: "Don't understand this arrangement." Discouraging.

The Journal's title page has a line for the owner's name, helpfully printed "Mr. ———" This has been crossed out and replaced, in not particularly assertive block letters, with "Philip. Prince of Greece."

The first ship is *Ramillies*, February 20 to April 12, 1940. He had joined and left her when he was still eighteen, and went through *Kent*, *Lanka* (a Colombo shore station), *Shropshire* and *Valiant* before his twentieth birthday on June 10, 1941. The log abruptly ends, in fact, just one day earlier. He then shipped for England to take his examination for sub-lieutenant.

He went, with four other midshipmen, from Port Said, down the east coast of Africa to Durban, in a Canadian Pacific liner, *Duchess of Atholl*. She was on trooping duties, and uncomfortably packed with soldiers, which his party found a bit overwhelming. As they were also doubtful about the state of her engines, they managed at Durban to transfer themselves to a sister ship, practically empty, and with less disquieting noises from the boiler room. She was on her way to Canada to load troops for Europe. The transfer wasn't the good idea it seemed. She crossed the South Atlantic and put in at Puerto Rico, where her Chinese stokers walked out, and the five midshipmen, up to then delighted at being the only passengers on board, found themselves nominated as volunteers to heave coal into her furnaces as far as Newport News, Virginia.[1] Then up to Halifax, and home. (It's to be supposed that England was regarded as home by now; he hadn't any other.)

Another good reason for staying in the first ship, not apparent at the time, was that when she later staggered into New York she broke down decisively and was there for three weeks. "I've resented this ever since." A spree in war-free America would have come in nicely. And his passion for seeing all that there was to be seen,

---

[1] The volunteers got certificates commemorating their sweating days down below, and the books all say that Philip framed his and has it hanging in his office. I asked. "Well, I probably should have," he said, "but I don't know where it is."

wherever the chance offered, was already strong. Even at New-port News he found time to rent a car and drive up to Washington. Earlier, in Colombo, bored with shore duties, he'd learned to handle the C-in-C's barge, gone out on a minesweeper patrol, attended the Festival of Pera-Hera at Kandy ("Buddha's tooth," he explains in brackets), visited a tea plantation, and then, "I heard there was a survey of Trincomalee harbour going on, so I asked whether I could be sent there to see how it was done." He could, and made the 160 miles there, mostly through "pure jungle," in an old, small car whose steering, when he was recalled a week later, "had definitely given up the ghost." All was dutifully recorded. The C-in-C's barge "was a 40 ft. Scott-Paine power-boat with twin engines, screws and rudders, and about the only thing one could not make it do was spread wings and fly off."

The complexities of mine-sweeping were stimulating:

> To get out the sweep each side is done separately, the leeward side being done first. The orapisa float is dropped, and veered until the required depth for sweeping is out, then the otter-board is slipped, and the sweep-wire . . .

And the write-up of Buddha's Tooth showed the power of observation coming on well:

> I counted 80 elephants in one of these processions all beautifully dressed with bright coloured sheets embroidered with silver and brass. All the old Kandy chiefs took part in these processions and they too were wonderful to look at. Four-cornered gold crowns on there heads then short beautifully embroidered jackets of purple velvet or silver and gold brocade. Then thirty yards of very fine white silk edged with gold, wound round their middles which

made them look as if they had enormous stomachs. They had close fitting trousers on with pointed red leather shoes on their feet. Each of these chiefs was preceeded by his dancers.

(Kandy, like so many other places, was one he'd be seeing again in different circumstances. On the 1953–54 Coronation tour with the Queen, which crammed a dozen Commonwealth territories into its 40,000 miles, the count of processional elephants was bettered—up to 140. That trip started on its last lap, in *Britannia*, from Tobruk, on the coast that *Valiant* had been tearing up with her bombardment twelve years before.)

But the powers of expression hadn't quite found themselves yet, and the spelling, as we've seen, could be wayward.[2] Buoys were a special nuisance. "We secured to a bow and stern bouy . . ." "A channel marked by four bouys about a mile apart . . ." "The ship swung around to starboard of the bouy . . ." Captains and other superiors also seem to have a blind spot for these. Their correcting pencils knock the spare "s" out of "misstakes," pop a "c" into "exept" and amend "Kali float" to "Carley float," but the bouys bob on unchallenged.

That phonetic rendering of Carley, an odd throwback to the Greek, might remind us not to be so damned superior over the orthography of a foreign national fighting our British battles. And when he writes "Italien" for "Italian" it's to be remembered that he spent the first eight years of his life, excursions apart, in Paris. Anyway, if other midshipmen's logs were better spelled, it's doubtful whether they showed the same dash and relish for everything going. From *Ramillies*, in port at Sydney in April 1940, a visit to a sheep station four hundred miles inland: detailed breakdowns of the topography, the vegetation, the climate, the sheep, the men.

---

[2] There are lapses even today. I have a note of his about the Chrystal Palace.

From *Kent*, anchored off Chagos Island in the Solomons, ashore by pinnace on an angling exercise that would have spun Izaak Walton in his grave:

> Before we left the ship the Captain had expressed a [universal] desire for fresh fish . . . so we proceeded to blow them up with small charges. We let go about four charges and collected about fifty or sixty fish. Four of us got into bathing suites and as the fish came to the surface we dived in and threw them into the boat. Eventually after a most interesting day we returned aboard at 1800.

There were other interesting days—at Colombo, Fremantle, Aden, Bombay, Mombasa, Alexandria, Port Said, Athens,[3] Durban. Especially Durban, which appears several times in the page headings, always earning the distinction of an exclamation mark, and sometimes running to three. "The grand unselfish hospitality with which we were welcomed by the people of Durban will live in our memories for years to come, and the fact that many hearts were left behind in Durban is not surprising." Parting was poignant:

> On Friday we heard that leave was only till midnight, and we sadly realised we were about to sail. At 0630 we were leaving the jetty, a grey, damp morning laden with hangovers. There was no one there to wave us goodbye, because nobody knew we were leaving. Outside, the convoy gathered themselves together in a slight swell, with the rain

---

[3] On leave, January–February 1941. Family reunion, with air raids and the Chips Channon rumor-party. The Italians were invading from the north. He records: "While in Greece I had ample opportunity for studying the campaign in Albania. Unfortunately I was unable to visit the front, and watch the fighting on the spot. . . . Considering the unequal balance of numbers and materials, the reason for the success of the Greeks is their magnificent morale, and the Italien's lack of it."

squalls moving over them at intervals, the rain obscured the coast, which quickly went out of sight, and we were at sea again.

As forlorn as the opening of a *Peter Grimes* Sea Interlude.

But things looked up. The hearts gone for good in Durban were mysteriously recovered, and from time to time quickened for other reasons. "We have something to look forward to, there is an enemy raider in the Indian Ocean, and there is just the chance that our tracks will cross." They didn't. Instead, the *Kent,* which he was now on, hit the Trades on the way to Colombo.

> Considering the amount of roll, which was often over twenty degrees, remarkably few people felt any ill effects. Seas were breaking over the foc'sle almost continuously. On one occasion a particularly heavy sea completely smothered the bridge and platform, and even the crow's nest felt the spray from it. Steaming with the sea on the beam and at twenty-one knots the rolling was greatly emphasised, and a lot of innocent fun was had in the mess, watching the Goancse stewards diligently laying the table, and then the plates, knives, forks, spoons, butter dishes, toast racks and marmalade landing in a heap on the deck.

The funnels were white with salt. Some of the upper works were smashed. If he was at all worried thirty years later, when *Britannia* took that beating between the North and South Islands of New Zealand, and the home headlines got so excited, it would only have been for the Queen. It was old stuff for him.

He'd been sorry to leave lumbering old *Ramillies,* but soon had a good word to say for *Kent.* He'd written of *Ramillies:*

> Nobody ever turns in. The most popular sleeping quarters are in the gunroom, where the midshipmen sleep in two

armchairs, two sofas and on the table. It gets very hot at night, since the ship is darkened and every scuttle is shut with deadlights.

In *Kent* these discomforts were diminished.

The ventilation is so much better that it is quite possible to sleep below decks in comfort. There is no danger whatsoever of hitting one's head on the deckhead or beams.

Kent took her amenities for granted. She was the flagship, and crack gunnery ship of the China station—headroom and ventilation were calm assumptions. All the same, not all her company was too happy in early April 1940. She'd completed a two-and-a-half-year commission the autumn before, with prospects of a return home and long leave. War had inconsiderately arrived and dished that. It would have been something if it had also made a dent or two in the ship's inflexible observance of regulations, which it didn't. Finally, the grim news that they were now to be lumbered with a prince of the Royal House of Greece seemed about the last straw. Among the ratings it cast a deep gloom. "You can imagine the comments," says one of them, looking back. "We'd already got a barrack routine, matchstick sentries, a change of rig five or six times a day, and an admiral in the quarterdeck. Now we had to have royalty."

They soon found they were getting into a state about nothing, and were the first to admit it. "I can honestly say,"—same man talking—"that when we first saw this gangling youth, running all over the ship trying to obey instructions from a host of gold braid, smiling and cheerful to everyone, no matter what their rank, he immediately became endeared to us." Fears were so far dispelled, in fact, that to stand a watch with the dreaded intruder soon became an agreeable exercise: "We had the pleasure of his company for long periods, and he often rolled and smoked our home-made cigarettes with us."

Most firsthand accounts of the time pick on the grin and the running. Both have lasted fairly well, though the first gets understandably extinguished at times, and the second has become more of a highly organized progress. Perhaps it doesn't arise so much these days, but he was one of those lucky people it's hard to be angry with.

In Alexandria harbor one night he was in charge of the last picket-boat bringing libertymen back to *Valiant*. The duty boat shipwright remembers having had a bad duty already that night. One boat got her rudder and propellers fouled by lines, and he was called to clear her; another snarled up in a nearby ship's torpedo net and had to be cut free. Then the first boat, back on ship-to-shore service, holed herself on a mooring buoy. (The launches were fast thirty-five-footers, and the harbor was blacked out and full of craft, so this isn't an exposure of Royal Navy incompetence.)

Feeling there wasn't much else that could happen, he was thinking of turning in and chancing it when the loudspeakers again called him out with his bag of tools, this time to the starboard ladder. "Now what the hell have you done?" He looked down into the gloom, where the last boat was stuck against the side, the two stanchions of the ladder platform rammed through her bows. It was an insubordinate remark, even to a midshipman who wasn't a prince. "Very sorry, Chippy," said the voice from below, genuinely remorseful, but in a cheerful key, all things considered. Philip then joined the rescue party in the two hours' work of clearing and hoisting inboard, and the duty shipwright found his natural resentment seeping away.

Philip hadn't been at the wheel, but as the only officer aboard it was his responsibility, and he had his shore leave stopped for a fortnight until the launch was repaired. Mysteriously, or perhaps not, the episode doesn't appear in the log.

The same man remembers a time when the cheerfulness failed. *Illustrious* was being dive-bombed off Malta. In nearby *Valiant*, stationed in one of the fifteen-inch turrets, the midshipman was watching the fun from the hatch—the heavy armament naturally having nothing useful to do in an air attack—and was ordered under cover by the gunner's mate because he'd lost his steel helmet ("Get the hell out, we've enough to worry about without any headless princes"). He was then observed pacing and muttering on the Marines' mess deck, where a repair party was working. One of them thought he was frightened by the din—there were fifty anti-aircraft guns firing for a start—and said a comforting word: "It's all right, Sir, it sounds worse than it is." It didn't go well. You want a front seat for a show like that.

One thing that strongly appealed to him about *Kent* was her improved facilities, over *Ramillies*, for cocoa brewing, a duty that seems to have dominated life a good deal and gets several references, mostly unenthusiastic. On a page headed "Middle of Indian Ocean, Germans in Paris, Italy Enters War," he notes with satisfaction:

> Have been changed round with one of the senior Midshipmen. . . . We keep three watches up there and we are not relieved for instruction. There is the advantage that you are your own master . . . and no cocoa to be made.

He'd added, "And no one to bother you," but prudently scribbled it out. Other people were going to read this, after all. People for whom cocoa had to be made. (One of his early sea duties in *Ramillies* had been "Captain's doggie.")

Over any chronicler of these times, the little-did-he-think syndrome inevitably threatens. It's tempting to hark forward, if there is such a thing, to the day at Spithead.

There were other preoccupations, besides the required flow of cocoa. Midshipmen lived at the run, and the Journal pants behind, trying to get everything in: practice shoots, paravane streaming, searchlight exercises, manning action stations for real or imaginary alerts. The convoys were met, marshaled, escorted, delivered—sometimes such resounding protégées as *Queen Elizabeth, Andes, Orcades; Empress of Canada, Viceroy of India;* sometimes "Dutch passenger ships with completely unpronounceable names." Other British ships on other escorts flit in and out of the record, soon sounding like old friends. From *Kent* he would see *Shropshire*, from *Shropshire* he would see *Kent*. "The next day we were joined by *Orion, Ajax, York* and *Perth* . . ." "That morning we met *Barham, Eagle, Orion, Perth, Ajax* and *Gloucester* . . ." "At about 0800 we put to sea in company with *Warspite, Barham* and *Formidable*, who has come out to take the place of *Illustrious* . . ."

Shore leave wasn't always up to expectations. "Aden even before the Italiens came in was not over exiting, but now with most of the civilian population evacuated, and a blackout, there was nothing doing at all, and they had run out of beer!" (Italy had come in on June 10, 1940, his nineteenth birthday.)

Unbelievably, the shine could even be taken off the delights of Durban:

> We soon discovered that the person responsible for our late leave being all-night was not as humane as we thought. There was field-training for all Midshipmen on the wharf, from quarter past nine to quarter to twelve.

The fact that one feels rather weak at that time after a run ashore on the previous evening, and that the temperature in the shade hovered around 80°F., and that the gunner's mate was also recovering and anyhow displeased by our efforts to manipulate an oily rifle in a military manner, did not help the rebirth of the "joy-of-living" which had ebbed away during the spell in the red sea, and was only just becoming apparent again.

The entry of Italy had brought prospects of action nearer. There were reports of Mussolini's ships and aircraft. In London those concerned with the risks to a foreign and royal midshipman must have been anxious. Though they had other things to be anxious about. In one of his periodic surveys of the wider scene, the diarist wrote, after Dunkirk:

The situation in Europe seems rather bad. The Germans have marched into Paris and there seems no way of stopping them. Knowing what the atmosphere was like in certain circles in London before the German offensive I should hate to think what kind of a panic they must be in now. However, we are assured that although the situation is very grave indeed the home front is taking everything very calmly, although the politians are doing their utmost to beat all previous tonge-wagging records.

There are noticeable prefigurations of character and attitude. An independence—that bit about being your own master—but an acceptance all the same, of things as they are, and no repining. Granted, a midshipman hasn't a lot of option, but this impatient spirit might have found other sources of dissatisfaction besides poor cocoa-brewing amenities and the elusiveness of the enemy. There's the

boundless physical vigor. Powerful curiosity. And the odd paradox, still discernible thirty years later, of a natural modesty, a
sparing use of the first person singular, and that touchiness over
others' shortcomings which smacks of knowing better. He'd only
been in *Ramillies* a fortnight when a practice shoot displeased him.
"The trainer was very bad, and kept moving the turret continuously as if he were driving a car. This never gave the layers a
chance to get on the target." In *Shropshire:* "We were visited by
the Italien air force, but it was frightened away by what appeared
to be very inaccurate shooting by *Carlisle.*" And in *Kent*, when
"friendly [and enemy] aircraft were expected," he kept his personal eye well peeled, "knowing the seeming incapability of look-
outs ever seeing anything." Sometimes there was a pat on the back
for higher authority. Instruction by gunnery officers in running
the air defense position was "an important step forward, as we
will now come into closer contact with the ratings." A blow for
fraternization, the closing of the rank gap? Or the cooler view,
that in this of all communities it was commonsense to know how
the other half lived?

Probably the latter. It's often thought today, even by those
close to him, that he hasn't a strong feeling for people as individuals.
The people, the race, yes, but people, not so much, though there
are one or two close spirits, and the rare off-beat figure can appeal.[4] But the log, covering a year of his life at an impressionable
time, with five postings and a lot of throwings-together, is strangely
thin on proper names. A C-in-C may get one, but that's about it.
(In his present life, of course, there's small chance of grappling
friends to his soul with hoops of steel, as recommended by Po-

---

[4] The Queen has softer feelings about individuals. Watching, with the family, a
TV newsreel of the Queen talking to an old bed-ridden dear who'd been brought
out of the house on to the sidewalk so that she shouldn't miss the great moment,
a guest ventured a mild commiseration at the poignancy of some royal duties.
The Queen missed the point but took another, saying quite angrily, "They should
never have done it. It might have killed her."

lonius: acquaintances and associates beyond number, but fewer friends. Anyway, there are all those affectionate relations.)

But there's an Able Seaman named. One of *Valiant*'s casualties, he "was buried at sea that night, after a short service on the quarterdeck in the dim moonlight." *Valiant* had been spouting shells into Bardia, and the Junkers 87Bs came back with bombs and machine-gunning. Bardia fell for the first time on January 5, 1941. Philip had joined *Valiant*, and the shooting war, three days earlier. Since October 1940 Greece had been in, and the embarrassingly neutral midshipman could now be properly exposed to fire. It suited him. From Bardia the Journal takes off with new gusto. The maps and diagrams fall off to nothing. Who's going to sweat over colored drawings of a capstan engine when you're in the middle of things at last?

> That evening at dusk the Battlefleet put to sea and shortly afterwards we were told we were going to bombard Bardia on the Libyan coast. We arrived off the coast on Thursday morning at dawn. In the dark the flashes of the guns could be seen a long way out to sea. We went to action stations at 0730, and at 0810 the bombardment commenced. . . . The whole operation was a very spectacular affair.

There was more spectacle to come. At first, a few days after Bardia, some liveliness off the south of Sicily:

> At dawn action stations on Friday gun flashes were sighted on the starboard bow. We increased speed to investigate, and by the time we were within five miles it was almost daylight. *Bonaventure* signalled that *Southampton* and herself were engaging two enemy destroyers. We could just see one of these destroyers blowing up in a cloud

of smoke and spray. The other escaped. Shortly after this the destroyer *Gallant* hit a mine and her bow was blown off, and floated slowly away on the swell. . . . At noon two torpedo bombers attacked us, but a quick alteration of course foiled their attempt, and their fish passed down the port side. Shortly after this sixteen German dive-bombers attacked the *Illustrious*. She was hit aft and amidships and fires broke out. Then the bombers concentrated on us and five bombs dropped fairly close.

The record is matter-of-fact. The page headings are laconic. One of them covers quite a bit of ground: "Dive-Bombers. Illustrious hit. Southampton sunk. Leave."

The leave was in Athens, where he had "ample opportunity for studying the campaign in Albania," but was unfortunately not able to visit the front. He stayed, naturally enough, with his royal relations, gathered there in family solidarity before the impending dash for the short-lived safety of Crete, then to Alexandria, then many separate ways—except for his mother, Alice, who hung on stubbornly through the German occupation, her home filled with fugitives from the SS (it took courage to shelter, as she did at one time, a family of Cohens) and her usual run of general lame ducks.

His sisters were in Germany, his father in Monte Carlo, so the reunion was mostly with uncles, aunts and cousins. The King was there, Crown Prince Paul (and Frederica) and second cousin Alexandra. There were parties, dancing, record-playing and bombs. They would go on the roof of the palace to watch the air raids, but accounts differ on whether he "showed off a bit by making knowledgeable comments on the action" or "never talked shop and never had a word to say on his personal naval duties." That he charmed everyone, and not only Sir Henry Channon, seems clear. But the impression, as so often, is that no one really got inside his head. Back to *Valiant*, and the Journal, and still no names dropped, though an ominous place name begins to crop up. Suda Bay.

Valiant began convoying troops to Crete. It was a belated reinforcement of that island's defenses, though the Battle of Crete, when it came, was over in little more than a week. It was from a blacked-out, embattled Suda that Alexandra and Frederica, with old Prince George, then seventy-one, left in the flying-boat with other less essential symbols of the continuing monarchy, while the King stuck it out to the last moment before making reluctantly for the south and HMS *Decoy*.

It's often said that Philip, in *Valiant*, was with the escort accompanying *Decoy* to Alexandria. He wasn't, which is tough luck on the dramatically minded. *Valiant* was busy to the north, trying with destroyers and cruiser squadrons to intercept German seaborne landings. Successfully, but at a price. The Journal entry for May 22, the third day of the battle, shows his powers of observation and expression much developed. Being in the thick of things also seems to have tightened up the spelling:

> Next day things began to get worse. *Juno* was sunk. *Naiad* and *Carlisle* were hit. A signal came asking for assistance, so we turned and steamed at 20 knots. . . . As we came in sight of the straits we saw *Naiad* and *Carlisle* being attacked by bombers. We went right in to within 10 miles of Crete and then the bombing started in earnest. Stukas came over but avoided the big ships and went for the crippled cruisers and destroyer screens. *Greyhound* was hit right aft by a large bomb, her stern blew up and she sank about 20 minutes later. *Gloucester* and *Fiji* were sent in to help them. . . . Three Me. 109s attacked *Warspite* as divebombers, and she was hit just where her starboard forrard mounting was. . . . When we had got about 15 miles from

the land 16 Stukas came out and attacked the two cruisers. *Gloucester* was badly hit and sank some hours later. The fleet then had some more attention, and we were bombed from a high level by a large number of small bombs dropped in sticks of 12 or more. One Dornier came straight for us from the port beam and dropped 12 bombs when he was almost overhead. We turned to port and ceased firing, when suddenly the bombs came whistling down, landing very close all down the port side.

Just the facts. The style rather puts the damper on more excitable accounts by people who weren't there. For example:

Then the *Valiant* sailed to take part in the Battle of Crete. In the smoke and bitter fighting of May 22 1941 *Valiant* was hit by a big bomb that shook up the ship and all on board. Philip was functioning at top efficiency. In spite of the horror of spattered blood and human flesh, and heart-stopping screams of wounded men, he had an exhilarating sense of power.

Or, as the Journal puts it:

It was only some time later that I discovered we had been hit twice on the quarterdeck. One bomb exploded just abaft the quarterdeck screen on the port side. . . . The other landed within twenty feet of it, just inboard of the guard-rails, blowing a hole into the wardroom laundry. . . . There were only four casualties.

Another writer got perhaps pardonably worked up as he reconstructed the midshipman's part in the Battle of Matapan:

Philip, controlling the probing shafts of light from his searchlight section, which caught the diving planes screaming shipwards with their loads of bombs, and unmoved as the cannon shell ripped down the pathways of the golden beams to smash his lights, was taking his baptism in the art of modern sea warfare. He survived unscathed amid his shattered lights, and he had done so well while the current lasted that his name appeared in dispatches.

His own account is worth giving in full, and not only because it differs in the more lurid details:

My orders were that if any ship illuminated a target I was to switch on and illuminate it for the rest of the fleet, so when this ship was lit up by a rather dim light from what I thought was the flag-ship I switched on our midship light which picked out the enemy cruiser and lit her up as if it were broad daylight. She was only seen complete in the light for a few seconds as the flagship had already opened fire, and as her first broadside landed and hit she was blotted out from just abaft the bridge to right stern. We fired our first broadside about 7 seconds after the flagship with very much the same effect. The broadside only consisted of "A" and "B" turrets as the after turrets would not bear.

By now all the secondary armament of both ships had opened fire and the noise was considerable. The Captain and the Gunnery Officer now began shouting from the bridge for the searchlights to train left. The idea that there might have been another ship, with the one we were firing at, never entered my head, so it was some few moments before I was persuaded to relinquish the blazing target and search for another one I had no reason to believe was there. However, training to the left, the light picked up another cruiser, ahead of the first one by some 3 or 4 cables. As the enemy was so close the light did not illuminate the whole ship but only about ¾ of it, so I trained left over the whole ship until the bridge structure was in the centre of the beam. The effect was rather like flashing a strong torch on a small model about 5 yards away. . . . She was illuminated in an undamaged condition for the period of about 5 seconds when our second broadside left the ship, and almost at once she was completely blotted out from stem to stern. . . .

When that broadside was fired, owing to the noise of the secondary armament, I did not hear the "ting-ting" from the DCT, the result was that the glasses were rammed into my eyes, and flash almost blinding me. Luckily the searchlight was not affected, so that when I was able to see something again the light was still on target. Four more broadsides were fired at the enemy, and more than 70% of the shells must have hit. The only correction given by the control officer was "left 1°," as he thought we were hitting a bit far aft.

When the enemy had completely vanished in clouds of smoke and steam we ceased firing and switched the light off.

Possibly a little underplaying. It wouldn't be intentional. Perhaps the oddest thing about it, considering everything, is that it's all so calm, so controlled, so—as we like to think—English.

Valiant took a week to patch up. They found another eight-foot hole, narrow but deep, in the starboard torpedo protection bulges amidships. In fact, though the Journal doesn't mention it, Philip was the one who found it. He noticed it when he went ashore at Alexandria; when he came back it had gone, but only because the ship had refueled and the gash had disappeared below the water line. It was a day or two later that he happened to mention it to the Commander, who said, "What hole?" No one else had seen it before it went out of sight. They spent the next week with a ten-degree list while the repair was done.

The ship was still refitting as the tragedy of Crete rushed to its close. *Ajax, Orion, Perth, Carlisle, Coventry, Calcutta* and the rest were running a desperate shuttle service, scooping off what battered Allied troops they could manage and bringing them into Alexandria. They could only be reported from hearsay:

> *Calcutta* was sunk. *Nubian* had her stern blown off but managed to return at 20 knots. . . . *Orion* was hit by two bombs, one of them completely wrecked "A" turret, the other went in through the bridge, down five decks and exploded making an enormous hole killing 140 sailors, and 200 soldiers who were being evacuated. For almost a week this went on day after day, ships coming in packed with troops, destroyers showing not-under-control balls, cruisers peppered with shrapnel from near misses.

Mountbatten's *Kelly* had already gone down (not that the name is dropped here). *Kashmir*, too. While *Kipling* was picking up survivors she ran over the submerging *Kelly* and "slit a hole in three compartments forward. . . . The same morning we heard that *Fiji* had been sunk with *Gloucester*. *Kingston* had an incredible list of survivors, about 200 from *Fiji* and 60 from *Greyhound*."

By comparison, Alexandria was dull. "During this period a few raids were made." The port's oil tanks were hit and blazed themselves out. The town was bombed. Parachute mines showered down on the inner harbor. And a pettish note crept into the log, with a relapse of spelling: "All Egyptians with famillies, and those who could afford it, evacuated themselves to Cairo. The result is that there are no taxis to be had, and very few Gharrys." The sort of thing that takes the fun out of a few hours ashore. However, he was shortly to be removed from these irritations. Early in June he was posted to England for his sub-lieutenant's examination. The Journal went with him to be produced to the examiners, as laid down.

The Coronation Review at Spithead wasn't his first naval appearance as Admiral of the Fleet. On board HMS *Devonshire*, in April 1953, two months before, he'd been giving away the prizes to naval cadets.

> "I would like to congratulate heartily all the prize-winners—and at the same time offer my sympathy to all those who were unsuccessful—an experience with which I am quite familiar."

Well, you have to get into a speech the best way you can. It was a perfectly admissible joke, and took the starch out of things as intended. But it wasn't true, and the next bit wouldn't have beaten a lie-detector either.

> "I'm afraid I'm in no position to offer you any advice about your future in the Navy, as I only served about half a Dog Watch myself."

He then went on, naturally, to offer advice.

Prizes and success hadn't noticeably evaded him. In his own days at Dartmouth he won the Eardley-Howard-Crockett prize as best cadet, and the King's Dirk as the best all-round cadet of his term. (The first of these awards involved more kudos than cash. The £2 book-token went on Liddell Hart's *The Defence of Britain*.) He hadn't excelled particularly at Cheam, it's true: he won a prize for French, nothing special after living in France for seven years, but the competitive streak didn't really show until the later schooldays at Gordonstoun. There he ended up as captain of cricket, hockey and the school—and his headmaster, the legendary Kurt Hahn, was no feather-bedder for rank. His seamanship earned him the rare privilege of sailing an open boat in the Moray Firth without adult supervision. And it mustn't be forgotten that the Dartmouth successes were under a handicap. He was up against cadets whose whole education, since preparatory school, had been at the Royal Naval College; he arrived late, at seventeen and a half, a Special Entry who hadn't been absorbing the feel of the place through his pores for four years or so as most of the others had.

In the sub-lieutenant's examination for which he left *Valiant* in January 1941 he came through with four firsts and one second. It meant that he went back to sea in the old destroyer *Wallace* with nine months' seniority out of a possible ten, and when he became her first lieutenant in October 1942, at the wish of his own captain, who knew a good thing when he saw one, he was one of the youngest second-in-commands in the Navy. He was twenty-one, and pitchforked into a long, thankless stint of east coast convoy work, shuttling from Rosyth to Sheerness and back, among the bombs and torpedoes.

He was determined that *Wallace* should be run better than any other destroyer in the squadron. There was another first lieutenant with the same idea, Lieutenant Michael Parker, on *Lauderdale*, an intelligent and engaging Australian who had transferred from the Australian to the British Navy in 1938. He was a year older than Philip, and a custom-made fellow spirit. In *Lauderdale* and *Wallace* they not only competed with each other at sea, for efficiency and smartness (the perpetual battle for paint was fought with many stratagems and wiles), but were continually raising, and playing in, ship's teams for sporting events on land. If it wasn't cricket or hockey or football it might well be bowls—the green outside Sheerness's Royal Fountain Hotel saw famous battles.

Out of the rivalry, which was at the same time intensely serious and a huge lark, one of the rare friendships grew. They had a lot in common. They were both mad about the Navy, enjoyed the war—not for its horrors but its challenge—and above all loved to laugh. Ashore together, or in each other's wardrooms, there was bound to be fun. More even than most, they were cut off from their own people. Parker's home was twelve thousand miles off. Philip hadn't got one. Both men were honest, direct, dynamically energetic; both had the trick of being serious about serious things but readily alive to the ridiculous. Both had the common touch invaluable in small ships, and would know by name a company of 250.

After *Wallace* and *Lauderdale* they were together again, in *Whelp* and *Wessex*, with the 27th destroyer flotilla of the Pacific Fleet, up against the Japanese off Burma or Sumatra, shelling the oilfields of Palembang; they were poised for what promised to be the bloodiest battle, the invasion of Japan, when the bomb fell on Hiroshima, and that was that.

Before then, there'd been leave at Sydney. Briefly, Parker was home. Philip met his family. There were junketings. With Mike's sister and other decorative companions they even had a day at the races. Mike at the time was wearing a full Player's Navy Cut beard (Philip had had one but removed it[5]), and the local press, getting wind of royalty, surged around the party yelling, "Which is the Prince?" "He's the chap behind, with the beard," said Philip. Parker was tempted to make a statement, but fought it down.

It was hardly surprising that when the marriage boiled up, two

---

[5] "Elizabeth soon made him shave it off," says one writer, rushing his chronology a bit.

years after VE Day, with all its weighty implications, it was Mike
Parker who was asked to join the strength. It was a great com-
bination. At first he was joint equerry to both husband and wife.
After the Accession, when Elizabeth came in not only for a kingdom but a wall of divisive protocol, he became Philip's own man.
The Queen had her own men in abundance. It was Parker's grim
task, when they were all in Kenya together in February 1952, to
tell Philip that the King had died. "I never felt so sorry for anyone in all my life. He looked as if you'd dropped half the world
on him." Both men knew that everything had changed.

"We got out of that place in an hour," he remembers. He
and Martin Charteris, then Princess Elizabeth's private secretary,
packed up, worked out timetables, sent a flood of signals, organized a plane at Entebbe, another from Mombasa to get there, and
timed a London airport arrival for 1600 hours. Though the King's
death was only a possibility when they left home, a Royal Standard
had been stowed in the baggage.

Until Michael Parker's divorce and departure in 1957, he'd had
ten years of service and friendship with Elizabeth and Philip. The
break was sad for all three, and was entirely his own decision.

They both urged him to stay (the Queen by radio-telephone to
Gibraltar, where Philip's world tour in *Britannia* was ending after
visiting many remoter specks of the Commonwealth). Prince
Philip drove with him to his plane for home, where he hoped for
a couple of hours' peace before facing the press at Heathrow.
Some hope. Every other seat had been booked by reporters.

Those close to royalty try to dodge the reflected glare, but this
was a direct light. For Parker it was the beginning of a bad time.
Journalists stopped his children on the way to school. One, claiming to be a naval officer, took up with his actress sister, and when
Mike, as a brotherly gesture, had them both to dinner, he found
the man had never sailed in anything more watertight than a Lon-

don evening paper. He came home one night to find a reporter going through his dustbin.

This seems a good time to say that Parker's conduct throughout the whole glum affair was honorable beyond all reasonable demands. He took all the mud-slinging that should properly have landed in other, and by no means obvious, quarters. Prince Philip's six-word summary, "He felt he had to go," could have run to some length. They still correspond, occasionally meet. Deliberately, Parker doesn't make the approaches. Philip is godfather to his elder daughter.

There was an occasion in Malta, HMS *Chequers* and the more free-wheeling days of peace, when Prince Philip had a failure. It was early in 1950, when his career as a husband went on in happy parallel with his career in the Navy. Later Elizabeth was to join him there, and live much as any other navy wife. It was her first and perhaps only complete escape from palaces, and she enjoyed it. Uncle Dickie, then flag officer commanding the First Cruiser Squadron in the Mediterranean, gave his house over to them, the Villa Guardamangia, with Philip's ship at the bottom of the hill.

The failure was earlier, and chiefly of interest because it picks out a thread that ran through all his time at sea, and has by no means faded since—his passionate desire to be valued as a man and not a prince. He's not against princeliness as long as it serves a purpose. But the trappings of grandeur, with blind obeisance, that's different. He may even be overobsessed with proving that he doesn't need them.

The occasion was his Command Examination, the big jump that lands a naval officer, with luck, on his own quarterdeck. There seemed no doubt that he'd walk it. Which he did, except for one subject, generally supposed to be his best. Michael Parker, now out of the Navy but in Malta with him at the time, was bidden to call on the Commander-in-Chief, Admiral Sir Arthur J. Power (known to all as "Arthur John"), and found him beetle-browing at his study window overlooking the Grand Harbor. He had Philip's flunked paper in his hand. "Who's this bloody examiner?" he said. "He's failed him in Torpedo and ASDIC!" Parker, who would now have to carry the bad news, got the alarming impression that the Admiral was thinking of overruling the bloody examiner, saying that he'd been through the paper himself and thought it was a damned good pass. He knew better than to hint at any such possibility when he reported back. Philip was furious anyway, when he heard of the interview. Not at failing, but at the Admiral's surprise that such a thing could happen. He had as much right to mess up an exam paper as the next man. There must have been a touch of telepathy too. He said, on an enraged premonition, "If they try to fix it, I quit the Navy for good!" They didn't. He sat again, and went through like a breeze.

As to that "half a Dog Watch," when he did quit the Navy in July 1951—it was called indefinite leave, but the King was already ill, and clearly there were going to be other things to do— the Navy had been more than a third of his life. As a profession he'd known nothing else. From Dartmouth to his own command, the frigate *Magpie*, in twelve years.

And a good deal in between. By the end of the war he'd sailed all the oceans, and got to know people all over the world, many of whom still feel, on his return visits in splendor, that they have a special claim on him. (It's odd, during some Australian motorcade, to see hairy-chested building workers cheering him and throwing streamers from the tops of buildings, thinking of him as a long-lost buddy.) He'd covered the evacuations of Greece and

Crete, the Canadian landings in Sicily, the Allied invasion of North Africa, survived a lot of battles, broken—or possibly just hairline-cracked—a few hearts (he tended to fade when pursuits got intense), had fun, lived down being a prince, grown to admire and respect the Royal Navy and all who sailed in her.

In its turn, the Navy had drawn out and bred up the modern, scientific, technological and practical[6] man, who was later to be endlessly questioning and suggesting in areas where applied science should be doing more both for the nation as a whole and for its individual citizens.

> You've got to bear in mind that the Navy is a techno-
> logical profession, and that the transition from that to
> commercial technology isn't very great. All service equip-
> ment has to be advanced, in the sense that it's worth while
> putting in a new technique, even if it's still experimental,
> if it will give you a slight advantage over everybody else:
> so that the services are very often the first people to feel the
> effects of scientific discovery and scientific application.

On September 2, 1945, *Whelp* was in Tokyo Bay, one of the first Allied ships to enter Japanese waters. Another was Admiral Halsey's flagship, USS *Missouri*. Aboard her the Instrument of Surrender was signed. The signatures were those of the frock-coated politicians. It was another ten days, in Singapore, before the defeated generals handed over their swords to Lord Mountbatten, now Supreme Allied Commander, Southeast Asia, and it was under his orders, however remote, that *Whelp* and the rest were sent off to collect and bring home prisoners of war, before making back to Portsmouth. There *Whelp* was decommissioned,

---

[6] Checking proposed arrangements for a Fleet occasion in which Charles and Anne were to be present, he came to an item saying they would both go aboard one of the ships. He crossed it through and wrote, "One each." Obvious really.

and her first lieutenant put in charge during the two-month process. In its anticlimactic way, it was his first command. It was 1946. In the summer he had some leave. If he hadn't been invited to spend it at Balmoral the matchmakers might not yet have begun to twitter. Or perhaps they might. They did, anyway.

Interviewer: Your childhood and adolescence were spent in the
                unsettled and unhappy circumstances of exile–
HRH: I don't think it necessarily was particularly un-
                happy. It wasn't all that unsettled.

His surviving sisters, Margarita and Sophie (or Princess Gottfried of Hohenlohe-Langenburg and Princess George of Hanover)
went to the pains of meeting me at the Hotel Vier Jahreszeiten in
Munich, which placed a room at our disposal containing a twenty-
foot boardroom table and sixteen green leather-bound blotters.
They managed to make it seem intimate all the same, and talked
about him fondly, mostly together, and competing with the sounds
of the Maximilianstrasse traffic and the city being dug up to sink
an underground railway for the 1972 Olympics. I asked about
the unhappy exiled child:
"We stayed at first in St. Cloud, because our Uncle George of
Greece and his wife, Marie Bonaparte, had two houses in this
big park and they gave us one . . ." "They had several houses
all round there . . ." "And our parents went to America that
winter to stay with my father's younger brother, Prince Christopher, who had married . . ." "So there were months in London
at Kensington Palace with my grandmother, Philip would be about
two . . ." "And at St. Cloud, Uncle George, who adored children, used to come over every single evening to say his prayers
with him and kiss him good night . . ." "On the Baltic Sea, where
the Landgrave and Langravine of Hesse had their summer house,
and Philip and our mother were there . . ." "He was older then,

he was very pugnacious and the other children were scared to death of him . . ." "It was close to there, about an hour away, where old Princess Henry of Prussia had a property, where he jumped off a hay wagon and broke a front tooth, of course he was a great show-off, he would always stand on his head when visitors came . . ." "We four girls were very afraid his mother was spoiling him. She wasn't, but we felt that as he was the youngest, and a boy, he might be spoilt, and we were all very anxious to prevent it and were all particularly strict and disagreeable to him. He must have suffered awfully, poor child, in those days . . ." "One very lovely year we were invited by Queen Helen of Romania, and her son Michael was three or four months younger than Philip, and was King, and we went to Sinaia, high in the mountains . . ." "No, but first in Bucharest, then it was getting rather hot so we went down to their house on the Black Sea, at the mouth of the Danube . . ." "Sinaia was lovely. I mean, a hideous castle, but baths all over the place, very comfortable . . ." "And we had horses to ride by the Black Sea and the children had ponies, and it was very funny, because Philip had never seen a horse and was a little bit nervous, but Michael quite accustomed to it, but at the seaside Michael had never seen the sea and was nervous, but Philip very much at home . . ." "And sometimes our father would be there, sometimes at Wolfsgarten, or Langenburg, or Salem, and they had a great great fondness for each other. They used to laugh together like mad."

9

Family Album

*"I think all one's previous experience tends to create
what you are at the moment."*

The childhood of Prince Philip of Greece, said someone, "would
have turned Dr. Spock's hair white."

Who shall escape hyperbole?

It had an early shake-up on *Calypso* day, perhaps when his
accommodation en route from Corfu to Brindisi was a cot im-
provised out of a fruit crate by resourceful British tars, but even
professors of child development could differ on the traumatic
effects of that, at eighteen months. It wasn't his first foreign excursion, though he'd had a softer ride before when Alice had twice
taken him to England, first, when three months old, for the funeral
of his maternal grandfather, Prince Louis of Battenberg (who had
died the Marquess of Milford Haven) in September 1921, and again
a year later as a nonplaying guest at the wedding of Louis Mount-

batten. They stayed at Kensington Palace with the widowed Marchioness, and Philip, as on later childhood visits, took the English air in Kensington Gardens, where nannies and prams were still as much a part of the scene as the Round Pond and Peter Pan. (When he told the *Newcastle Journal* that he'd been to England twice before he was oversimplifying.)

The birth at Mon Repos, on Corfu, went unremarked outside the family, though Alice lost no time in spreading the good news to those keenly interested parties. It had been seven years since her youngest daughter was born, sixteen since her eldest. The occasion wasn't accompanied by any ceremonial.

When Prince Charles was born at Buckingham Palace on November 14, 1948, "at 9.14 o'clock this evening" as the official announcement said, London and the world had been waiting. Since dawn, a crowd of thousands had been milling around the railings. The Harley Street limousines of Sir John Weir and Sir William Gilliatt periodically parted the mobs to roll in and out of the gates, until at last they stayed in and were joined by those of Mr. Peel and Mr. Hall of King's College Hospital. Though the Home Secretary, for the first time in history, wasn't in the palace—long held to be an essential safeguard against a switch of royal babies— the anteroom was well studded with suspense-wracked notabilities, the King, the Queen and Queen Mary among them.

The expectant father, never a good heel-kicker, eased his own tensions in a game of squash with Michael Parker, until the time came to see his son, bring his wife carnations and roses, and open champagne for the delighted relations and members of the Household. Telegrams flew to the four corners of the earth, the Trafalgar Square fountains turned blue for a boy (and kept it up for a week), and the citizens, now almost filling the Mall, cheered and sang into the damp small hours. They overdid it, in fact, and no one inside the palace knew how to stop the din and let Elizabeth get some sleep. In the end Mike Parker crossed the forecourt to the railings and appealed to the nearest intelligent-looking person to pass back a message. He then saw that it was David Niven. Somehow it worked, and things quieted down.

At Mon Repos on June 10, 1921, it was altogether a quieter affair.

The villa with the almost comical semi-detached name had originally belonged to Sir Frederick Adam; it was built in the 1820s when he was British High Commissioner of the Ionians, which were later restored to Greece as part of the deal that brought King George I to the throne. The King left it to his fourth son, Andrew, whose nephew, George II, helpfully bought it back in 1937. Helpfully, because in return for the title deeds Andrew was to have a tax-free annuity of 400,000 drachmas. It sounds bountiful. By the values of the time it was about £750. In Monte Carlo, even in 1937, it couldn't have gone far. The house was built in elegant neo-classical English style, and would have sat comfortably among the pillared porticos and wrought-iron balconies of John Nash's Regency terraces, though they have less and cooler air around them, no blue gulf below, and no olive trees, cypresses, oranges, lemons or eucalyptus. It's still a summer home, at least in theory, of the present, yet absent, King. The cruise brochures list it among the island's attractions: "Birthplace of Prince Philip." But there's nothing much to see, and the coaches don't stop.

Beside the elaborate preparations for the arrival of Prince Charles, those on Corfu were modest. The one doctor was the local general practitioner. In the Buhl Room at the palace nothing was lacking by way of equipment. At Mon Repos, Philip was delivered on the dining-room table, not for want of beds but because Alice, who was thirty-six and in a high state of nerves from other than natural and immediate causes, was thought by the doctor to stand a better chance. There was some local fetching and carrying help. There was Nurse Roose (who had prudently stocked up with English baby foods). Also the daughters, the two elder ones, at sixteen and fifteen, capable of being useful.

Alice was entitled to her anxieties. Almost to the day, Prince Andrew had sailed for Smyrna with his brother King Constantine in the battleship *Lemnos,* for what was to be his last absence at the wars. He was always in her mind. Earlier in her pregnancy the Turks had announced, either as propaganda or a genuine mistake, that he had "died of wounds near Broussa." It couldn't have helped.

Philip soon turned out to be fat, cheerful, snow-blond, belligerent, and much loved. The picture of his early years in Paris as the lonely child of a broken home has been somewhat overpainted —all those tales of no toys, patched pants and times when, says one determined tear-jerker, he stayed after school on wet days and explained that he was "saving up for a raincoat." This was the infant school at St. Cloud, oddly named The Elms. Its alumni were mainly the children of the Diplomatic Corps and of wealthy expatriate Americans, with a stiffening of royalty: Prince Philip's classmates included Prince Jacques de Bourbon and his sister Princess Anne, who later married King Michael of Romania. The fees were stiff, but Andrew's brother Christopher took care of those. He was another of Philip's uncles to have made a prosperous marriage, to Mrs. Nancy Leeds, widow of an American tinplate tycoon. (She was his first wife, and he loved her deeply, bank balance apart; but she died tragically soon, and in 1929 he married Princess Françoise of France.)

Alice, it's often said, struggled along by running a little shop, selling Greek embroidery and works of art. The shop is true enough, but what small profit it made didn't go to keep the Andrews in groceries; as usual with her, it was the poor and needy, mostly Greek refugees, that she had in mind. A friend who was in Paris at the time said, "Yes, I remember her shop. Her lady-in-waiting took me to see it." This was overpainting things the other way. The "lady-in-waiting" was a companion, friend and fellow refugee who lived with them, and if she did any waiting she probably didn't get a bean in return.

Still, "We weren't well off," says Philip.

But these things are relative. Nurse Roose was still in the counting. Far from Philip's being fatherless, Prince Andrew was at St. Cloud with the rest of them, and had a valet to shine his good shoes. Naturally, it was all a bit of a comedown, and the younger princesses tended to inherit the older ones' party dresses, but that's been known in other families not exactly on the bread-line. And, as with all Royals ousted by republicans, pro-monar-chist friends were ready and eager to help when things got too tough, rather than see the precious gilding tarnish.

The children's holidays weren't only with queens or Landgraves, in Romania or Germany. Sometimes at Blakeney, on the Norfolk Broads, which sounds strange. Sometimes back to Corfu, where the sisters dunked Philip determinedly in the sea (and once thought they'd overdone it and he wasn't going to bob up again. He bobbed). At Marseilles, where Alexandrian–Greek friends had a farm, a house and beach on the Mediterranean, and three suitably small children; and with the same family at Berck Plage, near Le Touquet, where they took a house when one of the children was ill and under treatment there. Among the rare authentic stories of Philip's childhood is the account of how an insensitive grown-up arrived one day on the beach with toys for all but the invalid child, assumed to be ruled out for playthings. Philip, who was five, went into the house and collected all his personal treasures and presented them to her, the latest acquisition on top.

It could have been showing off. It was more probably an early glimpse of character. One of his equerries recently came out with something on this: "What people don't realize is that he's immensely kind. No one has a bigger heart, or takes greater pains to conceal it." Pretty sentimental, for a military man. He'd been talking, in fact, of another aspect of character that gives his staff headaches, a sort of mischievous perverseness ("He knows he's *doing* it, don't worry") that likes to unravel a subordinate's decision, which has usually been taken with the idea of saving him trouble. That day a fairly cranky letter had come in, enclosing a pop record, and saying that if it got a princely push into the charts its message could work wonders for human concord. Not the kind of thing he would want to be fretted with. It got a polite letter from the office, and the small, closed file went upstairs in the usual way, showing the action taken. It came down again with a jotting. "Can't we do better than this?" And instructions to send it to a showbiz friend. "Ask her if it's any good. P."

The friend, as it happens, had been one of the Berck Plage family, all those years back, her parents staunch Greek Royalists. Her mother was at school in Athens with Philip's eldest sister. He's now godfather to her two children.

There's one other reliable tale of those times. It was at Berck Plage that Philip, having observed nomadic salesmen of oriental works on the beach, dragged out a couple of his hostess's carpets and tried setting up business on his own. They were repossessed before he made a sale.

Later, when he was at school in England, and his sisters were married, he could spend the long summer holidays with them. They'd all moved into German castles of varying impressiveness, but none of them was cramped. Often in the thirties, before the war came to freeze the family comings and goings, Andrew would manage to join the party. What with these reunions, and the earlier days at St. Cloud, father and son saw much more of each other than anyone seems to suppose. A deep understanding developed. Philip was not encouraged to forget that he was a prince. As he grew older there was a strong physical resemblance. When in 1946 he went to his sister Sophie's wedding in Germany—her second, to Prince George of Hanover, brother to Queen Frederica of Greece—the likeness was a shock. "I hadn't seen him for nine years, not really grown up at all. My father died in 1944. He was so like him. I shall never forget that moment when I saw him again."

They had the same mannerisms, movements, ways of standing, walking and laughing. "The colossal sense of humor, really seeing the funny side of things always, and making everybody else laugh. And so has Charles. He's not like Philip physically but very like him in some ways, in his ways of laughing, and his quick way of saying something."

Apart from his mother, the chief Battenberg influence in the boy's early days was probably his Uncle George—not the Uncle George of Greece who kissed him good night at St. Cloud, but George, second Marquess of Milford Haven, Prince Louis's eldest son, elder brother to the more dazzling Louis Mountbatten, and younger brother to Alice. He was also a sailor, but without Louis's obsessive upward drive. He had fought under Jellicoe and Beatty, through the great clashes of Jutland, Dogger Bank and the Heligoland Bight. Lynden Manor, his house on the river near Maidenhead, was Philip's home, as far as he had one at all, during the shorter holidays from Cheam School. It was George who had entered him for Cheam, and who turned up *in loco parentis* for the sports days and prize-givings. An earlier toehold in the bleak and boyless Kensington Palace, with his grandmother, had seemed less and less suitable as he began to grow up. At Lynden he had his cousin, David Milford Haven. He remembers fooling about with old two-stroke motorbikes. There were duels of roller-skate hockey, one of which cost him another broken tooth in a collision, later repaired for the royal smile. There were canoeing trips on the river. And it was from Lynden that they made the much-chronicled cycling expedition down to Dover, and decided, saddle-sore, to hitchhike back by Thames barge, sleeping a couple of nights on the grain sacks down below.

Was this the first sniff of salt water that drew him to the sea? It's as good a theory as some. There's talk of the maritime hered-ity, from both his grandfathers. Prince Louis of Battenberg had been First Sea Lord, after all, and Prince William of Denmark, before transferring to the throne of Greece, was already well into his Danish naval cadetship. The popular assumption, inevitably, is that Uncle Dickie was the one to fan the spark, though one or two theorists strike out boldly and pin it on Uncle George. The boy, it goes without saying—or would if everyone didn't keep saying it—had brine in the blood, and it only needed Uncle George to give it a stir. As one account puts it, the lad "never got tired of hearing his uncle tell what it was like in the forward turret of the *New Zealand*, on that dangerous afternoon at Jutland, when the two great twelve-inch guns under his command were firing so fast that they got red-hot, and three sister battle cruisers blew up from shell hits on their turrets. Quite naturally, too, George never got tired of telling about it." Well, could be. Though Philip in the rapt role of little Wilhelmine is hard to take, espe-cially during the repeat performances. It also makes George sound a bore, for which there's no evidence.

Or was it the schooldays at Gordonstoun, with all that sailing, rowing and boat-building, the waters of Moray and Pentland Firths slapping giddily under the bows? His sisters come out emphatically for this, throwing in the double heredity for good measure. Some say that it was Prince Andrew who wanted his son to go to sea, though he had the Greek Navy in mind, and hoped, in vain, that George II of Greece would come across with an invitation.

A handout biography from British Information Services said:

> In choosing a naval career he was following the tradition of the Mountbatten side of his family. Prince Louis of Battenberg was an Admiral of the Fleet and First Sea Lord; his son, the second Marquess, served in the Royal Navy, like Prince Philip's cousin, the third Marquess, and his uncle, Admiral Lord Mountbatten of Burma.

Prince Philip personally amended it:

> In choosing a career in one of the services he was following the tradition of both sides of his family. Both his grandfathers served at sea. His father was a career officer in the Greek Army, and both his father's and his mother's brothers served in the Navy.

It dropped the Battenbergs and got his father in.

Uncle George had got out of uniform in 1930, when Philip was only nine. He went into business, first on the New York Stock Exchange, then at the English end of an American gyroscope company and into a few directorships, of Marks and Spencer among others. It was a matter of money. Prince Louis hadn't left much. He had sold his castle at Heiligenberg, where all those blithe Battenbergs had lodged for the Andrew–Alice wedding, and German inflation had exploded the proceeds into worthless paper. And George's wife, a daughter of Grand Duke Michael of Russia, remembered the pre-Revolution splendors of Tsarskoe and St. Petersburg. By comparison a British naval officer's pay was on the thin side.

But in 1938, at only forty-six, he died. Philip was seventeen, in his last year at Gordonstoun, and it was the second time that his headmaster, Kurt Hahn, had had to break agonizing news. The air crash that killed Cecile was only the year before. Inevitably, Philip came more closely into the orbit of his other, more famous, Mountbatten uncle, and on leaves from Dartmouth, and later from the wartime Navy, the Mountbattens' small London house in Chester Street was the nearest to a home he had. It was less luxurious than you might expect. He slept on a camp-bed in the sitting room.

Sometimes there was a variation. He would stay in his grandmother's grace and favor apartments in Kensington Palace. That was pretty bleak, too, with the pictures stored against the bombs and the furniture sheeted. It had its compensations when his cousin David, companion of the schoolboy larks at Lynden and now also in the Navy, happened to have a coinciding leave. They cheered things up by painting the blacked-out town, and would creep back in the small hours, with stealth and by unaccustomed entrances, respecting the dowager's sleep.

David died, the third Marquess, in April 1970. This time Philip heard by cable during his Australian tour with the Queen. They'd known each other for forty years. David had been best man at the wedding, and prominently hilarious at the bachelor party the night before. But there'd later been a cooling. No valuable stabilizer, such as a royal marriage, had come his way, and he attracted a terrible lot of paragraphs in the juicier gossip columns. Too many for the sterner elements at Court. Not that that in itself would have cooled Philip. But he was badly shaken when David, after the wedding, wrote a piece for the *Daily Mail* which seemed, to say the least, uncalled for.

Philip's last borrowing of a Mountbatten address appeared in the

London Gazette of March 18, 1947, with the announcement that he had finally achieved British citizenship and sworn allegiance to the British Crown on February 28. "Mountbatten, Philip. Greece. Serving Officer in His Majesty's forces: 16 Chester Street, London, S. W. 1."

Of his married sisters' addresses, Schloss Salem, near Lake Constance, whose eastern waters lap a cozy conjunction of Austria, Switzerland and Bavaria, with stately white ferry boats trundling from shore to shore, was the most impressive, beating Buckingham Palace for size if not for treasure. There Princess Theodora had moved in as the Margravine of Baden.[1] Not only the most impressive, but the most significant. In it, or in parts of it, in 1918, was tucked Kurt Hahn's legendary Salem School, founded by the castle's earlier owner, Prince Max of Baden, Theodora's father-in-law and the last Chancellor of Imperial Germany. Philip was to go there as a pupil in 1933, after Cheam. In 1934 its foundations were rocked out of all recognition, at least for more than a decade, by Hitler, the first, and last, Chancellor of the Third Reich. And out of Salem came Gordonstoun.

---

[1] I asked the present Margrave, one of Prince Philip's many nephews, how he heated the place. "Oh, we don't." We were echoing along an interminable stone-flagged corridor. "If you threw a few pails of water down here in winter you'd have a skating rink. We warm our own rooms and treat the corridors as streets." Finding the private apartments at all had been difficult, but the school is still there and I haltingly accosted a wandering boy in the wastes of the courtyard. "Sprechen sie Englisch?" He thought. "Oui, oui, un peu." On the arts side, perhaps. Later an attendant in an alpaca overall beckoned me into a barnlike room, completely empty. We stood silently in opposite corners, until a faint jerk showed it to be a lift.

"Any nation is a slovenly guardian of its own interests if it does not do all it can to make the individual citizen discover his own powers: and . . . the individual becomes a cripple from his own point of view if he is not qualified by education to serve the community."

—KURT HAHN

"School life should be so ordered that it is in a real sense a preparation for life in a larger community. The schools therefore have this further duty, to teach the young to live as members of a community, with all that that implies in learning to give and take and play their part in a common life."

—PRINCE PHILIP

"There are three ways of trying to win the young. There is persuasion, there is compulsion and there is attraction. You can preach at them, that is a hook without a worm; you can say, "You must volunteer," that is of the devil; and you can tell them, "You are needed." That appeal hardly ever fails."

—KURT HAHN

"For some reason it is perfectly respectable to teach history and mathematics, electronics and engineering. But any attempt to develop character, and the whole man tends to be viewed with the utmost suspicion."

—PRINCE PHILIP

"Our educational system is chiefly concerned with the trans-

mission of knowledge, and accepts no responsibility for the training
of character."

—KURT HAHN

"It cannot be given to many to have the opportunity and the
desire to heap honors upon their former headmasters."

—PRINCE PHILIP, as Chancellor of
Edinburgh University, making Kurt Hahn
an Honorary Doctor of Laws

I didn't go to see Hahn. There was always a risk, with him, of
being snapped up and enlisted in something. One writer, David
Wainwright, who saw him to collect material for a book on great
headmasters, found he'd agreed instead to help Hahn realize another great educational dream, the Atlantic Colleges (providing
two-year residential courses for boys of different nations, before
university). The book never got written. When T. C. Worsley
called on him to fix a Gordonstoun place for a boy he was tutoring,
he ended up with a rum job as nonworking master. "At the end
of the term you will tell me, frankly and fearlessly, what you think
of the school." He did, and they finished by slinging books at each
other.

Hahn's recruiting instinct was one of the things that rubbed off
on Philip, who ruthlessly co-opts for any favored cause, from
saving the *Cutty Sark* to finding homes for old pub-keepers. As
late as 1969, then eighty-three, Hahn was urging his ex-pupil to
work at reducing road deaths by getting first aid included in the
driving test. (A Hahn aphorism: "Life saving is the job of the
layman: less serious matters we can leave to the doctors.") Correspondence on that still continues between the Prince, the AA, and
the Medical Commission on Accident Prevention—he's a committee
member of one, and president of the other.

(*153*)

The Duke of Edinburgh's Award was Hahn's idea, though it was adapted and modified:

> It would never have started but for Hahn, certainly not. He suggested I ought to do it, and I fought against it for quite a long time. Because you know what the British are like in relation to that sort of thing. And I said, well, I'm not going to stick my neck out and do anything as stupid as that, and everybody saying, "Ah! Silly ass," you know?

CHAPTER

10

Made in Britain?

"I'm one of those stupid bums that never went to a university, and a fat lot of harm it did me."

Old Etonians sending their boys to Eton can rely on the old place not having changed much. (If it's been wrecked in a fit of student unrest since this writing, that's too bad.) But the Gordonstoun that welcomed Prince Charles in 1962 had changed a good deal since his father went there in the mid-thirties. Hahn had retired as headmaster in 1953, and nothing survives a change at the top without modifications, though Prince Charles's headmaster, Robert Chew, had come with Hahn from Salem to be in on the start of Gordonstoun in 1934. Perhaps the guiding principles haven't wavered much, but material expansions have occurred on the grand scale. Philip went to a school of less than thirty boys, with no playing fields and all contests away, mostly in nearby Elgin. Now it has the lot, indoors and out: a spread of games pitches, tennis and squash courts, a chapel, science blocks (eight laboratories), sports hall and the heated and covered swimming pool opened by the Queen in 1967. Warm, sheltered swimming suggests a softening. But the sea and cliffs, a mile away, and the mountains to the north and south, which Hahn had spotted as a God-given flexing area for the developing young, continue as before.

One advantage of a school in the north of Scotland, more significant in the famous son's time than the (then) obscure father's, was simple remoteness. Four hundred miles from Fleet Street as the reporter flies. Eton would have liked to have Charles. Well, naturally. The arguments against it included family doubts on the desirability of that closed-circuit, ruling-class ambience in an age of social levelings when royalty was beginning to muck in with the people, but it was also just over the bridge from the Windsor home, and highly accessible to photographers.

Cheam had been bad enough, at least to begin with. Some diligent statistician has noted that in Prince Charles's first term of eighty-eight days there, the papers had stories on sixty-seven of them. It was hard on an eight-year-old, and with a more self-important child could have been disastrous, to find what you had for breakfast sharing the front page with Suez, Ike's re-election or the Hungarian rising. Royalty, torn between needing publicity and evading it, develops, with experience, a protective shell. (Inside the palace, on days when headlines are plangent and aides should be rushing around white-faced and with their neckties undone, all is comparative calm.) But this was too soon. Charles's schoolmates were somewhat in awe of him as their future king, never mind being news all the time as well, and he was shy, not yet having his father's gift of instant social penetration. It was probably no joy ride for the other children either. They'd been told to treat him like anyone else, which sounded easier than it was. One penalty of rank that he became aware of, though less at Cheam than at Gordonstoun, was that nice people kept their distance, for fear of seeming to court glory, while the less nice latched on and loved it. It was a problem at the time, though as he later said, "It's one of those things you learn, how to sense who are the ones that are sucking up, and who are being genuine."

He turned out genuine enough himself, as nobody will deny. Helped to some extent when, after that first print-riddled term, the Queen's press secretary, Richard Colville, invited a clutch of London editors to the palace and frankly asked them to lay off the lad. Cheam's headmaster was there to back him up. Things had reached the point where the whole school was being disrupted, and the first great royal breakout from private tutelage looked as though it might collapse miserably. In the main, the point was taken.

For Colville it was almost an unbending. He was often thought to be an overzealous guardian of the Family's personal lives. But he'd begun the job under George VI, and had had more than twenty years at it before he retired in 1968. "I am not what you North Americans would call a public relations officer," he once told a Canadian writer who called in for some research information and asked if he might see over the palace. It was a private home, said Colville (a view that the occupiers wouldn't entirely go along with, possibly). However, for those who like happy endings, the writer asked the keeper of the Royal Philatelic Collection if he might have a look at it, was graciously permitted and saw most of the palace on the way. But if Colville was a door rather than a window, it was from old custom and loyal motives. His successor, William Heseltine, an Australian, came in at a time when the mystery of monarchy was already losing a veil or two in the natural course of things, and he's since had a discreet hand in removing a few more dust-collecting drapes. Besides, Colville was an ex-Navy man. They never did say much.[1]

There had been no need to soften up Fleet Street for Prince

---

[1] The Queen's press secretary, though a member of her Household, is also Prince Philip's.

Philip's schooldays, either prep or public. Only long afterward was something of the sort done, and then not by the palace, but by his uncle. In February 1947 the chairman of Beaverbrook Newspapers and the editors of the *Daily* and *Sunday Express*, Arthur Christiansen and John Gordon, were unexpectedly bidden to Chester Street for drinks. Unexpectedly puts it mildly. They'd always gunned cheerfully for everything Mountbatten, and even then were laying into the head of the clan as a betrayer of Empire: wasn't he just off to India as Viceroy, to give it back to the natives? But this was why they'd been picked, naturally, rather than the less captious editors of other Fleet Street heavies.

Lord Louis was at his most winning, humbly seeking advice from those hard heads. His nephew, Philip (who was amiably self-effacing in a corner, said nothing, and didn't even get a drink), was intending to become a British citizen. What, in their distinguished opinion, would be the public feeling? They said that it ought to go all right, what with the young man's war record and his convincing impersonation of an Englishman born and bred. Faced with such confidence in their judgment, they could hardly say otherwise. Beaverbrook, when he heard of the meeting, was more amazed than enraged. Three tough old war-horses out-maneuvered like that? When the official announcement came out a month later their comments could only be indulgent.

Colville's strategy over Cheam and Prince Charles, though less subtle in conception, also paid off. And when Gordonstoun loomed, four years later, he made a more general plea for the communications media to do the decent thing. The Queen and the Duke of Edinburgh were grateful for past favors, and "hope that this happy state of affairs may continue. . . . Her Majesty and His Royal Highness fully understand the very natural interest in the Prince of Wales's education, but they feel that he will only be able to derive full benefit from his days at school if he is not made the center of special attention."

Again it worked pretty well. Helped by geography. There was the exercise book story, but that was blown in Germany's *Der Stern* and America's *Time;* and the lady journalist who got the cherry-brandy scoop was an astute free-lance, in ambush at the Stornoway end of a school sailing trip. Memories mercifully dim. Some bright sharper got hold of the exercise book and hawked it around Europe's more excitable magazines, and it all got so out of hand that the palace had to deny that the Heir to the Throne had made the sale personally because he was kept short of pocket money. As for the cherry-brandy affair, the ketch *Pinta*, out of Gordonstoun for the Isle of Lewis, Prince Charles on board, off-loaded its crew for lunch in a Stornoway pub. He was spotted, and the window darkened by the faces of peering locals. "So I thought, 'I can't bear this any more' and went off somewhere else, and the only other place was the bar." (He was underage for bars.) "Having never been in a bar before, the first thing I thought of doing was having a drink. It seemed the most sensible thing. And being terrified, not knowing what to do, I said the first drink that came into my head, which happened to be cherry-brandy, because I'd drunk it before, when it was cold, out shooting. And hardly had I taken a sip before the whole world exploded round my ears."

Prince Philip's exercise books wouldn't have raised a bob, though they'd do better now—and if he'd been found holed-up with a covey of meths drinkers it would hardly have made a king-size story.

Charles certainly got no special attention in the school itself. An early out-of-class assignment was emptying the dustbins. (His father had built a pigsty.) A mild interest in refuse collection seemed to stay with him, right up to Cambridge and his well-received dustman sketch in the Trinity Revue. This, it's fair to say, was well at the shallow end of his acting talent. He'd played Macbeth at Gordonstoun, and disgraced neither himself, Shakespeare nor his father and mother, who dutifully turned up in the audience with familiar parental flutterings.

Prince Philip says, or pretends, that his own acting reputation at the school nearly ditched his son for the lead in *Macbeth*. Hopes weren't high for a boy whose father had managed only Donalbain's two-lines-and-a-spit in the same play, and then because it was an open-air production. "There was nobody else who could be trusted to enter on horseback and not fall off."

The dustbins suggest that Gordonstoun was that sort of school. But the Prince of Wales emptied dustbins only because everybody emptied dustbins, as the roster came around. It wasn't part of that public school system, held by many to be so pernicious, which believes in giving newcomers hell to mark their insignificance, until they achieve enough seniority to give hell to the next lot. In an appeal brochure on the school's coming of age in 1955—taking, as always, the larger view, it asked for £250,000—a photograph of Hahn is captioned: "In the words of my late Chief, Prince Max of Baden, 'A nation has no greater treasure than the human nature of its citizens.'"

Humanity, on the whole, is the thing. And individual fulfillment. To "discover his own powers"—which needn't be those of an Aristotle or a Hercules. A boy who finds he can jump four feet when he didn't think he could jump at all comes well inside the specification. The school's motto says most of it. "*Plus est en vous.*" (And a boy who thought he couldn't do French, but managed that bit, was already on his way.)

"It's somehow got the reputation," says Prince Philip, "of being a Spartan, tough, rigorous, generally body-bending sort of organization. In fact it isn't at all, and never has been. It's a misunderstanding of what it's all about. I think it rationalizes the whole of the physical activities. Instead of this obsessison with games, which is the standard public school thing—the idea that you've got to be good at football or cricket or whatever it is to get anywhere —we in fact had a great many more activities. This is why it got that reputation. Because if you say that there's sailing, and Rugby, and mountain climbing and all these things, it's bound to sound as if. . . . But these are alternatives, they're not necessarily absolutes, not everybody does everything."

Q: Were you any good at cricket?
HRH: No, not particularly.
Q: But you were in the Gordonstoun eleven?
HRH: Yes, but remember there were so few of us, anyone who could hold a bat was in.

There were getting on for 150 boys there when he left, and he was captain of cricket and hockey, but you have to find out that sort of thing elsewhere. He was also head of the school. Though now it's hard to imagine his not being, his contemporaries don't remember him as anything very special. He certainly got no favors out of Hahn.

The appeal brochure has a reproduction of his portrait, painted and presented to the school by Edward Halliday, whose son was there. It shows the most eminent Old Boy in naval lieutenant's battledress, reveres immaculately curled, white scarf at the throat, binoculars held lightly at the ready in the large, strong hands. Against a background of sea and storm clouds he gazes, perhaps a thought too handsomely, into the middle distance. "The Guardian, Gordonstoun, 1938–39." There's a message underneath:

I must confess that I enjoyed my days at Gordonstoun and, as the dates above show, time has hardly had a chance to soften my recollections. I hope the appeal is a great success, because I would like as many other boys as possible to enjoy their schooldays as much as I did.

It isn't a rave, but then he'd be concerned to deflate the heroics. He hasn't been back much, and hardly ever runs across another Old Boy—though Jim Orr was one of them.

Kurt Hahn's influence, however, was considerable. It says something for his powers and prestige that Gordonstoun's first board of governors (assembled by a German in a foreign land) included the Archbishop of York, the headmaster of Eton, historian G. M. Trevelyan, and John Buchan—later Lord Tweedsmuir and Governor-General of Canada. (A quirky thought on Buchan: it was in one of his elegant spy stories that the frightfully British hero was alerted to danger by spotting that the head of another man, apparently just as frightfully British until then, had a German shape.) When, in June 1964 the Friends of Gordonstoun met at the Dorchester to honor Kurt Hahn with a dinner, the American and German ambassadors were among the guests, also Prince George of Hanover, two dukes, two earls, a viscount, eight of your ordinary lords, and fourteen knights and baronets. Top billing went to Prince Philip.

During his year at Salem he hadn't enjoyed himself much. It was one of the few periods of his life when he didn't. After Cheam, he was beginning to feel English. And at Salem, from which Hahn had already been removed by the Nazis, the loose-limbed life was giving way to an irksome regimentation. There was a great deal of "ghastly foot-slogging." No cricket, naturally. He'd been in the second eleven at Cheam, and might have got further if he hadn't left a year early for the German experiment. Besides, going to Salem was a "family" decision, which he vaguely felt had coerced him. His sister, Theodora, though in token consultation with the two Mountbatten uncles (and with the best of intentions) was all for the school so closely tied up with her recently acquired husband. And wasn't it in her own home? It seemed obvious.

There's a curious pattern of ifs, buts, echoes and parallels. If Theodora hadn't married Prince Max's son, Berthold, Philip would never have gone there. If Ramsay MacDonald hadn't scooped Hahn out of a Hitler gaol in 1933 (as George V, in effect, had scooped Andrew out of a Greek one in 1922), there would have been no Gordonstoun School to educate Greek royalty in Scotland's Moray. Oddly, the house that Hahn eventually took there for the school had royal associations of a kind. It belonged to the Gordon–Cummings family, participants, long before, in the great Tranby Croft cardtable affair that landed the future King Edward VII as a witness in a common libel action. Of no more practical significance than another faint thread in the design, revealing Moray as Ramsay MacDonald's birthplace. But odd, again, that Kurt Hahn, with his Plato-impregnated philosophies, should be the German schoolmaster who went to Scotland to impart Athenian theories to the Greek, if now increasingly English, Philip; and should himself have got his ideas from a couple of English boys he met in his teens when they were on a German holiday from Abbotsholme School and full of the "free" attitudes of their own remarkable headmaster, Cecil Reddie (whose German university, at Göttingen, was to be later one of Hahn's). It would be nice to say, for the student of these patterns, that Hahn's English tutor had come from Oxford, Hahn's English university. Alas, no. He was from Queens', Cambridge. Too bad. But he also was a Platonist and, as David Wainwright says, "linked together the academic ideas of Plato with what would today be called 'commitment' in society." So the circuit keeps feeding back.

A contemporary of Prince Philip's at Gordonstoun was Jocelin Winthrop-Young: in 1949, by Hahn's energetic manipulations, he founded the Anavryta School in Athens, and was for eleven years personal tutor to King Constantine II. A Briton, reviving in Greece, by way of Germany, the precepts of Plato. The Greeks, who might have got pardonably touchy about the German influence, after the events of 1941, instead became resentful that Athens's most prestigious school, as it grew to be, should be run by an Englishman, and their future king taught by one. (Makarios, as another intriguing twist, had sent his nephew there, away from the baneful British influences in Cyprus.) Winthrop-Young had to go, and went back to Salem, where he now has several royal European children of both sexes on the books.[2]

More echoes. Hahn, gaoled by Hitler for "the decadent corruption of German youth," and smuggling out his liberal principles to Britain, home of the free, found himself in World War II the object of British mistrust, not only as an undesirable influence on British youth, but even as a possible German agent. Didn't his boys man a coastal lookout station, one of several peculiar "services" in the school's curriculum? Who could tell what secret signals were flashing out over the Moray Firth? Hadn't the Gordonstoun schooner once actually sailed to Denmark, now in Wehrmacht hands? And with Prince Philip on board, too? Whose uncle, come to think of it, was the suspect King Constantine of World War I . . . when we had that Bosch Battenberg at the Admiralty, remember?

Not, of course, that Philip's name came into it. Who knew him then? But it's just the way things could have gone. Hahn's German masters who'd followed him from Salem were interned.

---

[2] Princess George, on the day we met in Munich, had just driven her daughter, Princess Frederica-Elizabeth, down there for beginning of term (Prince George, her father, had once been Salem's headmaster). Tangled skeins. Salem has long been co-educational. Gordonstoun's plans to go the same way made news in November 1970. "How many of the boys," asked a *Daily Mail* columnist, "want their masculine world disturbed by petticoats in the locker room or frilly undies among the Rugby togs?" But that may not be the system.

Hahn himself was a British citizen by now and beyond the reach of the Defence Regulations, but his school was given over to the Army, and he had to reassemble its tattered remnants in Wales. He got back after the war to find the buildings had taken an even worse beating than buildings usually do from the military. They'd been set fire to.

H. L. Brereton, a master in the 1930s–40s, and later Warden, wrote:

> For us, British masters and the older British boys it was a strange experience. We had given our loyalty to Hahn not only because we admired him as a man, but because we knew the story of his struggle against the common enemy. He seemed to us one of the few Germans who had fulfilled his obligations of citizenship.[3] If any German was on our side, then surely he was. Ever since his arrival in this country he had tried, by every means in his power, to open British eyes to the true menace of the situation, and make audible the cries of the tortured in Nazi concentration camps. . . . But in 1939 our association with this vigilant friend of democracy earned for us the suspicion of our countrymen.

This isn't a discourse on Hahn, though like anything that mentions him, it wants to be. He casts a spell.

Like a lot of great men, he had his smaller side. He could be a trial to work with. His habit of calling a general assembly at the drop of a hat, on the frequent occasions when he had a fresh truth to impart, was a dramatic disrupter of teaching schedules. And his truths, true or not, were unbudgeable. Most of his staff,

---

[3] His public outcries against Hitler had been doubly courageous in the Germany of 1933. He was a Jew.

notably those who'd been with him at Salem (not all of them were German), worshiped unquestioningly. Later-comers were sometimes assailed by doubts, or maddened by methods, and didn't stay. From time to time, a master or boy will proclaim his disillusionment. One ex-Guardian (his name for head boy was a borrowing from Plato) hinted in the Cambridge *Granta* that in spite of the high thinking and hard living designed to keep the ignobler passions at bay, they sometimes got a look-in all the same.

During Worsley's short time there, he was landed with producing the school *Hamlet*. The boy playing the lead, who was clearly going to be brilliant by school play standards, ingeniously extended some sick leave to take in a short binge in Edinburgh, releasing his ignobler passions on an accommodating local typist. Hahn's displeasure over the moral lapse was nothing to his fury at having personally cast the lad as Hamlet—"a fine character, a noble character. How can we expect a true performance from such a weakling as that?" Opening night was nigh. Worsley got nowhere with his argument that it was a mistake to confuse life with art. Hahn (who also maintained that Shakespeare went better in German than English) gave the part to the school's morally impeccable Guardian of the time, who couldn't act and wrecked the play.

Some may hear, again, an echo of Prince Philip's dogged attachment to the formed view, and of his occasional eyebrow-raising assertions.

Hahn probably couldn't have got away with the Award Scheme. There were still those who saw him as a sort of intellectual scoutmaster. Do-gooding for the young is a tricky exercise in Britain. All that running and jumping, digging, building, messing about in boats, rock climbing, playing at coast guards and fire brigades— these things alarm the islanders. Organized youth. Hearties. A master race in the making. Prince Philip was properly wary about getting mixed up in it, at any rate on that scale.[4] But once he did, Organized Youth—which isn't organized in the offensive sense at all, the emphasis being on the individual—got its biggest single leg-up into acceptability. The whole faintly suspect picture of youth work, the goody-goody earnestness, the whistles and lanyards and overlong shorts, went out of the window. The Scheme spread beyond Britain to the Commonwealth—it's a sight to see gold medalists from, say, Fiji, assembled with their loved ones on the quarterdeck of *Britannia*—and even to foreign parts, where they'd like to cash in on the name and call it the Duke of Edinburgh's Award too, but hardly can. No one's said "Ah! Silly ass." The thing's been hooked up into rightful and sensible recognition. He has that touch. No one knows it better than the award-seekers themselves. To set your sights on practically any achievement not actually criminal, and to achieve it, is more of a lark than glooming around in the so-called amusement arcades, or wrecking the shelters and frightening the old ladies along Brighton front.

They don't all make it through to a Gold Award, or even a Silver. (Plato's ideal city-state planned for graded citizens: gold, silver and, rather defeatistly, "others.") If they manage only a Bronze, it's something attempted and done.

Anything goes, from clearing overgrown churchyards or walking across the Isle of Skye to making a pair of Elizabethan rapiers or teaching yourself Chinese Mandarin. Boys have climbed Snowdon, learned stage-lighting, plowed through the *Seven Pillars of Wisdom* to produce a 5000-word commentary; girls take up numismatics, geological surveying, fire-fighting, building shacks in refugee centers. They don't all come through the Bronze, even. But those who hit the Gold turn up at Buckingham Palace for a

---

[4] Though, strangely enough, the first thing he ever lent his name to was the London Federation of Boys' Clubs. As a patron, which he still is. It was in 1947, when he was a modest Lieutenant, RN, instructing at Corsham.

handshake, a word, a flashing smile and a diploma. The presentations come off four times a year, once in the gardens, twice in the
ballroom. And once at Holyrood.

The ballroom presentations are spectacular, as four hundred or
so winners file under the clustered chandeliers, and a Guards band,
in the gallery with the gilded organ pipes, provides one of those
peculiarly unmilitary programs ("If I Were a Rich Man," "Moon
River," selections from *Gigi,* "Just My Bill"). Some of them forget the handshake, and Philip, knowing they'd never forgive themselves, reaches down and grabs it. Some of the girls forget the
curtsy, and come scuttling back for a quick one. He makes most
of them laugh, which takes some doing in half a dozen words. A
few of the boys, resolved to take the palace in their stride, stroll
up defiantly, meaning to keep a hand in the pocket, but can't go
through with it in the end. They haven't bothered a lot about
haircuts. The girls have primped a bit, and run to obviously unaccustomed hats, but those in cadet uniforms can't do anything
special. A curtsying young policewoman is really something.

It would be easy to see a patronizing grandeur behind it all, and
a useful shot of the monarchic mystique—impressionable young
minds going off to spread the glittering word. This particular
afternoon, as it happens, his next engagement is to visit drug addicts
in Camberwell: the other end, you could say, of the achievement
spectrum. His persona travels well, unsupported by gilt, plush,
red carpets or a Guards band. He flops down in a rickety treatment center chair and wades right in with the rickety patients.
What does one say? No trouble. He smiles at the nearest. "How
did you get hooked?" And we're away. Afterward, as the car
moves off (not the Rolls, too offensively opulent for the East End)
he waves and beams. There are cheers from the doorsteps, and
an urchin of about ten runs alongside whistling loyally with two
fingers in his mouth. Philip winds the window down. "That's

very good. Can you do it without the fingers?" Then he settles back to worry, but realistically, about drug addicts.

It's hard to say how much Gordonstoun made the Philip we know, or how much was there already. But Hahn's part, perhaps more as man than schoolmaster, must be great.

To take a last look at the ifs and buts, if Hahn hadn't defied, and in fact publicly attacked, Nazi doctrines in 1933, and got himself ousted from Salem, Prince Philip might have finished his schooldays there. His English relatives would have been just another fringe of the far-flung family, handy for the occasional visit and that's all. The British would have known no more about him than they know today about his fund of foreign cousins. If a war had come, even without benefit of Hitler, he would have served in the German Navy—afterward, perhaps, married some archduchess or other.

That it sounds so preposterous only marks our complacent acceptance of the way things actually turned out.

"It was in the romantic setting of the Highlands, amid the great mountains and wide moors that stretch around Balmoral Castle, the King's home in Scotland, that the Princess and Philip really decided they were in love and would marry. In August 1946 a fair-haired, tall young man in well-fitting sports clothes went out with the King and other guns on the 'Glorious Twelfth.' . . . It was his first appearance at Balmoral, where he had been invited by the King and Queen to stay for a few weeks, and among the ghillies and keepers the news that 'Philip's here' spread quickly. Princess Elizabeth holds a place of her own in the hearts of the proud and independent men who tend the King's Scottish estates . . . so when they found that this year her eyes seemed even brighter, her smile even readier, her happiness more infectious, because of the presence of the young naval gentleman, there was nothing too much that a ghillie or keeper could do for Philip. And, as anyone knows who has spent a shooting or fishing holiday in the Highlands, to establish that happy relationship with the men who know the forests and streams is to ensure a good holiday. For the deep hearts of the ghillies are not easy to win."

That's from Louis Wulff's *Elizabeth and Philip*, published in 1947. I'm afraid I missed it at the time, and my copy is second-hand. It's inscribed on the flyleaf, "Florrie and Bert, with every good wish from Lottie."

July 10, 1947. The engagement was at last announced officially.
(*The Royal Family*, Odhams Press, 1950)
The navy went on, if only ashore: instructing at HMS *Royal Arthur*, petty officers' school at Corsham, Wiltshire.
(*Radio Times Hulton Picture Library*)

November 20, 1947. "I had the extreme good fortune to get married."
(*Radio Times Hulton Picture Library*)

bove: Honeymoon, with bene-
t of photographers, at the
Iountbattens' house, Broad-
nds, near Romsey, Hampshire.
The Times) *Right*: And two
arter Knights, Windsor, 1948.
The Royal Family, Odhams
ress, 1950)

Tragic recall from Kenya, February 7, 1952. With the sudden death of the King, "the whole thing changed, very, very considerably." (*The Press Association*)

Above: 1949. Official duties were already claiming time. Visit to a hospital in Guernsey (on the far left, Michael Parker): and a youth club in Fulham, *left*. But his patronship of the London Federation of Boys' Clubs was one of the earliest associations, beginning in 1947, before the wedding. "It's rather like being involved with something local in your village."
(Radio Times Hulton Picture Library)

Gambia, February 1957, toward the end of his first world tour. The beard modifies a bushier specimen grown in the Antarctic.
(*Syndication International*)

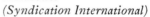

Later that year a crammed audience of children in the Festival Hall heard a lecture on his travels, and he presented an adapted version on television.
(*British Broadcasting Corporation*)

Good with children. Royal Tour of Australia, 1963.
(*Mirropic*)

"I have to make speeches as a matter of duty. But the line I take is my own."
(*Above, London Express; below, The Press Association*)

Above: Students of Salford University informally petition their chancellor. *(Syndication International) Below:* There are grimmer occasions: at the Welsh mining village of Aberfan in October 1966, where a collapsing coal tip engulfed houses and part of the school. *(Syndication International)*

Natural Selection

"I had the extreme good fortune to get married."
—Speech at Edinburgh on receiving the Freedom of
the City

The Danish dynasty alone has produced eighteen kings of Denmark, four of Sweden, six (by adoption) of Greece, seven tsars of Russia, and queens to kings of Britain, Germany and Romania. There were liberal injections from elsewhere, notably by the efforts of Victoria, whose great-grandchildren come out at a rough count of seventy, and great-great-grandchildren baffle amateur accountancy. Multiplications continue. All things considered, it's surprising that the birthday reminders on Prince Philip's weekly engagement cards only tot up to about 150 a year. You have to draw the line somewhere. And that he can lay out his Christmas presents before dispatch on a mere couple of six-foot trestle tables—

there's a minor host of godchildren to be got in as well.[1] It's less surprising that he and Princess Elizabeth, two of the great-greats, should have collided in the ordinary course of kinship, long before the breathless commentators of 1947 were treating him like an unknown bit-player suddenly sprung through a trap and blinking in the spotlight.

As with other families, the weddings and funerals were the special rallying times. And coronations, which the rest of us aren't exposed to on a comparable scale. His first two brushes with the English branch, at Prince Louis's funeral and Uncle Dickie's wedding, came and went before he could walk, so they didn't impress him much. But at the wedding of his cousin Marina in 1934, and the Coronation of his second cousin George VI in 1937, he was standing up and taking notice. His third cousin, Elizabeth, was by then doing the same. Not that they noticed each other particularly. She was eight the first time, and eleven the second—when Philip was in his rising teens, fresh from the diverse pursuits of Gordonstoun. It was nice to have time off for these affairs (among the few concessions the school ever gave him) but he probably wanted to get back to finish building a boat, or catch up on his javelin practice and metal-work.[2]

No spark was struck.

He was a cadet at Dartmouth when they next met. There are sharp divisions of guesswork on the details. Certainly it was in the summer of 1939, on a Sunday described by some as wet. The occasion was a visit by the King, the Queen, their daughters, and the King's personal ADC, Captain Lord Louis Mountbatten (whose

---

[1] The last week in June is bad for birthdays. The Duke of Windsor, Prince Kraft of Hohenlohe-Langenburg, the Earl of St. Andrews, Princess George of Hanover and Lord Mountbatten.

[2] In Athens, in 1936, at a strange reunion of the Greeks when the bodies of King Constantine, his mother, Queen Olga, and his wife, Queen Sophie, were brought from their exiles' graves in Florence for reburial in the Tatoi gardens, he said to a quorum of uncles, "What would you like made in iron?"

naval cap, from the photographs, had less gold filigree than the King's but a larger and more jauntily cut peak to support it). Some say the yacht was *Britannia*, which wasn't built at the time, others rightly identify it as the old *Victoria and Albert*—though the account telling how she "pointed her elaborately gilded figure-head into Weymouth Bay" and anchored in the River Dart seems to be about fifty miles off course. No matter. Biographers and geographers have these little differences: a report of the Battle of Matapan sets it "near the toe of Italy," which is about five hundred miles out.

The visitors were to join the cadets for morning service. But mumps intervened. If it wasn't chicken pox. Some say both. "The Queen was told that seven cadets were in the College sick bay with mumps." Put it another way, the doctor said to the King: "Your Majesty, two of the boys have come down with mumps." Or another (out of actual earshot): "Many of the younger cadets had become the victims of a twin epidemic of mumps and chicken-pox." It was decided, anyway, that the princesses had better not risk it, or them, and should cut church—though this naturally doesn't appear in the version that cuts church for everybody and sets the whole action on a Saturday afternoon, the centerpiece a tea party, and "Cadet Prince Philip, as a distant relative of the Royal visitors, selected to be present."

It seems clear that he was told to entertain Elizabeth and Margaret. "They had a glorious time," says one authority. Another says the whole thing was a flop, and that "Princess Elizabeth repeatedly asked, 'When are we going home?'" Did Philip "proudly show the Princess round the College"? Or was he, as a grumpier reading has it, "sullen-faced," and "entirely unamused at the prospect of attending all day on two small girls"? In the end he "suggested a game of croquet"—or, for those who prefer, took them on the tennis courts and "showed off by jumping over the net," whereat Elizabeth exclaimed, "How good he is! How high he can jump!" (Or possibly, "When are we going home?" It's hard to say.)

"When the *Victoria and Albert* sailed that afternoon . . ." Several accounts agree that there was a dinner party on board that night, to which Philip went, but still ". . . half of Dartmouth College followed her out in all sorts of craft, from launches to sailing dinghies and rowing boats." Then all but one gave up. And who would you guess was in it, alone and still rowing, as "Elizabeth watched him fondly through an enormous pair of binoculars"? Right. He was "extremely attracted to his pretty little third cousin who looked at him with adoring blue eyes." Through enormous binoculars. And she, in turn, "had caught a disease more dangerous than mumps: she had an advanced case of puppy love."

The solitary oarsman was ordered to put about. Whether by megaphone, general bellowing, or "Uncle Dickie's high-pitched but commanding voice" we are free to choose. Did the King say, "Damned young fool"? Or "This is ridiculous, he must go back"? Hindsights are blurred. However, there's a fair consensus that this was the day when romance first struck, at Dartmouth on July 21, 1939. Or July 22. Could it have been both? Not all the historians bother with the date, perhaps wisely. You can trip up with too much detail. For the record, the nearest Sunday was actually the twenty-third. Always supposing we've got the right year.

Prince Philip himself doesn't claim total recall. It was a long time ago. The silver wedding comes up in 1972, which somehow seems surprising, in spite of his recent recognition that "we're getting a bit old hat now," and the delicate beginnings of a handover to Charles and Anne. (The Prince in the headlines isn't necessarily him these days. "Prince Eats Piece of Buffalo," a report from Canada's Northwest Territory in 1970, didn't mean the same chap any more.)

The wartime visits to Windsor, when he had nowhere particular to go, are well documented. Dates are shaky, but Christmas is a fairly safe bet, and much is made of those larky pantomimes; George VI rich in rehearsal hints, the princesses in plum roles, naïvely visible wig-joins for the Widow Twankey, and the young naval gentleman from Greece rolling in the aisles at the appalling jokes. But that one sounds true. His laughter is very near the surface, and on the whole more responsive to banana skins than to a mere Homeric twinkle. It makes for great amiability, if you can tap it. Charles inherits the fondness for what he calls "awful sort of groan jokes," and when he gets the British Film Institute to dig out those hoary silent comedies for family showing he can rely on his father for sound-track, mostly yells of mock anguish as the long-dead comics disappear down manholes or battle with squirting hydrants. If it isn't quite on a par with the Punch and Judy audience screaming "Look out, he's behind you" as the crocodile creeps up, it has the same quality of rapt involvement.

"These film shows are a great mistake, my in-tray's overflowing," he says, settling happily in his deep armchair all the same, with the Queen adjoining. They tend to sit together in the front row (notorious in public cinemas as the worst seats in the house). During more serious presentations, judging by the Queen's occasional reproving raps, the *sotto voce* comments from the next chair can have a certain extravagance.

Films provide the easiest hour or two's switch-off from the pressures of the daily round. There's a sixty-seater cinema in the palace, on the west ground floor next to the Queen's Gallery. At Sandringham they use the ballroom. Also at Balmoral. In *Britannia* twin modern projectors with automatic reel change operate from the servery to fill a wide screen in the dining room, though the ward-room programs, when royalty isn't aboard, come nearer the home movies mark: the single projector means a blank screen between reels, and just nice time to collect another gin from the bar. "Do you see a lot of films?" an officer asked me in one of many thirst breaks during the two hours plus of *Funny Girl*. The yacht was newly back from the 1970 Australia and New Zealand trip. I said not a lot. "Lucky for you," he said. "I've just seen thirty-seven in sixty-three days."

However, all that equipment isn't for exclusively frivolous purposes. Wedged in among Prince Philip's more public engagements, films with a closer bearing on the job are always cropping up. Previews of Award Scheme films, wildlife films, NPFA films, Outward Bound films, films about Service training, the Central Council of Physical Recreation, Industrial Design; with a lot of them he's had some sort of finger in the planning pie, and even if he hasn't it's as well to take a look. When an organization banners your name on its stationery you like to know what it's telling the world. The world, given the chance, will be quick to link you with a boob. Sometimes the films are just pre-recordings for TV, and have to be seen somehow because he's said he'll join a studio discussion after transmission.

At least in *Britannia* and other domestic auditoriums he doesn't find a couple of thousand pairs of eyes riveted on him when the lights go up. Those Windsor pantomimes, translated to the London Palladium, scene of so many royal sufferings in good causes, wouldn't have been half the fun; nor would Mack Sennett two-reelers at the Odeon, Leicester Square. This isn't to pan, even at this remove, those teen-age interpretations of Aladdin or Cinderella. All the same, did Philip dash around the back at curtain-fall with cries of darling-you-were-wonderful? Anybody's guess. And later, during the ghost stories by candlelight, was there any degree of hand-holding? Cousin Alexandra of Yugoslavia's book puts the question.

"We settled ourselves to be frightened," wrote Margaret, "and we were not. Most disappointing." But was it so disappointing for Lilibet and Philip, close together in the shadows for perhaps the first time?

Answer comes there none.

But there's some agreement on Balmoral, 1946, as the time and place where things took a turn for the altar. One historian is categorical. "It was at Balmoral that Philip proposed and was accepted. Several years later the Queen revealed in an unguarded moment that this took place 'beside some well-loved loch, the white clouds overhead and the curlew crying.'" To be accurate, the moment was hardly unguarded, but came at a large public luncheon in Edinburgh. The words were part of a polite passage on the beauties of Scotland.

What happened, and where, and when, doesn't much affect the fact that it did. Some people worry about who hooked whom. Cousin Alexandra has to hand it to Elizabeth, and gracefully on the whole, if with a dab at the eyes. Girls, it appears, had always thrown themselves at Philip's head, and the list of throwers is quaint but imposing.

> Daughters of publishers, sultry-eyed steel heiresses, girls with strings of huge department-store and farming fortunes, all crossed Philip's path. . . . But it was the shy, timorous, secluded one, who captured and held fast his heart.

Enough to make strong ghillies weep.

After Balmoral, he went back to work. In Wiltshire. Instructing hard-bitten petty officers at Corsham. HMS *Royal Arthur* was a cluster of unseaworthy huts at the back of the town, where instructors and instructed shivered through a winter of blizzards and power cuts and lectures on naval strategy and current affairs. "Only officers with a high record for leadership are selected for these duties," says the British Information Services' biographical broadsheet. Or said, until he removed it in his recent revision, cutting down the eulogy content.

In fact it was true, though the blackboard, pointer and map of the world were a trifle static after livelier times in HMS *Whelp*, and the Corsham shacks a dreary contrast with Balmoral's granite splendors, Sandringham House (where, to general public interest, he spent the next Christmas) and Buckingham Palace's mystic rectangle. He was still a lieutenant and still a prince on eleven pounds a week, but somehow managed a small, fast car that covered the ninety-seven miles from shack to palace in impressive time when occasion arose. After the engagement there were motherly gasps from the papers. "Philip: Take It Easy!" (*Sunday Pictorial*). "Lt. Philip Hurt in Car Crash" (*Daily Mail*). This was to do with a skid and a twisted knee a month before the wedding. Nothing sensational, compared with a modern motorway pile-up, and the comments were on the whole doting, as on a cherished but naughty son. They got a bit sterner after the marriage. One accident dented only the fender of a taxi at Hyde Park Corner, but Elizabeth was with him. Ten years later the *Daily Express* was able to scrape together a total of seven incidents, headed "Should Philip Drive the Queen?" (Three of them were only reports of high speeds, none in this country, clocked by someone at 70, 85 and 75 mph.) Wrote Anne Edwards: "It is a commonplace that this love of speed which the Prince shares with so many men might one day be serious for the Queen. . . . I feel bound to point out (in a very small voice, of course) that it worries me too that if I were on the road—it might very well be serious for me." But they all loved it really.

From February 1, 1947, public anxieties were reduced for a bit. The Royal Family embarked in *Vanguard* for South Africa, which removed Elizabeth from passenger hazards. They didn't come back until the middle of May, when the Princess, on stepping ashore, "noticeably had an inner radiance."

He wasn't there to meet her, as he hadn't been there to see her off. The palace was still bravely denying the romance, and it wouldn't do to make its work more difficult. When the engagement was at last announced, Press Officer Colville, like the racing tipsters, quietly forgot any earlier misinformation, and the news agencies of the world ratified with rapture, too excited for an I-told-you-so. The face of Philip, now plain Lieutenant Mountbatten but at last unexceptionally British, came smiling off every front page in the world. So did Elizabeth's, but that was less of a novelty. Both appeared on picture postcards, a popular tribute of a kind that had lapsed since the younger days of Gladys Cooper. "Elizabeth and Philip—Official," said several headlines, probably as near I-told-you-so as they could be bothered with.

He waved, in unmatchably smart company, from the palace balcony, from royal limousines, from flower-decked royal boxes, Lord's pavilion and Ascot's Royal Enclosure; appeared in "an informal engagement photograph," painfully perched on the gilt arm of his fiancée's chair; walked briskly past the serried lenses, sometimes in uniform, sometimes in double-breasted civies with immense lapels; beamed blindingly in ballrooms, on Clydebank launching platforms, at supper tables, from the suddenly renowned skittle alley at Corsham's Methuen Arms; applauded soberly as the girl "whose heart he had wooed and won" received the Freedom of Edinburgh. ("Lieutenant Mountbatten is on the left," said the caption writer, still fearing, in these early days, confusion with the Lord Provost, on the right.) Really diligent newshounds, with their keen nose for private albums, dug back further, and presented him as a chuckling, gap-toothed tot, an under-twelves high-jumper at Cheam and a boy sailor up the rigging at Gordonstoun.

One of the supper-table photographs showed "Lt. Michael Parker, RN, who was one of the royal party"—but only just got in the picture. He'd been one of the first to be in it, figuratively speaking, and was to be in it for nearly ten years. He had been asked down to Corsham before the news officially broke, and was there let into the secret, and offered the job. It came as a surprise. They'd known each other since *Wallace* and *Lauderdale* (bowls at Sheerness), and became pretty close during the friendly rivalries of *Whelp* and *Wessex* (racing at Sydney). There weren't many things they hadn't chewed over at one time or another. But Prince Philip's matrimonial plans had never come up. He didn't seem to have any. If, even in the later years, Elizabeth was in his head, she stayed there. Other considerations apart, he wasn't the kind to parade his distinguished relatives.

The impression is of a coolly reasoned view: that wartime was no time to marry. Girls, yes. Wives, no. And what was the rush? On V-J Day he was still only twenty-five. If he'd been holding back for greater things, and it's one of those theories so wildly easy to trot out after all this time, nobody knew but him. It seems improbable.

Looking back on the big surprise unwrapped at Corsham that day, Parker realizes that the name of the girl wasn't too surprising a part of it. He doesn't know why. Perhaps the news, when it came, was followed so fast in his mind by its recognition as a great idea, that it all fused into obviousness. But of course. Who else? Suddenly it seemed the only possible arrangement.

Frightfully disappointing, of course, for all those other heiresses. But we must harden our hearts about that, and count ourselves lucky. Though the range of eligible husbands for the royal heiress wasn't all that wide, picking a loser could have been easy all the same.

A fringe benefit was a home of his own at last. Clarence House had a delayed start, while the Minister of Works spruced it up into a suitable residence, and for more than a year they camped out in an extension of the bride's old unmarried quarters at the palace. (It was eventually largely furnished with wedding presents.) They were immensely happy there, and when Elizabeth became Queen, and had to return to the palace in full possession, it was depressing. "Now we've got to live behind railings," she said.

There was also to be a weekend pad, Sunninghill Park, near Ascot. A picture spread in one of the Sunday papers went joyously to town over the amenities. "A solitary swan glides past the tree-fringed, grassy banks of the lake, under the white stone bridge with its guardian griffins . . ." "Among the finest interior features is this magnificent marble staircase . . ." It was Crown property, and would have been a grace and favor home. Unfortunately, and despite the ready wealth of water and the incombustibility (you might think) of marble staircases, the house was mysteriously burned down before the decorators could get in, and Sunday readers, if their memories lasted that long, may well have shed a tear.

Indeed, the setting-up of the happy couple drew nothing but approval from the war-shabby public. It seemed only right that the Commons should vote £50,000 to put Clarence House in order, £10,000 a year for the Duke and a rise of £50,000 for his wife, and this in 1947, when utility and austerity were the grinding watchwords. If you couldn't have a fairy tale of your own, you got your fun out of somebody else's. A house now had to be rented for the weekends, Windlesham Moor, in Berkshire. Though this was no two-up and two-down either, dwellers in the bomb site prefabs were delighted. It was only in the affluent society of twenty years later that people began asking whether the Queen and her husband were giving value for money. (Even then there were some compassionate hearts. When, in 1969, Prince Philip talked of having to give up polo, dockers in the Fellmongers Arms, Bermondsey, started a fund to buy him a pony. He didn't let it get that far, but suggested, in an appreciative letter, that they should do something "for the young, rather than the middle-aged.")

For much of this time, he didn't see much of his new homes. The Navy went on. It's true he wasn't yet at sea again. But for the first few months of his married life he did a nine-to-six job at an Admiralty desk in the Operations Division. ("I was just a dogsbody, shuffling ships around. It was quite interesting.") But the obligations of royal as opposed to naval rank were already eating into the engagement book. After a day's ship-shuffling there was often only time for a quick wash and brush-up before haring off to open an exhibition, chair a committee, present a cup, dine with some men. Demands for speeches were rolling in, and they had to be written as well as delivered. Sometimes his wife was with him, often not. Even before the full effect of the Accession, some separation of duties was inevitable.

After the Admiralty, a staff course at the Royal Naval College, where he actually lived in at Greenwich, with only weekends at home. He found it absorbing, as near to a university as he'd ever got. (If he sometimes seems to make deflating remarks about universities it's only because he sees a danger of their becoming "a fetish, and an end in themselves," thinks we should be more realistic about their true value and purpose.)

In the autumn of 1949, by now a father, he again went to sea, as First Lieutenant in HMS *Chequers*, leader of the first Mediterranean destroyer flotilla. *Chequers* was based on Malta, and from time to time Elizabeth would join him there. For the first and last time they were free of civic receptions, provincial tours, presentations, centenary celebrations and the procession of vellum-paged visitors' books. Practically like an ordinary married life. Naturally, the governor was bound to honor them with a ball. There were formal occasions with the British community. Elizabeth had conscientious twinges, felt she must show herself at the schools and hospitals. The prescribed detective tagged along.

But by home standards, it was the simple life. There were swimming, dancing, picnics, excursions to the still uninvaded coves and beaches of the island, and to its smudge of a sister, Gozo, within easy launch distance to the north. If they wanted their friends in they had them, and no demon protocol showing its barbed tail through the curtains. Elizabeth went shopping, and had the exhilarating experience of actually going out to get her hair done. She swapped calls and gossip with the other navy wives, watched polo—it was in Malta that Philip first caught that persistent bug—and other competitive navy larks. She enjoyed herself, laughed a lot, looked blooming.

From her husband's point of view things got even better: in July 1950 promotion to Lieutenant-Commander, and at last his own ship, the frigate *Magpie*. There'd been a slight confusion on *Chequers*, where his commanding officer had felt a painful urge to call him "Sir." The First Lieutenant, with great respect, insisted that a ship's captain was "Sir" to all his officers. (The ogre of special treatment loomed dangerously after the marriage, and he had to spell things out once or twice. If the Navy couldn't read his rank badges properly he'd have to leave the Navy, which neither party wanted. The message eventually got home.)

Magpie solved that one, anyway. Some remember her as the happiest of ships. Cousin Alexandra's ghost writer recalls an officer "glowing with warm enthusiasm as he told me how popular Philip was with his crew." One of the crew said, "He worked us like hell, but treated us like gentlemen." One of the gentlemen claimed that he'd rather die than serve in that ship again. Another that he "stamped about like a ——ing tiger." Still, they privately called him "dukey," and that sort of tiger doesn't usually attract the inoffensive nickname. When his launch left for the last time they gave him a twenty-one-gun salute. It was only in smoke flares, but it sounds more like good luck than good riddance.

He commanded her for less than a year (nothing left of her

now but the glassed-in model that decorates his *Britannia* study). Perhaps not with universal acclaim, Gordonstoun's "Plus est en vous" was impressed on all who served on her. She had to be the best. Star of maneuvers, she hoisted the proud plywood rooster. In the annual regatta she won six out of ten boat events, and her Captain rowed stroke in one of the winners. None of your detached exhortations from the sidelines. If javelins were to be thrown, he was in there throwing.

She dropped anchor in many harbors during his short command, often serving Whitehall as a convenient instrument of international courtesy. A call from a friendly British warship (the unfriendly are gunboats) has always been a fine thing. With a royal duke on the quarterdeck, unusually well-connected by marriage, it could give pause to a lot of that loose chat about second-class powers. When *Magpie* came in, scrubbed, taut and shining, and the Captain was piped ashore in white and gold, first-class was the only word. Just swanning around, some said, in what they liked to call the Duke of Edinburgh's private yacht. Well, it's too bad, but you can't get along without prestige in this world. Ask the advertising profession. He swanned around Jordan and Iran, calling on their kings, dined with the presidents of Turkey and Iran. In November 1950, representing his father-in-law, he opened Gibraltar's new Legislative Council. Glimpses of old glory irradiated the Alexandrians, the Venetians, the Algerians, the Cypriots.

Perhaps it's harder to make out a working case for Monte Carlo, but he's said to have navigated out of the millionaires' marina there in conditions when other ships weren't putting to sea, which could rank as a valuable exercise. And even a nostalgic stopover at Corfu drew some goodwill ceremonial. On a meltingly hot day, walled in by broiling functionaries, he received a hero's welcome from his island birthplace. Mike Parker, who was then still equerry to both Prince Philip and Princess Elizabeth, and present on one of his regular courier hops from Clarence House, remembers sweating right down into his shoes. "Were you as hot as I was?" he murmured to the boss as they left the town hall. "Was I? I'm positively squelching out of this place."

There was a frankly business-with-pleasure jaunt to Athens, in the early summer of 1950: the right time for Greece, before the dust has coated the olive groves and the sun fried the first freshness off the oleanders and bougainvillea.

The C-in-C, Arthur John Power, made over his dispatch vessel for the Princess. This was HMS *Surprise*, from which, unexpectedly soon, she was to review her fleet as Queen. *Magpie*, lacking suitable accommodations for its commander's wife, escorted her, with a destroyer, from Malta westwards across the Ionian Sea, into the Gulf of Corinth and through the tight squeeze of the Corinth Canal. Signals of great gaiety passed between the ships. Some were in clear. *Surprise* to *Magpie*: "Princess full of beans." *Magpie* to *Surprise:* "Is that the best you can give her for breakfast?" Others were in those biblical codings, much favored for inter-flotilla messages. Authentic examples aren't, alas, on record, but a ship enjoying another's difficulties would make, say, Isaiah 33:23 ("Thy tacklings are loosed," etc.) and probably get in return after flippings through the good book, Samuel I, 15:14 ("What meaneth this bleating of the sheep?") Not top-line wit, perhaps, but a reflection of those lighthearted times. Comic messages weren't necessarily ecclesiastical. When Philip, nipping home by air on some piece of official business, flew over HMS *Vigo*, she signaled up enviously, "All right for some." He sent back, in a radio catch phrase of the day, "*Vigo*—ve come back."

On the Athens trip, Michael Parker, on *Surprise* as equerry, devised most of them at that end, with some assistance from Christopher Bonham-Carter, then commanding the second frigate flotilla (and when Philip got his own ship, *Magpie*, became his CO).

Parker remembers him in those days as "the funniest man alive." Like called to like, and nearly ten years later he became Treasurer to the Duke of Edinburgh's Household. After eleven years at the palace his sense of fun got smothered a bit under the pressures of the job. It was still good for an occasional firework to ease the boredom of a Program Meeting—but no one in that office has a lot of time to wade through the Testaments for the Word. Ecclesiastes 1:8: "All things are full of labor."

On *Surprise*, Elizabeth soon caught on to the signal joke, and got pretty good at it. Indeed, there were buoyant spirits all around, even when, in the Gulf, they hit one of those sudden storms for which Greek waters are feared and famous. The seas became short, steep and nasty, bad enough for Parker to stay watchfully up all night.

Contrary (as usual) to most of the stories, the Queen is as good a sailor as most people, and better than a lot; it was only on Parker's insistence that she came down off the bridge and went to bed. He had told her meanwhile that the sunrise in those parts wasn't a sight to be missed, particularly as it would be coming up in the morning as they passed the towering crags of god-hallowed Parnassus. She agreed she oughtn't miss it. The navigating officer, who may blush at the recollection still, miscalculated the sunrise by an hour, and Her Royal Highness came up for the show in a pitch-black pre-dawn. There are royal personages who wouldn't have taken it kindly. She and Parker went into the galley and brewed tea until the display came on. It was gratifyingly up to standard.

Philip showed off his homeland to his wife, like any other husband pointing out the that-was-where. They stayed with his cousins, King Paul and Queen Frederica, in the Royal Palace. The Parthenon was floodlit for them; this isn't laid on for everybody (except, nowadays, for the tourists' *son-et-lumière*, when the English version of the script disquietingly personifies Solon, Homer and Pericles in well-known accents from the BBC Drama Repertory). But it was mainly an informal occasion, a family rather than a Family affair. There were the inevitable picnics, not always al fresco. In royal terms a picnic isn't a matter of jam sandwiches and wasps, particularly for Philip, who likes to cook. On rare free evenings during starchy official visits he takes eagerly to the hot stove and the striped apron, and there's often a pot-luck threesome, when he, his valet and duty detective, all rank abandoned, champ through delicious if sub-Beeton menus. (In what can only be called a rumpus room next to his study at Windsor, where Andrew's and Edward's train sets are laid out, and the walls covered with specimens of their father's camera work, an electric grill stands in a corner, ready for instant transfer to the south lawn.)

One of the indoor feasts on the Athens trip was mounted a few miles along the shore, at the British Ambassador's beach house. His wife, Lady Norton, had obligingly handed over the key, so that a small group from *Magpie*, after a demi-official reception on board, could boat along in the evening and thrash around with the pots and pans. The party climbed the cliffs from the beach, carrying its food at the ready, and the key had no sooner rattled in the door than an upper window burst open to a fiery shout of "Who's there!" Even ambassadors' wives can forget to mention arrangements they've made with third parties. His Excellency heard of the projected picnic without enthusiasm. What with one thing and another, he could hardly tell the invaders to beat it, but he mentioned that he was trying to get some sleep, and would be obliged by as little uproar as possible. The picnickers, not too seriously chastened, got on with it. Enticing fumes pervaded the house. Presently the kitchen door opened to admit Sir Clifford Norton, KCMG, CVO, a small figure in pajamas, rumpled but alert, and carrying a knife and fork. It's doubtful whether he or the cook recalls the moment with greater joy.

July 1951 saw the end of Malta and *Magpie*. Indefinite leave, a privilege that couldn't be got around for once. No more larks (or so it seemed, though in fact there've been plenty). It was good-bye to the Navy in everything but the letter.

The King was ill. There were a lot of things he couldn't take on: fairly imminently, an east–west tour of Canada, with a rounding off in the United States. (It was to be Philip's first exposure to American security arrangements. The turnout of police, guards and FBI men was on an alarming scale, and he found it absurd. President Harry Truman, who regarded a flock of detectives on his morning walk as a quite enjoyable part of the trappings, said, "I suppose you haven't got the tradition of nuts that we've got." They stayed at Blair House, the White House having the painters in, where Mrs. Truman's deaf and aged mother was bedridden in a top room. She would never forgive him, he said, if Princess Elizabeth left without a meeting. They toiled together up many stairs. Harry yelled, "Mother, I've brought Princess Elizabeth to see you!" Winston Churchill had become Prime Minister again in the course of the tour, and the old lady came back with topicality and charm: "I'm so glad your father's been re-elected.")

The tour had been planned as a moderate exercise, as such exercises go, but was now elaborated by additions and interpellations at the Canadian end into a 15,000 mile journey studded with stops like suckers on an octopus. Whitehall had decided that the Edinburghs, as Malta society had called them, should do it. The grand departure was to be by sea; it was fixed for September 25. The date was almost around the corner when the King's doctors announced that he must undergo a grave operation. Could the Heiress to the Throne leave the country at such a time? Put it another way, could Elizabeth leave her much-loved father? It was one of those private agonies just as real for royalty as for the rest of us, though we mysteriously tend not to think so. The surgeons got to work only two days before the due sailing date. The operation was declared a success. But even so. Could they go? Certainly not by ship. Time had run out. It's hard to believe now, but flying the Atlantic wasn't on. Businessmen, other royalties and statesmen were boldly buzzing to and fro. Princess Elizabeth must not. But how else to beat the calendar, and avoid disruptions and disappointments at the other end?

Typically opportunist, Philip hatched a plan to beat the barrier —and once beaten it could hardly come back. He needed the King's connivance. It would be announced that the visit was off. Alexander of Tunis, then Canada's Governor-General, would lodge horrified protests. The British Government must respect his feelings. It would be the perfect time to advance the airborne solution. The ploy succeeded. It involved a call by Prince Philip on Clement Attlee—almost worse, Winston had to be talked around. Though he wasn't in office, he was the elder statesman most vigorously against the Princess's risking a transatlantic flight, but now gave in. The safety conferences at London Airport, with BOAC's Miles Thomas, were in enough depth to make an air traffic controller's hair curl. But on October 8 they roared off for Montreal, leaving the flying ban shattered behind them.

The tour was a triumph. The understudy ambassadors were considered qualified, and it was decided that they should again stand in, at the end of the following January, for the visit to Australia and New Zealand. Again they flew. It already seemed obvious. The King, bareheaded in the cold wind, waved from the tarmac. On their eighth day away, Elizabeth became Queen, and they both came home to the new and different life.

To approach him with preconceived ideas is a mistake, and one I kept making.

Q: How much do you think Gordonstoun influenced you to go into the Navy?

HRH: Not very much.

Q: Oh. But didn't all the sailing . . . ?

HRH: I always did any expeditions by boat if I possibly could, simply to avoid all that ghastly foot-slogging, which I was made to do at Salem and hated every minute of it.

Q: But you already felt an urge towards the sea?

HRH: I had to find something to do for a living.

Q: There's a suggestion that your Uncle George, the Marquess of Milf—?

HRH: Not really.

Q: (Floundering) But there was the seagoing heredity?

HRH: I don't think that played any great part. I may have been more easily persuaded as a result of it. I remember thinking, well, I'm certainly not going into the Army.

(Well, naturally. After the deal his father had had from the military, he wouldn't. But it wasn't that.)

I mean, I wouldn't have minded if there'd been horses. But the idea of walking about, which I hated, or driving around in a tank or a lorry or something, it struck me as an unpleasant way of existing.

Q: (Regrouping) But with the Navy, was it Lord Mount—?

HRH: He may have persuaded me. Or said that it would be easier to get in. I just sort of accepted it. I didn't feel very strongly about it. I really wanted to go into the Air Force.

Q: (Shot down) Into the—?

HRH: Oh, yes. Left to my own devices I'd have gone into the Air Force without a doubt.

CHAPTER

12

Children to Bless You

"Training isn't necessary. They do on-the-job training, so to speak, and learn the trade, or business, or craft, just from being with us and watching us function, and seeing the whole organisation around us. They can't avoid it.
"What is much more difficult is bringing them up as people."

He has a streak of self-indulgence, at least in the sense that he likes doing what he likes doing, so it's a reasonable inference that in finding so much time to spend with his family he gets as much fun out of it as they do. If they'd been stupid, boring or merely uncompanionable it's safe to say they'd have seen a good deal less of him. From the beginning, both parents were determined to see as much of the children as possible; the long holidays were kept clear of outside commitments with that very much in mind, and even on working days there were always inviolate times for talk and play. This is not to suggest the stock picture of the English nannied classes (now rapidly thinning), with Mama and Papa graciously receiving the little ones for a short spell before dinner, provided that they're well-scrubbed, only speak when spoken to, and will be removed at the first droop of a mouth corner. It's always been much more than that. Speaking only when spoken to, in particular, was never on with this family.

Q: Did you encourage them to take their own line, and argue with you about it?
HRH: They didn't need any encouragement, I can tell you.
Q: They'd automatically take the opposite view?
HRH: Oh, absolutely, yes, without fail.

That would suit him very well. In court circles a good knock-down argument is sometimes hard to find, can cave in respectfully at the other end just when the battle is truly joined.

Also from the beginning, all the children have been offered the widest possible range of things to get interested in. The Queen saw to it that they all learned to ride, and Anne to drive pony-traps. Prince Philip, with a broader range of personal pursuits, introduced them to swimming, sailing, shooting, fishing, go-karting, polo for Charles. . . . Does it smack of those overmanaging fathers who can't wait to involve the kids in their own pet pursuits, whether they like it or not? This wasn't the idea. The idea was to open up the widest possible choice of interests. If only one of them stuck and seized the attention the plan would be working. In Charles's case, for instance, fishing and shooting stuck hardest, and he's marginally better than his father at both (music and acting were his own discoveries). "I've always tried to help them to master at least one thing that they enjoy doing, because as soon as a child feels self-confidence in one area, it spills over into all the other areas. You even notice that if they feel they've made a real personal accomplishment of that kind, then this is immediately reflected even in their academic performance."

Academic prowess hasn't been much fussed over. Like any other parent, he went through the school reports, and still does with the two younger boys, but without the pulse-racing anxieties, on both sides, that can often attend this grinding ritual. "I don't really take them frightfully seriously. I say, 'Look, I'm only going to bother if you're permanently bottom, I really couldn't care less where you are. Just stay in the middle, that's all I ask.'" He deplores, with many, the tyrannies of the examination system, thinks it's crazy to worry, when a child's eleven years old, about what he's going to be like when he's thirty. How can you tell, anyway? "Children go through enormous changes. For a time they're in phase with life around them, then they go out of phase and become unliveable with, and everything they do is wrong and cross-grained and maddening—then suddenly it all comes right for a bit—then they go off on another tack. It's impossible at any point to say, 'This is what they're going to be like.' The pendulum's got to swing quite a lot before it settles down."

These pronouncements, like others quoted here, don't pretend to be oracular, though this much understanding of the younger generation, if spread around more than it is, might do much to close the well-known gap. With him, it springs partly from an intuition for getting through to the young, on a wavelength unblocked by the superiority of years or the diligent condescension of those TV uncles whose head-patting approach must surely turn many a juvenile stomach. To treat children as people seems to him obvious beyond comment, except to recall that he's been surrounded by children, mostly relations, all his life, because of his late arrival in a houseful of older sisters. "Remember I was only ten when my first nephew was born. I mean, you were in a room with grown-ups, and you talked to the grown-ups, and children wandered in and you talked to the children, you just didn't think about it. . . . ." It's made for immense companionship with his own brood.

Their behavior has been average to good. "I think they do silly things occasionally, but it's nearly always satisfactorily arranged, more by discussion than anything." Dishonesty would be his idea of a major crime. "By that I mean that if you ask them a question they must give you an honest answer." Equally, he's against those needless parental inquisitions practiced by so many. "There are often questions you'd like to ask, but it's much better not to unless it's really necessary."

So the hand on the reins is unexpectedly light. Fathering a future king could in itself seem to carry awesome overtones: if he hasn't been deaf to these, they've never sounded predominantly on his inward ear. When Queen Victoria's first son arrived, and her doctor congratulated her on a fine son, she corrected him, faintly but with spirit, to "a fine prince." And there are other families where baby's first cry, given the right gender, means above all that the proud addition "and son" will one day be tacked on to the firm's brass plate or factory gate. Charles was a son first and Heir to the Throne afterward. He'd have no choice about going into the business, but its very inevitability made cautionary reminders superfluous. The situation would simply dawn, gradually and naturally, just as the specialized techniques of public behavior would seep in by a kind of osmosis. No textbooks on when to shake hands, what to say to mayors, how to look as if you're enjoying yourself when all you want is to go home.

If Charles was irrevocably planked down on the constitutional rails at birth, he has always been consulted about the route, and the stops by the way. His father's overpainted reputation for laying down the law as he sees it and dismissing the dissenting view has given the impression, for instance, that Charles went to Gordonstoun because he was told to go, and similarly to Timbertop in Australia, another of your Spartan educational establishments;

that he was later packed off arbitrarily to Cambridge, with an uncomfortable interlude in Aberystwyth at the University of Wales—all as part of a stern, cold-blooded plan to put a bit of backbone into the lad and fit him for the role of a modern prince. Not so. For one thing, the backbone was there anyway, and much more of his character that had gone entirely unsuspected in the earlier years. With a memorable radio broadcast in March 1969—when listeners who switched on in the middle couldn't wait to learn the identity of this composed, agreeable and amusing young man—Charles seemed to explode on to the public scene out of nowhere; all the doting and drooling which had made such hard reading during his childhood and schooldays might have been about someone quite different.

Other unsuspected qualities were to be demonstrated during his tour of Wales that year, when he came, saw and conquered the people on their own ground. He was alone, with only his own instinct and resourcefulness to see him through. And courage. In the 1966 general election more than 60,000 Welsh Nationalist votes were polled, and the spirit of mistrust for London and all its works was still mounting. There was a degree of dynamiting: and if no one actually threw a bomb at Charles, well, that isn't a thing you can rely on at the time.

He had to face out the Welsh, simply because it was a situation that couldn't be blinked, had to be met head-on and dealt with. He was under no obligation, however, to go to Gordonstoun, or to Cambridge, and certainly wasn't directed there by an imperious father. Prince Philip's part, as in so much, was simply to state the options. Gordonstoun was by no means preordained. Charles is said to have been "put down" for Eton at birth; if so, it wasn't by his father, who gets some quiet amusement out of the suggestion, on the ground that if Eton had been decided on, even much later and without the formality of advance booking, the school wouldn't have been very likely to have said no. But in any case . . .

"From the beginning I was careful not to make a rigid plan— I haven't for any of them—until some sort of foreseeable situation. I said, 'Well, here are the alternatives: you've seen Eton, you know the place, it's right on our doorstep [at Windsor], you can more or less come home any time you like. Its disadvantages are that every time you hiccup you'll have the whole of the national press on your shoulders. . . . Also, Eton is frequently in the news, and when it is it's going to reflect on you. If you go to the north of Scotland [Gordonstoun] you'll be out of sight, and they're going to think twice about taking an aeroplane to get up there, so it's got to be a major crisis before they actually turn up, and you'll be able to get on with things. On top of that it's near Balmoral, there's always the Factor there, you can go and stay with him— and your grandmother [Queen Elizabeth, the Queen Mother] goes up there to fish, you can go and see her.' And we had a general discussion, and I said, 'Well, it's up to you.' "

Of course, there were other schools. The problem would have been to pick one offering such sound and intelligible reasons for picking it that the press and the public—and the schools that didn't get him—wouldn't raise a pother of query and speculation.

There was a small, select dinner party at the palace in December 1965, when the Queen and Prince Philip entertained the Prime Minister, the Archbishop of Canterbury, Lord Mountbatten, Sir Charles Wilson (Chairman of the Committee of University Vice-Chancellors), the Dean of Windsor and Sir Michael Adeane. Object, to plot Charles's course after Gordonstoun, where he still had two years to run. A university? If so, which? A broad decision, first, between old gray-stone and new red-brick, or even newer plate-glass. If new, the choice must again be for sound and intelligible reasons, not a gesture of expediency to suit public opinion.

Or there were other forms of further education. A period of

voluntary service overseas, perhaps. His father saw predictable snags there. "It sounds all very well, going off to teach for a year in Borneo, or somewhere, but in practical terms it would defeat its own object, be just too newsworthy, you know what I mean?" (Something of the sort was later considered for Anne, when headlines would have been milder; it was dropped because of her passionate involvement with horses and horsemanship; she was getting within reach of championship standards—not that anyone really believed that, since she only got a mention if she fell off— and it would have been brutal to interrupt it all.)

Charles wasn't at the dinner. Once more it looked as if the poor, defenseless lad was having no say in his affairs. But he'd actually had his say already. It would be indiscreet, perhaps, to suggest here that the small, illustrious gathering had been convened to be informed rather than consulted, thus deflecting the appearance of responsibility from the family . . . but it was odd that their decisions coincided so snugly with those of Charles and his parents, reached in private discussion long before.

The family has been raised "on a committee basis," which doesn't mean a committee of just two. Once they were old enough to have sensible views, the children have also had a vote. "It's no good saying do this, do that, don't do this, don't do that. You can warn them about certain things, that's about the most you can do, or you can say, this is the situation you're in, these are the choices, on balance it looks as if this is the sensible one, go away and think it over, and come back and let me know what you think." Needless to say, there are times when the junior committee members get over-ruled, but their feelings never go unconsidered, nor their reasonable requests denied. Taking time to think is something he believes in on either side. "It's very easy, when children want to do something, to say no immediately. I think it's quite important not to give an unequivocal answer at once. Much better to think it over. Then if you do eventually say no, I think they really accept it. If you start by saying no, and they persist in the argument until you realise you could perfectly well have said yes, you can get into a situation where they won't ask you any more, or you find you're stopping them from doing things which in fact it would be perfectly reasonable for them to do."

He has adopted these methods with others than the immediate members of his own family, notably the late Duchess of Kent's children (whose father died in a wartime air crash in 1942). But then, the interplay of family consultation has always been great. He cherishes his vast regiment of relatives, and has encouraged his children, who have known a lot of them as long as they remember, "from their grandmother, sideways and downwards, I suppose you could say," to talk things over with them. The span of generations is a boon, especially in the middle range, where some of the many cousins, for instance, being older than Charles and Anne but younger than their parents, can sympathize as well as advise. "So that they were never dependent on us absolutely for everything that went on, and we've always tried to make them feel that members of the family stand in a special relationship to them." He added, disquietingly, "Mind you, this happens anyway, in the children's situation, because they soon discover that it's much safer to unburden yourself to a member of the family than just to a friend . . . you see, you're never quite sure . . . the pressures are a bit . . . a small indiscretion can lead to all sorts of difficulties."

A chilling glimpse of life on the royal high wire. To have to think twice before being frank with a friend? Alarming, the essential cultivation of such delicate private footwork, and a sharp reminder that these are unnatural lives. Though it's been the concern of both the Queen and Prince Philip that the children should be hampered as little as possible by the circumstances of birth, yet at the same time prepared as much as possible for exposure to public view, the compromise is far from easy. So much has been written about parental plans to provide "ordinary" lives, and there has been so much gleeful acclaim of Charles and Anne as a pair of "ordinary" children, going to parties, dancing at discothèques, indistinguishable from the children of any other couple, that the futility of the exercise is lost sight of—particularly by those who mistake its purpose, which isn't to de-royalize them (absurd and impossible), but to help them to be royal in their own socially shifting times. When Charles went to school at Cheam, for an ordinary preparatory school education, no one was likely to forget that he was the Queen's son, and would be king one day. When Anne arrived for her first term at Benenden, it was hardly an ordinary experience to find the entire school, three hundred strong, paraded for a ceremonial welcome in the forecourt. It's true that she'd been accompanied by her mother, but that's a loving gesture an ordinary schoolgirl can expect to enjoy without a fuss on this scale.

The people want it both ways, that's the trouble. A Prince and Princess of the Royal House, separate, special, revered, remote; and yet, in the title of an archetypal newspaper article in 1965, "The Royal Teenagers: A Thoroughly Nice ORDINARY Couple of Youngsters." They're tough assignments for the journalist, up against the eternal dilemma of presenting the ordinariness as something extraordinary. If the remarkableness of the unremarkable is worth celebrating in two thousand words, our court correspondent must be wasting his time, because the remarkableness is bound to come out on top anyway. Anne, as Princess, means tiara, satin ballgown, long white gloves, and hot policemen linking arms to hold back the very crowd who keep reading that she's really one of them, loving to dress in "rib-knit socks, loafers, sloppy jerseys, chunky sweaters, gamin caps." Charles, as Prince, means the sixty-fourth heir to the Throne, with towering dignities and splendors; yet "Charles has become so used to being just one of a crowd at school that he no longer sticks out in a crowd, there or anywhere else."

It's all nonsense. To be an ordinary couple of youngsters, in the sense so dear to popular commentators, simply can't be done. Charles's most casual observations become public utterances (his father has the same problem, and once said that when he sees himself quoted in Sayings of the Week columns he usually can't see why, and assumes something's being read into it that he never meant to be there). All Anne's hats are public hats, and proliferate instantly into millinery for the masses; if she's caught without one, that's public too ("Her hair is combed slickly to the left, with no attempt to encourage its natural kink into conventionally pretty waves.") Ever since they could read, they've read about themselves. There's been no parental bar on this. It's no good hoping the facts of life will go away. The most to be hoped for is that they can sustain the public glare without damage to the private character. But it's the chicken and the egg. Without the character in the first place they couldn't carry things off as they do, whether it's Charles representing the Queen at the Fiji independence celebrations, or Anne, as if it were the most natural thing in the world, handing out St. David's Day leeks to a parade of the Welsh Guards. Try putting an ordinary couple of youngsters into this line of work and see how they get on.

Yet, in its way, pretending not to be a prince and princess is just as demanding. Charles's Australian excursion, two terms at that rugged outstation of Geelong Grammar School, living rough on the fringe of Mount Timbertop's gum forests, was in his own words an exercise in "enlightened masochism." He once did seventy miles walking and climbing during a long weekend, and often because of the risk of forest fires, was living on uncooked food cold from the can. All very different from the comforts of home. But he warmed to the Australians, as his father had done so long before. They came up to you and said what they thought. Back at Gordonstoun, much expanded in body and spirit, he finished his time there as head of the school,[1] and soon afterward began taking on public engagements. One of the first meant a return to Australia just before Christmas, 1967, as the Queen's representative at the memorial service, in Melbourne, for Prime Minister Harold Holt. He was just nineteen.

Anne's engagement book lagged behind her brother's for a time —the year and three-quarters age gap—but soon after Benenden things began to pile in, and by the end of her first "official" year she'd launched ships, presented cups, opened youth clubs, day nurseries, swimming pools, animal centers, visited the Western Fleet, dropped in on a North Sea drilling rig, christened a Hovercraft, driven a tank, lunched at Scotland Yard, toured innumerable hospitals, housing schemes, furniture exhibitions, been appointed colonel-in-chief of two distinguished regiments . . . and remained a thoroughly nice, ordinary youngster? Well, if it's possible, she did. And if she did, and Charles did the same, Prince Philip's part was great.

Q: Do you see your own heredity coming out in them?
HRH: (Laughing) Yes. All the worst parts.

In fact, he thinks that Charles has his mother's serenity, and concern for individuals, but also her unsuspected inner toughness: that Anne has a lot of his own abrupt directness and practicality. Andrew is between the two, softer than Anne but not yet showing Charles's imagination and flair ("Still, he's got a long way to go"). Edward, at seven, "has tremendous charm, as children of that age often have, but I also think that, of all of them, he might well develop the highest artistic sense."

---

[1] I rather stupidly said to the Dean of Windsor, who mentioned this, that it looked like a bit of a put-up job. "No, no," he said, "he was streets ahead of the lot of them." Too bad that laurels in high places are bound to be suspect.

Bringing them up has been a close-planned yet somehow relaxed exercise. Asked about crimes and punishment, he can't remember much under either head, but points out that the minor misdemeanors were taken care of in the nursery, and by others: no confrontations, at the end of a hard day, with the natural tantrums that fray domestic relations elsewhere. But later disciplines, says an observer of long standing, were likely to be by disapproval. And effective enough, it's to be imagined. Not only because Prince Philip's disapproval, fall where it may, can have an edge like an ice ax, but because the disfavor of those we love and admire, and whose approbation we seek and prize, makes other penalties sheer nonstarters.

He could hardly not be pleased with the way they've turned out. Admits to "nothing but admiration" for Charles's disarming of the Welsh, and is seldom in better spirits than when he and Anne are doing something together. There's great affection, no sentimentality.

"I don't goo over them. I think they're just people. But I think they have nice qualities, and not, on the whole, nasty ones."

Q: Had you a policy for giving the children a normal upbringing? I mean, considering their unique circumstances?
HRH: Yes and no. People talk about a normal upbringing.
What's a normal upbringing? What you really mean is,
was I insisting that they should go through all the disadvantages of being brought up in the way other people are
brought up? Precisely that—disadvantages. There's always this idea about treating them exactly like other children. In fact, it means that they're treated much worse,
because they're known by name, and by association. For
instance, everybody says that Charles went to a prep
school and was treated like everybody else, but before
you know what's happened it turns out that the school
barber was in the pay of one of the newspapers. . . .
How many boys would you think of pinching their
schoolbooks and flogging them on the market? And
then being accused of doing it yourself? Which is what
happened. It's all very well to say they're treated the
same as everybody else, but it's impossible. I think that
what is possible, and in fact necessary, is that they should
realize that they're not anonymous. This has got to come
at some stage.
Q: Do they feel that they suffer disadvantages because of
their special situation?
HRH: Oh, I think they would certainly agree with that. For all

their advantages, they have very considerable disadvantages.

Q: Do you think they would have wished to be born into some other station in life?

HRH: That's a hypothetical question.

13

Call Sign "Rainbow"

*"I fly because it's useful for getting about, but I also
enjoy the . . . intellectual challenge of it all, if that's
the right word."*

☙❧

"Prince in Air Miss," said the front pages early in August 1970.
The Prince was the Prince of Wales, but his father was with him.
It was hardly a near thing, but near enough for flutterings in min-
isterial dovecots. They'd be nothing new.

Getting Prince Philip into a pilot's seat had been nearly as hard
as getting Princess Elizabeth into a passenger's. The idea of princes
of the Royal House in charge of those dangerous flying machines
has always alarmed the denizens of Whitehall, politicians and air
marshals alike. He's been flying for eighteen years now, but still
fumes over what he regards as excessive safeguards for his happy
landings. He wants to be treated like any other pilot, as he wanted
to be just another naval officer. What enrages him as much as any-

thing is inconveniencing other fliers, for which he usually gets the blame:

> Members of Reading Flying Club are complaining that the Duke of Edinburgh spoilt their Saturday morning sport.
> The Duke made a trip to White Waltham to practise flying a Turbulent plane—and the order went out to ground all planes at Woodley airfield, the club's headquarters. . . .

The headline said "Duke Upsets Fliers" (*Daily Sketch*, October 1959), but they weren't half as upset as he was. His office shot off a letter to the aggrieved members saying he'd no idea that any such order had gone out, and it certainly hadn't come from him. "His Royal Highness would like you to know that if you think you have difficulties getting into the air, they are nothing to what he has to go through."

It doesn't often lead to impatience in the actual pilot's seat, or he wouldn't be the good pilot he is; but once, shortly after taking off with a civil airline crew, the panel warning light showed an engine on fire. He looked out, saw no smoke, diagnosed an instrument fault and went on flying. The co-pilot, fearlessly correct, stopped the engine and filled it with foam, leaving him to circle on one and come down again to a maddening delay. Indefensibly, he took a poor view of the whole affair. That he'd been right, as it happened, was no excuse. (Still, he tells the story himself.)

He can get rough with over-conscientious ground controllers, and even rougher with incompetent ones. It's an insensitivity, a failure to realize what pressures come homing in on even that imperturbable breed when they pick up the call sign "Rainbow," which attaches to any aircraft the moment he's actually driving it.

"If you kill him," said Flight-Lieutenant Caryl Gordon's CO, late in October 1952, "you realize what it will do to the Queen?" Well, it was one way of putting it. Gordon, then instructing on

Meteors at the RAF's Central Flying School, and picked to teach Philip to fly, was alive to his responsibilities without this sort of thing. But the administrators always seemed to be making their own flesh creep. The following Whitsun, a week before the Coronation, it was Mike Parker who found himself on the carpet, and a rather particular one, in front of Winston Churchill's desk at No. 10. He'd been sent for. Churchill kept him standing for some time before looking up from his papers. "Is it your intention," he rumbled, "to wipe out the Royal Family in the shortest possible time?"

He'd had an alarming report: that Prince Philip had been flying by helicopter. Not at the controls, it's true; that wasn't to happen for another two years, though inevitably he'd been casting envious eyes. The report was accurate, all the same. Helicopters were convenient, practical, quick. To rule them out for royal transport seemed absurd. That apart, the crisp, modern image needed them, just as it was no day and age for the Queen to be getting around the world by battleship.

The facts were, that with less than a week to go to the Coronation, and Commonwealth and Colonial troops at Pirbright and Woolwich promised a welcoming visit from the Duke, a Royal Navy chopper was the obvious way to squeeze them in. So he whirled cheerfully off from the palace, did the job and was back for lunch. By car it would have meant all day. The Prime Minister wasn't impressed with Parker's explanation, and had plenty more to say beyond his dramatic opening. It was typical of both men that the exchanges took a rosier turn toward the end. "By the way, Sir," said Parker, "I understand that you have an engagement outside London tomorrow. The commanding officer of the Royal Naval Helicopter Squadron has asked if he might put a machine at your disposal?"

Winston was rocked by the sheer cheek of it, and agreed. (He was seventy-nine.) Afterward, meeting Mike Parker on various formal occasions, he would snarl in his ear, "Helicopters!" With the accent on the hell. But it was the breakthrough. Prince Philip has since logged some three hundred helicopter hours.

His impatience to fly, as against being flown, had already turned him to the idea of being instructed by the Navy, even for fixed-wing aircraft. It was his own service, and its uniform the only one he had, at the time, to stitch the enviable wings on. It wasn't until early 1953 that he sprang overnight to top rank in all services. He enjoyed himself one morning soon after that, arriving at White Waltham to get in a lesson on the way to some RAF engagement, by appearing in the full finery of a marshal of the Royal Air Force. It had been tweed jackets and flannels before that, (though his aircraft had the five-star symbol of a MRAF painted on its side), and the eyebrows of his lowly flight-lieutenant instructor shot up gratifyingly. "I'm wearing it to shake you," said HRH. Rapport between teacher and taught had soon been established, and was sustained companionably through three years of work.

Rumors of Royal Navy instruction had at least lit a fire under the RAF, who weren't going to see this distinction go elsewhere, whatever damp palms and sleepless nights went with it. Of course, it was a nuisance to be landed with the royal whim—there seems to have been an idea, in the early days, that a bit of token tuition up to wings standard would be all that was needed, and if so they'd got the wrong man—but they'd bend their best resources to the job. Meanwhile, the important thing was not to kill him. When Gordon reported at HQ Home Command on October 20, 1952, he was greeted by an air marshal, two air vice-marshals and an air commodore, all anxious to make the point, and a few days later was bidden to wait upon the Secretary of State for Air, Lord De L'Isle and Dudley, who made it again on behalf of the government. He began to catch on.

It was all rather different from his pupil's own style when the time came. He was out to enjoy himself, and at the same time work like hell. Relaxed and ready for a laugh, but knowing a lot already—navigation and VHF were no problem after the Navy—stuffed with required reading, and with privately concocted mnemonics as an aid to remembering pre-flight checks. (In January, at Sandringham, he showed Gordon the model aircraft he'd been making—swept wings, deltas, crescents—nothing fancy by way of materials, but they all flew. Much later he designed an instrument to simplify flying approach patterns, and had it made up: it's now been long overtaken by technological advances.) From the start he was alarmingly eager to get on with the next thing but one, whether it was spins, rolls and loops that the syllabus wasn't offering yet, or fresh and more sophisticated airplanes.

There were always renewed official alarms each time a change-over loomed, and exasperating hold-ups for an updating of safety equipment. It made sense, naturally, but sometimes the precautions got almost literally topheavy, until a machine could hardly part from the runway for the weight of built-in security. Gordon's blackest moments were breaking the news of delays and prohibitions. With Squadron-Leader Peter Horsley, then the Duke's equerry, Mike Parker, and above all the Duke himself, he was all for getting on with the job, but there would always be someone at the top, often hard to identify, treading with sluggish caution.

Gordon wrote in his diary one day in April 1953:

> When we finished, the C-in-C was in the office to apologise to HRH for certain extraordinary contradictions that have taken place recently. Firstly, permission has been refused to transfer to the Oxford [he was just finishing on the Harvard] until the Chief of Air Staff has consulted the PM. Second, night flying may not be done until the same procedure has been gone through. HRH has now been flying for six months, and during all this time it has been known that night flying and Oxford flying were to be done,

and it therefore seems incredible to him that at the last minute an objection is lodged. . . . The problem seems to be that nobody is willing to take the responsibility for these decisions on themselves, but what I fear is that in their anxiety to see that no harm comes to HRH the whole of his training can be brought to a halt. HRH explained his views in no uncertain terms to the C-in-C, and there is now hope that in future these delays will cease. As far as I can see, the only person who can get any action at all, and who appears to know what is wanted, is HRH, and whenever I am in serious difficulty I tell him.

One of his difficulties was to strike a working medium between keeping the rules and bending them. He managed to strike it. Earlier in that entry he'd written:

HRH could not stay late, nor fly tonight, because it is the Queen's Birthday, so we confined ourselves to ¾ hour instrument flying, followed by an hour solo, during which he went off to practise aerobatics. I told him that the C-in-C wished him to do no more of these for safety's sake, but on such a glorious summer day if he did just a few and I didn't see him, nobody would know. He did quite a few, I think!

Anxious times for the Flight-Lieutenant (now Group Captain), and few MVOs can have been better deserved than the one he collected at the end of it. His pupil would turn up at odd hours (once at 6:45 in the morning "complete with sandwiches") or with only a phone call's notice, when a canceled engagement opened the prospect of an hour or two in the air. He would arrive when there was snow on Smith's Lawn,[1] or weather forecasts of the gloomiest

---

[1] Windsor Great Park. Early flights by Chipmunk were often from there. A

kind. The authorities, as might be expected, had been all against his learning to fly in winter anyway; they didn't get far with that one.

He first flew the Chipmunk on November 12, 1952. On December 20, Gordon decided to send him up for the first time alone, from White Waltham, and neither the decision nor the vigil from the ground could have been much fun. He'd had only ten hours flying, wedged into the implacable round of official duties. A week gone in Malta, presenting Colours to three Royal Marine Commando units.[2] More days lost to fog, rain, snow, high winds (though he often flew in the last three). Sometimes he'd roll up in hopeless weather and never get off at all, but instead talk flying inexhaustibly, with questions, questions. But on December 20, for the solo, he got both up and down. Not just that, either: "His take-off, circuit and landing were beyond reproach, the landing a beautiful three-pointer." Gordon wasn't invariably complimentary. He said what was wrong as well as what was right, and once had a stern word about the hazards of overconfidence. It was received with humility. A month later there was a somewhat alarming solo spin. Noting it down, Gordon kept an iron grip on his understatement. "I was perturbed at the number of turns he completed before recovering." You bet.

Prince Philip, under the laughter and leg-pulls, had a fair idea of what it must be like to be his instructor. There were more personal recognitions than the eventual MVO. At Christmas 1952 he gave Gordon a silver locket, engraved "A reward for diligence," and with the date of the first solo. That had probably been a headache, he said, and wouldn't be the last. "You can use it to keep pills in."

wind-sock had been rigged and the cricket pavilion turned into a makeshift briefing room.
[2] But he managed to get himself on to the flight deck of the BEA Ambassador, flew her part of the way, and came back with ideas for improving the readability of its altimeter.

But on the whole they were relaxed and cheerful times. When the weather got finer they would often come down at Smith's Lawn to find the Queen there, fondly critical or approving. Or Charles and Anne, as full of questions as their father, if on a more elementary level. Later he'd be flying them regularly up to Aberdeen, for the Balmoral holidays, and later still taking Charles back for the new term at Gordonstoun. As in any other family with a newly airborne member, there was much waving from gardens: from the palace, from Sandringham, from the Royal Lodge at Windsor, or, as wings spread further, from the Queen Mother's Castle of Mey. There were times when the Duke was more anxious to fly people than they were to be flown. "We flew off down the coast in the Devon [July 1954, a weekend at Arundel Castle with the Duke of Norfolk]—Portsmouth, Southampton, Isle of Wight, Selsey Bill and back to Tangmere. It was too bumpy for house party passengers, so HRH excused them."

The Devon was his fourth training aircraft, the last before he got the Queen's Flight Heron, and the first to yield any real bulk of pilot hours. The flying was now becoming functional, a way of getting to places where he had to be: to visit the Cameron Highlanders at Inverness, the coal mines at Cardiff, Marines at Plymouth, to Syerston as a guest of the Trent River Board—to Frankfurt, Luneburg, Oldenburg (to present a standard to 26 RAF Squadron).

He was entertaining to fly with and still is, full of talk on the usual range of subjects, alert for landmarks of interest below. He got special amusement, during the longer training flights, from the aerial views of old or familiar haunts, and even in foreign parts would shake Gordon with his geographical or topographical surveys.[3] This isn't to say there weren't unsmiling moments. Mal-

---

[3] "That's Maya country," he told me, looking down on the red-brown inhospitable terrain of Yucatan. But I couldn't pretend I was well up on pre-Aztec civilizations, and he kindly let it go. After the Commonwealth tour of 1953–54, Churchill

functioning equipment was never very popular; he was meticulous
with his own checks and inspections, worrying out the last technical details of a fault, and not short of ideas on how to avoid it
in future. When a Chipmunk had engine trouble he got the full
dope on it from the De Havilland mechanic,[4] so that when he next
met Sir Geoffrey de Havilland he could tease him from strength.
Laughter usually broke in soon, even in matters of communications,
notoriously a thorn in an airman's flesh. He suffered one day from
a stream of superfluous VHF chat by a couple of Yorkshire radio
mechanics, testing on the ground. "I can't hear thee down 'ere,"
one of them kept saying. HRH pressed his transmit button: "Tha
sounds bloody fine from oop 'ere!" He's loosed off some colorful
rockets at ground control in his time, and a marshaller at Luneburg
who landed him downwind, and with crash vehicles placed almost
on the runway, can probably still remember the exact words.
Crowds collected to watch him land always embarrass him—what's
so special? Haven't they seen an aircraft put down before? And
certainly in the early days a battery of waiting cameras would get
well under his skin. Press attitudes, once it was announced that
he was learning to fly, were predictably jokey. More fodder for
the Philip headlines, always in demand even then. A Brockbank
cartoon in *Punch*, based on gleeful reports of a bouncy landing,
showed the Chipmunk coming in on a series of hops, and an RAF
sergeant noting for the record, "Time of arrival, 14 hours, 31 minutes, 6 seconds . . . 11 seconds . . . 15 seconds . . ." (But the
original drawing was soon in the Duke's collection of—largely
insulting—cartoons at Sandringham.)

---

joined *Britannia* and came up the Thames in her with the royal party. He said
to Lord Moran the next day, "I had never been up the river before. The Duke
knew everything about its history." That tour, incidentally, snipped nearly six
months out of his flying, but he was up doing night flying on the Sunday before
they left, and again in the air the day after they came back.

[4] His early planes, though RAF owned, were maintained by the makers (and
brilliantly—any engine can have trouble). It was only with the Heron, and later
the Andover, that full responsibility passed to the Queen's Flight.

"Wings" day, May 4, 1953, changed most of that. The wings were presented in a Buckingham Palace drawing room by the Chief of Air Staff, in the presence of the Queen, the Secretary of State for Air, C-in-C Home Command, the Captain of the Queen's Flight, and such lesser but intimately interested parties as Squadron-Leader Peter Horsley, Flight-Lieutenant Caryl Gordon and Mike Parker. That morning the press, newsreels and television had descended, by unavoidable invitation, on RAF White Waltham to see if he could actually fly. Gordon wrote, "He did three solo take-offs and landings—all excellently done." It was an ordeal. Not just because of the reporters and cameras, poised to record any delicious boob, but because it was, had to be, a performance, a personal display for its own sake. There's nothing he hates more.

It would be hard to say whether he or Gordon was more pleased with the wings. There was still work to be done. Gordon stayed with him, part instructor, part co-pilot, for another two years, by which time HRH was able to declare in his log:

This is to certify that I have read and understood the appropriate Pilot's Notes, that I know the fuel, oil and emergency systems and that I have been instructed in the action in the event of fire, and the method of abandoning, the following aircraft:

1.	Chipmunk	4th December, 1952
2.	Harvard	23rd February, 1953
3.	Oxford	6th May, 1953
4.	Devon	20th June, 1953
5.	Heron	19th January, 1955
6.	Provost	11th April, 1955

PHILIP

A year later another certificate was pasted in, headed "705 Squadron (Helicopters) Royal Navy," and noting that Admiral of the Fleet HRH the Duke of Edinburgh had successfully completed his helicopter conversion. So the naval uniform could have Navy wings. He got a private pilot's licence in 1959, and later took a civil pilot's conversion course to fly the Andover. Only the Army was left out in the cold. They got a bit fed up with seeing him fly in for visits and inspections wearing Air Force wings on his army uniforms, and in May 1955 the Army Air Corps at Middle Wallop persuaded him to qualify for a pair of their own kind.

By then he'd flown jets: Meteors and Vampires. During his first stint with Gordon in a Meteor 7 he did stalls, turns and six landings at RAF West Raynham. He seldom failed to talk civil airline captains into letting him "pole around" when he found himself, a frustrated passenger, in Viscounts, Comet IVs, Boeing 707s, Tridents, BAC 1-11s, HS 125s—but jets for his private use have never broken the official caution barrier.

Throughout the training there had been an extra complication for the instructor, though agreeable for all concerned. At the kick-off, Prince Philip had said, typically enough, to Parker, "Why don't you learn too?" Done like a shot, though it's not quite clear how; Parker was only an ex-RN civilian. (Gordon at first wrote him up as "Commander Parker"; he was "Mike Parker" in about a week, and "Mike" from then on.) In a way, it became a repetition of the old competitive days in *Whelp* and *Wessex*, and if Philip forged ahead it was only because he was better placed to squeeze in an hour or two's flying on demand. But Mike, too, became pretty good in the end. There were times when Gordon had them both going solo at once, watchful down below or, sometimes, flying above them, noting points, and hoping that no telepathy of high spirits would lead to anything rash.

And all the time, ever present but out of sight, "their Airships," as they called the RAF top brass, were also watching, praying.

As a wry passing note, Peter Horsley, the squadron-leader equerry who from 1952 to 1955 was so much on the side of the angels, is now an air marshal at the Ministry of Defence. "I can't believe it," he told Parker when they recently met—"I'm an Airship!"

They remembered things. A proving flight to Helsinki together in an old and dubious Anson. Prince Philip was to go there for the 1952 Olympics, not yet as a pilot, but all royal flights into unfamiliar airports are "proved" beforehand. As they were warming up for the return take-off an engine died, and a mechanic, sticking a hand in, pulled out a bird's nest. "Put it back," yelled Horsley, "she'll never fly without it." There was the time when they'd successfully rocked a distinguished Airship, and an Earl to boot (the 5th, of Bandon), who was Assistant Chief of Air Staff, Training, when the Prince was learning to fly. He and Buckingham Palace were much interlocked over it all, so it was simple for him to ask one day if he could send a fly-past of fighters over the building, which was a useful navigational fix for a formation exercise. Agreed. As the machines went over, Parker and Horsley called him up at the Air Ministry on their loudspeaker telephone.[5] "Listen to this, Paddy, something perfectly frightful's happening, one of your chaps is beating up the palace!" And they played into the microphone a record of a Battle of Britain dogfight that Mike happened to have. "What?" gasped the Earl, as the zooms and whines came through loud and clear. "My God! He's gone off

---

[5] One of Prince Philip's first innovations at Clarence House was an intercom installation, linking all its "operational" rooms by direct line. An expanded version went into the palace in June 1953, together with a number of amplifying sets. Going down the corridor full of offices today, on the ground floor, Constitution Hill side, where all doors are open and all rooms talking, it sounds like a football match.

his head! Who is he? Get his number!" HRH must have enjoyed hearing about that. Gaiety was the thing.

But the wryest part, perhaps, is that Horsley is now one of the
men earnestly wrapping protective cocoons round Prince Charles
and his Queen's Flight Basset.

If you're flying an airplane, you can't think about anything else.
To that extent it's a great smoother of the brow. There's no doubt
that Prince Philip's fierce onslaught on the job, during the six
months before the Coronation, helped to take his mind off those
misgivings about how life would go as husband of the Queen.
(One of his duties, to be fitted around the circuits and bumps,
was to be chairman of the Coronation Commission. The opening
of his first and only address to the distinguished members, who included Churchill and the Archbishop of Canterbury, was pretty
true to form: "There's a tremendous amount of work to be done,
so the sooner we get down to it the better.") But even today, if
he's flying to some occasion that doesn't promise to be a load of
fun, or back from one that unhappily wasn't, he has to forget it as
soon as he settles to the controls. It may take a little time. The
co-pilot in the right-hand seat, usually one of the brightest gems
from the Queen's Flight crown, picks his moment before providing
any light relief. Wait for it. Eventually it will probably come
from HRH in any case.

One June 10, out of Addis Ababa, the crew had been affection-
ately inspired to prop a birthday card over the instrument panel.
Suitable designs being scarce in Ethiopia, it had taken some finding,
and they were pleased with themselves. But it wasn't one of his
sunniest mornings, and the tensions of take-off, not great with
this pilot but present with any, were laced with doubts about what
sort of reception the tribute would get. It got a grunt, was re-

moved and dropped on the cockpit floor. A bloomer of the first order, decided the co-pilot, and remembered with a nasty stab that somewhere aft there was a cake too. However, up to cruising height and the card was recovered and read, and went well. He presently handed over, and was back in the cabin cutting the cake. He remembers an even finer cake when he clocked up his 2000 hours.

The therapy bit is incidental. He simply enjoys flying an airplane. It embraces so much else that he enjoys, the exercise of skills, the command of marvelous mechanisms. Besides, there's the practical satisfaction of cheating the clock, whether you're chopping around Sussex for the Award Scheme, half a dozen well-distributed appearances between lunch and tea, or, farther afield, eating up India and Pakistan, hunks of Africa, or the various Americas.

Perhaps eating up is putting it a bit strong. The aircraft he now uses, the twin turbo-prop Andover, settles down happily at 230 mph or thereabouts. It means, to take a random example, that his spring tour of Australia and New Zealand in 1968, adding another 140 hours to his pilot's log, meant only a paltry 30,000 miles in the air. Yet, though he could go faster and farther by turbo-jet, the breathers between engagements would be shorter and less relaxing. Anyway, if you're piloting yourself over the Andes, from Chile to Bolivia (1962, but this was in a Herald) it's nice to take things at a stroll and enjoy the scenery.

Even if he flew faster it wouldn't mean any extra leisure on the ground. Organizers at the host end of royal visits circle like vultures over gaps in the timetable, whether it's Prince Philip's or anyone else's. Show them a couple of hours going spare, and they've plugged it with a smelting works or hydroelectric plant. It's what you get for always appearing to enjoy yourself. Unthinkable for time to hang heavy on royal hands. The palace planners try hard to keep the engagements apart, but whether for State or merely individual visits they often have to submit in the end. Both the Queen and Prince Philip are physically extremely tough, but not, as seems to be supposed, actually indestructible.

His total hours in the air are probably incomputable. On State visits he flies vast distances with the Queen—lately by BOAC Super VC 10s, internally tailored to the specific demands of the trip under close Queen's Flight supervision. (They're sometimes "re-roled" in between going out and coming back, extra dressing rooms will arrive or disappear, sitting rooms become conference-rooms.) His own pilot hours now top two thousand; and since the early 1950s call sign "Rainbow" has attached itself at one time or another to more than forty types of aircraft. Only a few hours in some, just that itch to be up front and get the feel of a Stratocruiser, Constellation, Shackleton, a Solent or Canso (flying-boats), a carrier-borne Gannet, the occasional executive jet or light sports job, a selection of choppers; but the really heavy mileage piled up in the Heron and later the Andover. "Rainbow" has crackled over the R/T into a global distribution of control towers, from Greenland's icy mountains to India's coral strand.

In these footloose days no one's going to be dazed by talk of Heathrow, Prestwick, Gatwick, Turnhouse, Lossiemouth, Shannon or an exhaustive directory of RAF airfields; or even, perhaps, by Athens and Rome, Oslo and Orly and Munich; Ottawa, Christchurch, Auckland, Sydney, Brisbane; Kennedy, La Guardia, Chicago's O'Hare. But how about Luxor, Bangkok, Katmandu? Lima, Rio, Acapulco, Brunei, Bogota, Caracas, Asuncion and a choice of several Santiagos? See any good gazetteer for full list. It will need to be especially good for Mui, Malakal or Tandaho, Lodwar or Hara Meda. It's impressive, a word that doesn't go down well.

The Andover is a small airliner. The civil version seats about thirty-six. HRH's party is usually very much smaller, though the plane, like those used by the Queen, gets a certain amount of re-roling for any long trip: wardrobe and dressing-room space is bound to vary. His suits and uniforms travel in the fully hung position from home to aircraft and are clipped rumple-free on the wardrobe bar; a long mirror, aft, faces him before he comes down the steps, in case the headphones have messed up the hair style, but because of his height he has to stoop a bit for the last quick comb. (Neatness is a habit. Out shooting he'll have a snap check on his reflection in a brake window: blame the Navy—and a conditioning to photographers.) The steps are released from the aircraft, none of your hanging about for that tedious ground-staff wheeling. Sometimes two loos, mostly one. Usually an office nook with electric typewriter; work goes on, static or mobile. There's a telescopic flagpole, if you can call it that, slim aluminum and forked to break out double on touchdown, with his own standard and the flag of the destination country. (The flag room at the Queen's Flight looks like an orderly preparation for a carnival of the world; not only the personal standards of all the Royal Family, but the national flags of everywhere from Sweden to Swaziland.) There are facilities for coarse cooking, but prefabricated meals to ordinary air-travel standards come aboard as the program requires.

As the Andover is a small airliner, so the Queen's Flight is a small airline. A fleet of six: three Andovers, two helicopters, Prince Charles's trainer. Answers to parliamentary questions, not infrequent, give its yearly cost to the taxpayer as £450,000. Cheap at the price, some say—we spend £50 million on the Diplomatic Service, whose function, in part, isn't all that different. Critics forget, perhaps, that this isn't just a set of convenient toys for the Queen and her relations: they're also on call for the Prime Minister, leading members of the Government, Chiefs of Staff and others deemed to qualify for rapid moving around at the drop of a hat with topline concern for life and limb. As between royalty and the rest, the use percentages come out at about 60–40.

The captain of the Queen's Flight, Air Commodore Archie Winskill, CBE, DFC, RAF (retd.), is a member of the Household, and also claims the letters MBIM after his name, for Member of the British Institute of Management. He needs them. For a start, his organization at Benson, crammed into one immense hangar with enough supporting equipment to service Cape Kennedy, has twenty officers and 140 other RAF ranks. It's well stretched. He turns down twenty or thirty requests for flights in an average year, mainly because of the depth of maintenance. Before each use a machine is gone through with the minuteness of an income-tax investigation; all is double tested, the floorboards come up, not a murmur gets past. Engines are changed when they've reached half the manufacturer's recommended life. Tricky trips aren't only proved, but timed, in advance. Red tape, if not cut, can be un-knotted and conveniently re-routed. (It's even cut sometimes. The makers of Charles's plane went bust, and their assets, including spares, were seized by the Official Receiver pending settlement. Well, you can't send up the Heir to the Throne without his altimeter. A word from Winskill to the Board of Trade achieved an unfreezing.) On long flights there can be a densely equipped escort plane at a discreet distance. Though Prince Philip has become resigned with a groan to this sort of thing, he did object to the escort's description, in official papers, as a "shepherd." If you have a shepherd, doesn't that make you a sheep?

Strictly, Queen's Flight aircraft are available to him for any purpose he fancies, but he always takes care to incorporate a working destination somewhere in the program. A trip that ends up with his sisters in Germany will take in some legalizing duty on the way. All those airports listed above sound like a fair old frolic, but business is combined with pleasure, and the first is well in the lead.

(*222*)

Some may think that even the pleasure is combined with business. On the whole, when he steps out of the plane and breezes into the inevitable reception party, they're as delighted to see him as he is— or always appears to be—to see them.

Ten-thirty in the morning, Buckingham Palace, and I'm asking him about his part in getting the Crystal Palace sports center set up by the London County Council, also the difference between the National Playing Fields Association and the Central Council of Physical Recreation.

HRH: Just a minute, the top of my head's coming off.

It isn't his own head, despite dinner last night with the Younger Brethren of Trinity House, but a replica, being modeled for the Royal Yacht Squadron at Cowes, and he's spotted a crack in the clay. The country's full of his heads and portraits, continually commissioned by other people. It all takes time. The sculptor closes the crack and smooths the clay.

This began at ten, the first engagement of the day. To come: two audiences, an official lunch, two annual general meetings, a speech to write, an official cocktail party, an official dinner. From time to time he flexes his right hand, where the old polo injury has blown up again. The recurring weakness affronts him more than he pretends, and he's sent out Joe Pearce, twenty-three years on the staff and eleven as valet, to see a chemist and get a wrist support. Pearce is small, brown and unerringly tuned to the royal wavelength. When he presently knocks and enters he's obviously got a secret joke.

HRH: Any luck?
Joe: He says he'd have to come and fit it.
HRH: When could he do that?

Joe: He says he could come at eleven, but he says he's very
        busy and can't hang about.

His laughter stays walled in behind the eyes.   The sitter's bursts
out in full yell.

HRH: (Recovering) Oh, well, that's all right.   You can tell him
        I'm a bit pressed too.

Exit Joe, still under control, but you can see from the back view
that he's hugging himself at the fun of it all.

14

Pies and Fingers

"You get involved and then you get more involved."

There'll be a comprehensive book someday, and thick.   This one can only select.   If the six box files on his work for the Commonwealth Technical Training Weeks don't get a fair look-in (partly because they came with a note from the office saying there were four more when that lot was done with) it's a pity but can't be helped.   The same goes for his sixty or so overseas visits in the last twenty years—on his own account, as distinct from Commonwealth and foreign tours with the Queen, though he made some on her behalf, attending, for instance, the independence celebrations of Tanganyika, Zanzibar (since united as Tanzania), Malta, Malawi, Kenya.

There's a true Kenya story.   The place was wild with impending liberation.   As the official motorcade crawled through the hopeless jam to the stadium there were rifle shots, and Jumbo

Thorning, in the front seat of the royal car, felt more than usually alerted. Might only be *feux de joie*, but still, it had been Mau Mau country not many years before. He decided to stick close, especially when the ceremonial in the floodlit stadium reached its climax, and everything went out but a single spotlight on the two leading figures, Jomo Kenyatta and the Admiral of the Fleet in brilliant white. Some target. That's how he came to hear Philip, as he set out with Kenyatta for the flags, one to come down, one to go up, say in a calm aside, "I suppose you don't want to change your mind?" It doesn't look much on paper. Given the circumstances, however . . .

"Gentlemen," he told the committee of the National Playing Fields Association at his first meeting as president, "I want to assure you that I have no intention of being a sitting tenant in this post." He followed with a practical demonstration, gutting and reconstructing an appeal drafted to go out with his name on it.

This was in 1949, an early hint that bodies capturing him for their letter headings needn't think that was all they were getting. Involvement is two-way. He identifies with the organization, and fights its battles as personal challenges. But if it lapses into any ludicrosities they reflect on him, and he can make life hot and uncomfortable for the officials and executives.

The affairs of the NPFA were in a mess, and he said so. The next thing was to get them out of it. As usual, it was largely a matter of money, which he set about raising. Having raised it, he was watchful about where it went. He'd shaken it out of the public pocket, by innumerable wiles and guiles, on both sides of the Atlantic, and it must be seen to be well spent. He wasn't even satisfied to be the driving force. He had to participate. When the staff course at Greenwich was over he did a stint in the NPFA office, walking from Clarence House to Buckingham Gate every day like any other nine-till-fiver. He attended the famous Variety Club midnight matinee—Frank Sinatra flew in especially and for nothing—rushed about the country making speeches, urging the snatching-up of derelict plots for recreation grounds, flailing the hesitant, straight-talking the municipal planners ("You may believe that you've designed the perfect playing field as seen through adult eyes, but I can assure you that it may prove deadly dull to a child of four"), playing cricket with top names, unabashed by a context of Comptons and Edriches, and beamingly accepting checks. At sea again, the NPFA presidency went with him, like other growing home responsibilities; in Malta he made an NPFA appeal film with Bob Hope. Back in England, after leaving *Magpie*, there were more and more playing fields to open. By 1953 they were coming along at a rate of two hundred a year. It has been his longest term of office, lasting until 1972. He doesn't ordinarily believe in prolonged associations, thinks they make for ossification at the top, but this seemed a special case.

It's conceivable that the organizations themselves aren't always too cast down at the idea of a change. During his tenure with the Automobile Association he bombarded its offices mercilessly. Honorary life membership had been pressed on him a month after the wedding. Accepting the presidency four years later, he wrote that he looked forward to "taking an active part in the affairs of the Association." No idle threat.

Proddings about insurance provisions, accident prevention, motorway landscaping, diesel fumes, standards of lighting on commercial vehicles, signposting, road classification and numbering poured out tirelessly for ten years. After the presidency he stayed on as a committee member. They still didn't get away with anything. In May 1962, formally notified that a new fellow member had been elected to the committee, the sort of thing that would get only a glance from most of us on its way to the waste bin, he wrote back asking who he was, why he'd been appointed and what were his qualifications.[1] Nothing remarkable there—except that he'd just done a two months' tour of South America, was now in Montreal to inaugurate his Second Commonwealth Study Conference, then off to visit the Seattle World's Fair and across to New York for a World Wildlife Fund dinner. Many people, similarly placed, wouldn't have noticed if they'd been landed on a committee with the Great Train Robbers.

He had also dashed off a line from Brazil, reporting that the buses had vertical exhausts. It was just a handy bit of leverage in his long-running campaign to get the fumes off the roads at home— a campaign that failed, as choking motorists will have observed.

All the doctors were for it, but, as he told the BMA, it was no good just passing "pious resolutions" (a favorite indictment of the faint-hearted reformer). Most of the technologists were against: vertical exhaust pipes would collect condensation, they said, and shower pedestrians with soot. "How do we know?" he came back. "Opinion was divided about the shape of the world until it was proved to be round." The press was sniggery, the police baffled —and at a high level. He slung off a two-pager at Commissioner Sir Joseph Simpson, Scotland Yard, asking him to take a look at the Road Traffic Act Regulations, 1931, Part I (No. 17), Part II (No. 67) and Part III (No. 79). Did they, or did they not, make it an offense to emit diesel smoke? Was it possible, easy or difficult for offenders to be hauled up? Er . . . well, replied the Commissioner, in effect. It was a question of—hrrrm!—if faulty vehicle design could be proved . . . or damage to property, injury to health . . . if the smoke obscured the view and rendered overtaking dangerous. . . . In the end the top cop fell back with relief

---

[1] In case of any hurt feelings, I should say that there was no cause for alarm. An impeccable appointment, as Fanum House hastened to say at some length. "That's all I want to know, sounds admirable," replied HRH.

on a parliamentary answer by Ernest Marples, then Minister of Transport, claiming that what little could be done was being done. It was one of the lost causes. He remains stubborn about it.

Q: Why didn't anything come of it?
HRH: They're insane, that's why.

Letters flooded in from the private motorist, the private citizen, the private loon. The sensible got sensible answers, were often used to put a bomb under the Road Research Laboratory, the Clean Air Council, the road safety organizations. The less sensible collected the familiar marginal comments. "Chump." . . . "How do you spell the sound of a raspberry?"

Not all his correspondents were fearful for the public's lungs. There was carping about the AA's maps. He sent for a set. "This one's out of date," he wrote. "The Maidstone and Ashford by-passes aren't shown." He went on to stir up the Association, the Secretary of State for Scotland, the chief constable of Aberdeenshire and the county surveyor over the matter of reclassifiying, for signposting purposes, a few Highland roads.

The AA stint ended with, though not as a result of, another of those outcries about his intrusion into political areas—almost worse, into trade union areas. It was all to do with a walk-out of girl secretaries at the Association's offices in Birmingham. They were then given their cards. It got into the news. And the local queen bee of the Clerical Workers' Union wrote to the president, stating the grievance. The AA, it seemed, didn't mind some of their girls belonging to the union, but, as not all of them did, declined to negotiate with it. The president—or, as some saw it, Prince—called for papers, studied both sides, told the AA that if they got this kind of publicity he caught the backwash, and set about sorting things out at the Ministry of Labour with the chief conciliation officer, who wasn't getting anywhere much. He requested clarification, under four heads: *a.* What was the position if . . . ? *b.*

Was there separate negotiating machinery for . . . ?   *c.* Should AA policy in the matter of recognizing . . . ?   *d.* What proportion of union membership . . . ?

It dragged on for six weeks, outcries and all.   The girls got their jobs back.   Related bugs were ironed out.   As for the beefs about the political Prince, he rejected them blithely.   In his presidential hat they had no relevance.

The hats are a godsend.   Without them, merely as the Queen's husband, the need for political detachment could be a paralyzer. As it is, though he must appear equally delighted in the company of either a yachting or a landlocked prime minister, he can get into the ribs of government departments with no holds barred. It's the only way.   When your lines are out in practically every reach of the nation's life, from the chancellorship of universities through every layer of industry and commerce, education, recreation and all the infinite permutations of youth, the arts, the armed forces, the Church, the learned societies, there isn't much the politicians don't loom over, if only because you have to get the money out of them, a subject on which Whitehall is notoriously coy.

Back in 1957, as a Trustee of the National Maritime Museum at Greenwich, he thought it wasn't getting enough.   At first, just that the director wasn't, but he dug a bit deeper, and found that three classes of museum are known to Whitehall: very large, large and small, with cash benefits accordingly.   The National Maritime, closer to his heart than most, was small.

He reached for his Trustee's hat and pad of ruled foolscap and drafted a letter to the Chancellor of the Exchequer.   By a stroke of luck, at the meeting where the poor state of the museum's finances had been discussed, he'd been acting chairman, the chairman being away.   He was able to write in that capacity.   "The

Trustees have asked me to inform you. . . ." Would the Chancellor look into the whole regrettable business, raise the status from small to large, with suitable financial adjustments?

The Chancellor, polite but firm, would not. An exhaustive investigation had been conducted two years before, finding that the museum was in its proper bracket, and should stay there. Pause, during which Mr. Peter Thorneycroft, the Chancellor of the time, probably considered the correspondence closed. At the palace end it wasn't. Researches showed that the exhaustive investigation was actually a morning visit by three eminent historians, who didn't stay long and didn't know a lot about museums. Other ammunition was collected.

"It seems to me absolutely astonishing," wrote the acting chairman, firing it off, "that this Museum, which houses the treasures of our maritime history . . ." (and so on). "I am amazed that three worthy Professors can demonstrate such a complete lack of understanding of all that ships and the sea have meant . . ." (and so forth). The case was again put. And again met with an unbending restatement of the Treasury position: the Chancellor's decision was clearly final, but with an audible whimper. "I pray that, with my clear conviction in the matter, Your Royal Highness will not press me further."

His Royal Highness pressed further by return:

> I am afraid that you have not convinced me that my case is in any way unsound. I see it as my duty as a Trustee to pursue the matter until a satisfactory solution is reached. . . . If this is in the least embarrassing to you or to the Treasury, I am quite prepared to discuss with the Prime Minister my giving up the position of Trustee.

A blow below the waterline, perhaps, but all's fair, and slowly the Treasury began to sink. It took time, and all available reinforcements. Friendly MPs were lobbied. At official meal tables the Trustee seemed to sit next to an extraordinary number of useful persons with ears worth dropping a word in, and would follow up swiftly with a written reminder that he'd dropped it. There was valuable intelligence work, as when, for example, Derick Heathcoat Amory moved in as Chancellor—Thorneycroft must have relinquished at least one file without a pang—and an alert agent reported that Amory was "the proud and zealous owner of a ten-ton cruising boat." It could have turned the course of the battle. Anyway, the Treasury surrendered in the end, after a long hard fight. It lasted, in fact, about three years, concurrently with the Trustee's other running commitments, and in its later stages he was bringing his guns to bear from India, Pakistan, Bermuda, and HMY *Britannia* off Rangoon.

Well, perhaps it was only a skirmish, but it's interesting to study the strategies, once he sets his mind to something.

It should be said that there are many other movers in a thing like this.[2] He's constantly saying so. "I don't mean I did it, I was just involved in getting it done." But you need the generalship. Most of them get caught up in only one or two battles, but the general fights the lot. At least he won't forget them, if that's a consolation. While the rest of us can't name our bank manager half the time, he can reel off a hundred veterans of campaigns long past. . . . Besides, you might want them again.

It's useful to have all the best doorbells to ring. "So I got on to David Exeter . . ." (6th Marquess, steel, banking, insurance, motorcars); "So I wrote to Ian Luke . . ." (2nd Baron, goldfields,

---

[2] Not to mention things unlike it. The Award Scheme, for instance, has full-scale offices in London, Edinburgh, Cardiff and Belfast, over 250 local award committees, and overseas branches busily beavering away in Australia and New Zealand, Canada, Aden, Hong Kong, Sarawak, Jamaica, Kenya, Nigeria.

electricity, advertising, sales management). Sounds pretty top-drawer. That isn't the point. And a lot of names without handles keep cropping up as well, anyway. But we all have our networks, and the members of this one happen to be the sort who often have networks of their own, and in a good cause are fearless exploiters of friends.

It would be absurd—crazy, he'd say—for the Duke, whose time and energy mostly go on one good cause or another, not to exploit them in turn. Setting up the Maritime Trust (not to be confused with bumping up the National Maritime Museum) he drew in practically anyone of influence who'd as much as seen a ship. It was another three-year exercise, 1967–70, and concerned with pre-serving historic hulks which were often falling apart in remote anchorages, and, once lost, would leave no other representatives of their time. Money, as usual, was the snag. He wrote to old friend Sir Solly Zuckerman, then chief scientific adviser to the Cabinet, probing the chances of a handout from the Exchequer, and got a gloomy reply with an alternative suggestion. Why not model ships instead?

"Dear Solly," wrote the Duke. "I take your point about models. How would you react to the suggestion that the Zoo could be run more cheaply if the exhibits were all stuffed animals . . . ?" (It wasn't a random analogy. Zuckerman, among much, much else, was honorary secretary of the Zoological Society.) A bit hard, perhaps, but he doesn't take too kindly to a modified response.

It's a tight-fisted world, and raising cash takes a lot of his time. If he devoted a hundredth part of it to lining his own pocket he'd have enough over to help the Queen make both ends meet. He's shrewd about it. Digging up funds to get St. George's House Conference Centre going at Windsor—and talking of the best door-bells, this involved all the Garter Knights—he noted on one corpo-ration proposed as a likely touch, "Not a good moment, they've just been taken over."

The St. George's House operation was enormous. It wasn't Prince Philip's idea, but the Dean of Windsor's, the Very Reverend Robert Woods, MA, Domestic Chaplain to the Queen from 1962 to 1970, when he departed, with a KCVO, to become Bishop of Worcester, where the diocese may at first have thought it had been hit by a cyclone. His energy comes near to matching Philip's own, and his laminated involvements have bred the trick of starting to talk before he gets into the room where the other half of the conversation is waiting. (The two men would have long discussions on the place of religion in a scientific society, and if a speech of Philip's had theological passages he would ask for professional criticism and get it. The traffic was reversed sometimes, with drafts of sermons; they got the treatment too.)

To oversimplify, St. George's College, founded in 1348 by Edward III, had always been meant as a meeting place of minds between clergy and laity, a function that had of recent years become somewhat obscured. Soon after his arrival, the Dean decided it was time to clear the cobwebs. He had to begin, practically enough, with huge restorations and rebuildings in the Castle precincts. It took five years, and the cost was prodigious. Now the courses, lectures and debates are many and continuous. Prince Philip didn't just come in on the financial side. He was the first to speak there. Subject: "What's Wrong with the Church."

There's not much he won't do for a good cause. In America once, where he was fund-raising for the Variety Club, a man of substance with a home at Miami Beach offered him $100,000 to go and swim in his pool. He accepted with grace and came away with the check—a useful slice went to the Award Scheme. It seemed a fair deal. When the incident cropped up recently he'd forgotten about the money, and remembered only that the house was "a mass of plastic flowers."

Though he gets some fun out of his association with the Variety Club of Great Britain—an offspring of the American parent and its golden showbiz heart—it's related firmly to the end product, which is cash, and more cash, to go where it will do the most good. As Patron and Twelfth Man of the Lord's Taverners, a band of benevolent cricketophiles heavily sprinkled with actors (who often have more time for cricket and good works than they'd like), he used to adorn their charity matches until it became "too much of a raree-show"; but he'll go on being His Royal Twelfthmanship, as they like to call him, until they stop piling up the financial runs. Reports of his attendance at their social shindigs suggest a rip-roaring night out with the boys, off the hook and loving it, but if there weren't to be a check at the end of it, and more playing fields to open, he'd probably rather go to bed.

He has a head start, of course. Buckingham Palace stationery does no harm; nor Windsor Castle, Sandringham House, Balmoral—*Britannia* in far waters—the British Embassy or Government House in Rome, Rabat, Kuala Lumpur, Ottawa, Canberra. The first batch of St. George's House letters, to prospective philanthropists, went out from Holyrood. They didn't, and never do, mention money. "I am myself closely concerned with this project" is enough, with a little reading between the lines. Even these days, a letter from a prince, especially this one, is still a great opener of coffers.

Not that they're all fund-raising operations. Not even most of them. The Royal Mint, for instance, isn't seriously short of the ready. He's president of its advisory committee on the design of coins, seals, decorations and, at a pinch, crests on government stationery. What with meetings, correspondence, observations on proposed new strikings as the commentary sheets come around ("I think it's dreadful"—new crown piece for the Isle of Man—) the flow of work is continual. Some of us, holding this sort of appointment, would claim it all-absorbing, and a great get-out for anything else. "Quite impossible, sorry—my commitments at the Mint, you know." But these commitments run to hundreds. Only half a dozen may be actively bubbling at a particular time, but a lot more are on the permanent simmer, and you daren't really take your eye off the stove. It all goes on behind the visible exterior, the public appearances that already look, from the daily Court Circular in *The Times*, to be taking all the time there is. And even allowing for what's seen and what isn't, there's still another layer at ordinary routine level: interviews, meetings, the estates to run, a girl from the office to say good-bye ("Medium framed photograph?" says Randle Cooke's reminder. "Good idea. P."), sittings for painters, sculptors, cameras—if a Commonwealth country changes its uniforms he must find time to pose for the official record in his various ranks.

Through it all, other strange threads: odd letters rushed off, something that's seized his passing attention—to a naturalist, on the possibility of establishing and artificially maintaining colonies of ants, now being extinguished by agricultural chemicals—to another, about a TV script on conservation ("What about putting in that Darwin finch using a twig to catch insects?")—to a lady who wants him to attend a cricket match at the University of Florida—to the author of a scientific paper ("I hope you will forgive me if I make one or two general criticisms . . .")—to a friend in California ("Your book sounds most interesting, and I enclose what may be useful as a short foreword . . .")—to a nobody in distress ("Contrary to your expectations, I have seen your letter. I deeply sympathise with your problem, which would not arise in an ideal world [and some comfortable words]"). Letters about African Horse Sickness (with side comments on the treatment of polo ponies with Butasolidine), about the creation of fishponds, a new Windsor traffic plan, the reclamation of derelict land, the future of world energy, the shortage of mathematics teachers, the application of holography to air-traffic control.

And somehow, in a year, eighty or ninety speeches get written and delivered. Sometimes delivered but not written ("NT" says the office record: "No text"). Speeches about sewage, Dr. Livingstone, dancing, coal, Anglo-Lebanese development, microscopes, astronautics, concrete, the Capricorn Beetle, libraries, agricultural engineering, cooking, cricket, insurance, plant diseases, education, the arts. Half of them never get reported. He couldn't care less. If they aren't all brilliant—who could be brilliant eighty times a year?—they all have the one indispensable element: they're tailored to the occasion and the company. "I've always worked on that basis. If you're speaking at a dinner, those are the people you're talking to. If anyone else wants to listen, that's their problem."

Q: You don't put things into speeches knowing the press will lift them?

HRH: No. (A laugh) I often take them out for that reason.

Despite side interests in ants, boats, cooking, design, education, farming, the Galapagos (in 1967 he made a film, *The Enchanted Isles,* for television) he's most at home with, and has most ideas on, scientific and technological matters. It's partly the Navy, partly because they're the stuff of modern life, and partly, perhaps, because his first speech about them, on any significant scale, grabbed public attention and shook it into realizing that this wasn't just a socially acceptable prince with a big smile, but someone of seriousness and intelligence. Not to say bravado. The speech was to the British Association for the Advancement of Science, and an altogether tougher assignment than the light after-dinner displays for City livery companies.[3] This was perhaps the most intimidating convergence of scientific scholarship ever gathered under one roof to hear the president inaugurate the year's meeting. The year

---

[3] During a thick patch of these he once began, "I'm finding it hard to remember whether I'm a fishwright or a shipmonger."

was 1951, and the year's president, who could have pleaded inade-quacy and trotted out a few acceptable bromides, decided instead to review a century of British science, to draw conclusions, make points, utter warnings.

It was in August, only a month after leaving *Magpie*. He'd written the speech mostly in his cabin, mewed in by stacks of ref-erence books, and it took seven months to get right. (He hasn't that much time these days, often sends a speech down to be typed at six o'clock, for delivery two hours later.) He endlessly scrapped and re-jigged, with blinding flashes of self-doubt over the idiocy of tackling two thousand crammed craniums on their own ground. If Sir Harold Hartley, FRS, described it afterward only as "a most discerning survey" it was because of personal modesty. He'd been instrumental in getting the president elected in the first place, and for the speech, as his protégé insists, "acted as tutor, editor, cor-rector and suggester throughout the composition." He was later to be a powerful mover in those other elaborate operations, the Duke of Edinburgh's Commonwealth Study Conferences in Britain (1956), Canada (1962) and Australia (1968), and his is today the one name Prince Philip is likely to concede when he gets that hoary old interview question about the influences in his life. They were still corresponding in 1970, when Hartley was ninety-two. ("In the long run," wrote pupil to teacher, "energy will have to come from renewable raw materials—water, or vegetable matter—or from nuclear breeder stations. The only trouble with the latter . . .")

He'd gained confidence since 1951.

It was the year of the Festival of Britain, that stout heave on our own bootstraps designed to hoist us out of the postwar gloom into Churchill's "sunlit uplands." Science and technology were getting a hopeful showing on the South Bank that summer. Just a century before, in 1851, they'd gotten the same at the Crystal Palace in Hyde Park. The idea of a hundred years' survey was inspired.

It could still have been a mere catalog of achievements. They came into it. Household names to be proud of: Eddington, Jeans, Rutherford, Lister, Fleming, Florey. But the trawl swept deeper. What about Patrick Bell's reaping machine? Or Perkin's mauve, the first of the aniline dyes? Ross and the anopheles mosquito? Appleton's pulse-ranging? Harington's synthesis of thyroxin? There were the major milestones: anaesthetics, internal combustion, plastics, the atom. But he didn't forget the technology of metals, the architecture of molecules, spectrum analysis, astrophysics, low-grade ores and high-speed cutting tools, synthetic fibers, superphosphates, the propagation of radio waves. Not to be overlooked, what he called "the youngest science and the oldest problem": the study of man's mind.

Themes of his, often hammered across since, got their earliest airing. Among them, the need to use discovery and development to improve the human condition; to educate the many in what the few had found out; nearer home, to keep the British brainchild from ending up with foreign foster parents. There were the warnings: that commercial laboratories pursuing profitable ends in secret were starvers of the general good;[4] that "the natural conservatism of laymen is a powerful brake on the adoption of new ideas." And, more grimly, that science could jump two ways. "We can either set the world free from drudgery, fear, hunger and pestilence, or obliterate life itself."

A stale ring? Only because it's since been said so often, and by so many. This was twenty years ago. He was just past his thirtieth birthday, and it was quite a performance—not a good way to put it, with him. It produced a brilliant effect, whether that's what he was after or not. A few predictable nit-pickers feared

---

[4] The original draft had attacked the practice of suppressing discoveries and buying up patents. George VI, either as the Association's Patron, or consultant father-in-law, recommended him to drop it. Stick your neck out, but don't actually pass the ax.

that he was showing an ability unfitted to his station in life; was he shaping up to run the blasted country, like clever-clever Albert? But Sir Charles Darwin, FRS, declaring himself "thrilled and amazed," summed up the broader feeling.

"We like the look of the lad," some jolly head-patting journalist had written four years earlier. Now there was more to it, and there's been still more since then. If it's led at times to less glowing comment, it hasn't stopped him emptying his well-loaded mind into people. Have there been temptations to pack it in, fire blanks or nothing at all, settle for the quiet life? Probably only a passing impulse. A fleeting despair, perhaps, as when at a 1970 press conference in Rome, after visiting an Italian national park, he opened with a discerning preamble on the whole conservation problem, invited questions, and got the first one from a BBC man who asked him the color of the European brown bear. All that the papers printed was, "What a Bloody Silly Question, Says Philip."

It's a handicap to know so much about so much. You try to underplay it. ("If, as I am often told, a little learning is a dangerous thing"—a lecture on Aviation and the Development of Remote Areas—"then you are in for a very dangerous address."

If it still shows, it's just too bad.

One of his incoming letters on August 9, 1963, was from a Mrs. Molly Martin, all about "Dad's book," which nobody would publish. Dad—actually her father-in-law—was a retired clergyman of eighty-six, who appeared to have spent most of his life doing paintings of wild flowers. Mrs. Martin told the story at length, enclosing a wide range of rejection letters. "I did wonder," she wrote, "if you could suggest any way by which we could try to get the book published, so that Dad could see one of his life's ambitions realised."

Many with less on their minds would have read three lines and floated it into the out-tray for noncommittal acknowledgment. Flower paintings by an octogenarian parson? You must be joking. Prince Philip sent it down to his equerry, then Squadron-Leader David Checketts (later made over to Prince Charles), with a handwritten note:

> I don't think I can do much about this. However, it's quite impossible to judge, or even interest anyone else, unless I have something to go on. Can this lady send one or two reproductions, or perhaps the earlier versions, to see what the pictures are like?

She could. And they were like, of course, the rest of the fourteen hundred exquisite paintings that two years later stormed to the top of the best-sellers as *A Concise British Flora* by W. Keble Martin.

During those two years a lot of wheels were set in motion, and creaked to a halt. First, a publisher of HRH's personal acquaintance was asked to come to the palace and consider the proposition. Like those before, and many after, he pronounced it economically hopeless. The cost would certainly be great, the sales almost certainly small. Most of London's leading houses told the same tale. The Folio Society was approached, the National Book League. There was talk of minor recognition, a trickle of samples by *Time-Life* or *Reader's Digest*. (The Pilgrim Trust, as possible fundraisers, had been approached already, and been cool.)

David Checketts, himself fired by the project, and prodded on by the Duke to try this, try that, speak to the other, show them to so-and-so, continued to hold out for the full treatment, and was soon accumulating a fattish file. It included his periodic reports to the Martins: they must be patient, keep their fingers crossed, there were "still some strings to the bow." There were nerve-racking gaps while publishers sat on it, debated, went on holiday, consulted their boards.

After eighteen months of pursuit (and there were a few other things, after all, claiming attention in the Duke of Edinburgh's office), John Hadfield, editorial director of George Rainbird, wrote to say that a way had been found. It was complicated, involving arrangements with the National Magazine Company and Michael Joseph, but Hadfield said he thought there could "hardly be any snags now."

The book came out the following summer, and exhausted its first printing of 50,000 copies, with two more, of 25,000 each, soon to go the same way. On the foot of Hadfield's letter Prince Philip wrote, "Tell them I'll take 24 copies."

He also wrote the foreword to the book.

Arts and Crafts

*". . . the arts world thinks of me as an uncultured,
polo-playing clot."*

✦✦✦

If you have to give a cup, which happens pretty often with him,
the easiest way is to send somebody out for one. They then devise
an inscription, get it engraved, send the thing down to Dispatch,
and all you have to do is sit back and wait for the letter of thanks.
It's a proved method with topline executives of a charitable bent,
whose secretaries' legwork earns lots of grateful letters.

It shouldn't now be necessary to say that this isn't his system.
For a start, he'll do his best to avoid an actual cup, or what he calls
a "Victorian pot," in favor of something more particularly apt at
the receiving end. And what finally arrives there is usually his
own idea. When the Grand Order of Water Rats—another band
of show-business philanthropists—proposed a Prince Philip Greyhound Trophy, he said, "What about a silver lamppost?" but having

had his joke, came up with drawings and specifications for a silver
dog collar. They were well detailed ("ring for lead optional") and
went through the professional silversmiths unchanged. He gave it
away at Harringay, May 7, 1962, all gate money going to the
Award Scheme. Successful ideas tend to repeat. In 1970 the
Auckland Greyhound Racing Club also got a silver collar, and the
New Zealand Award Scheme got the benefit. Checking the inscription—he was in *Britannia*, spring tour of Australia and New
Zealand—he gave it extra point by inserting "Captain Cook Bi-
centenary Year" before the date.

Other people's ideas sometimes appeal. Such as the Scottish
Tiddlywinks Association's suggestion of a silver wink. He was
much taken, but still had firm notions on form:

> It might be a plain silver coin, of about crown size, with
> "The Silver Wink" engraved on one side and my arms or
> badge on the other, with the words "Presented by HRH the
> D of E" round it. To be set either as a mobile or firmly
> fixed in a solid glass support in some sort of flowing, rather
> than cut, design.

By finals day of the great England–Scotland university knockout
there was £1000 for the playing fields.

Sometimes, but it's the exception, he enjoys the common privilege of giving something because he wants to, and no collecting-tin
rattling at the other end. He dashed down a memo to his treasurer in October 1966:

> You will be more than distressed to hear that I have
> offered the Argentine Polo Association a trophy for an
> annual 30-goal tournament. . . .
> ["I am," replied the Admiral.]
> We could get a nice miniature polo stick made, about

3ft long, ebony and silver, and then each winning team could add a thing like a wine label with their names on.

He made drawings, including the labels, which must be silver, and big enough for the team's name on one side and its four members on the other. He lettered the names on the label sketches. "1. James Snitch, 2. Augustus Bull, 3. William Clot . . ." and added a note, wary as ever of the serious-minded: "These names NOT to be engraved." It would have a case lined with satin.

The Admiral's alarm for the royal bank balance probably wasn't much allayed when the makers' first estimate came in. Assuming, as they said, that it could be regarded as an export, and therefore free of purchase tax, it would cost £187. (The shaft was cut by a foot, which helped a bit, but not much.) There were to be inscriptions on the head in English and Spanish. While it was particularly desirable to get the Spanish right,[1] he directed that it must lie in its case with the English side up, and quite right, too.[2]

There are golf trophies (silver tees, silver putters), sailing trophies, flying trophies, trophies offered as alternatives when people ask for hard cash, which they sometimes do with no great bashfulness. "Dear Sir," writes a forthright captain of sailing from the University College of North Wales, "the College Sailing Club needs £600 urgently. Will you help us to raise this sum?" Philip, the Chancellor since 1948, unaffronted, begins to think about a ship's bell, to be given as a team racing trophy. And not just any ship's bell, but one with Welsh associations. He gets on to a useful

---

[1] For those interested: "PRESENTADA A LA ASOCIACION ARGENTINA DE POLO POR SU ALTEZA REAL EL DUQUE DE EDIMBURGO."

[2] Sailing companion Uffa Fox, pressing for a trophy to mark the centenary of a French yachting club, wrote, "In a hundred years time, when you and I are flapping about aloft with a trumpet tucked under our wings, it would still be competed for, and remind the French of Prince Philip and the wonderful qualities of the British race."

old friend in the right spot, as usual, Sandy Gordon-Lennox, once commanding *Surprise* on that Malta to Athens trip so long ago, now an admiral who admits to being "Admiralty campanologist" (since then, Serjeant at Arms, House of Commons). He's soon ringing out a peal of discovery on the bell of HMS *Flint Castle*, a frigate scrapped in 1958. He'd get the Admiral Superintendent at Devonport to "buff it up a bit." Cost, a fiver. The donor, delighted for other reasons than the price (but it delights his treasurer for once) is cheated of any designing, however, and has to settle for planning a suitable mounting. Even he cools a bit when his sketches come back with an estimate of £347. 5s, and in the end the club finds one of its own. But he isn't happy until he's seen photographs. At least there's the engraving to play with. And what about incorporating his arms as Earl of Merioneth? Foiled here, though; the College of Arms reports, after some researches, that he hasn't got any.

Make do and mend is always a possibility borne in mind on the accounts side. Memo from treasurer: "Anything suitable among your own silver that you don't want?" Scribble from HRH: "Nothing at Windsor, I've had a look. Might be something at BP, but I'm not very hopeful."

The hunt was on for a suitable Royal Yachting Association trophy, not the first during his 1956–68 presidency, but this time for team racing championships on an Oxfordshire reservoir.[3] A silver "armada dish"? The last one had cost £52, and only a ten-incher at that. He had a thought. Hadn't someone, somewhere, sometime, presented him with a ship's wheel? Disposal of gifts, especially after a foreign tour on any scale, is quite an exercise. They go off to grateful schools and museums by the vanload. But

---

[3] Easily confused, though not by members, are the RYA and the RYS. The Royal Yacht Squadron is Cowes, outstripping all dreams of exclusiveness. Prince Philip became admiral in 1952, and commodore in 1961. As commodore he had more executive elbowroom, set about redrafting its constitution, gave a thumping check to its building fund, was authoritative on the proper design of changing rooms.

the wheel had survived. Circle it with a silver band, suitably worded, and it proves to be just the thing.

He says his feeling for the arts is strictly average. "I don't claim any exceptional interest or knowledge or ability." If he doesn't want to be thought of as "an uncultured, polo-playing clot" either, you can hardly blame him. The phrase is from a note to Bonham-Carter at the time when St. George's House, Windsor, was trying to get going. He was offering to put up the money for an organ or choir scholarship (he'd already given an organ for the refurbished music school, though it was one that he'd been given himself, and no one was using). He thought it might be "a very small counter" to the general idea, much fostered by intellectuals, that royalty and the arts go their separate ways. A minor lunge at the gripers about creative barrenness seemed worth a try.[4] His only complaint about a recent book on the Family was that it made him out to be "a total Philistine." This one has no intention of rushing off to the other extreme, but there are things worth mentioning, and one before we leave Windsor. It was he who thought of getting Benjamin Britten to write for the chapel there, at a time when St. George's, for six hundred years a front runner in church music, was still feeling pretty progressive with Walford Davies. No dishonor to that great man, but in 1958, when this happened, he had, alas, been and gone. Britten was in his eager prime. He was "extremely excited by this suggestion of Prince Philip's." They met and talked, and it was done. First a *Jubilate*, then a *Te Deum*. If it was as much a stroke of updating as of artistic imagination on Prince Philip's part, at any rate it was well in character.

---

[4] He misinterpreted something I'd written about this, and commented, helpful as always, "If you really want to criticize, you could point out how fatuous it was of me to imagine something like that would make any impression at all!"

"The people concerned with our collections," he wrote to Feliks Topolski in 1966, "view me with horror and suspicion." It was just the sort of thing to speed him further toward "contemporary" works. His official visits to galleries, which may look like just another formal walk-around with an expression of intelligent interest, can be followed by a call from the palace saying he's interested in Nos. 3, 28, 91 . . . Holyrood is full of pictures by living exhibitors at the Royal Scottish Academy. In 1948 he and the Queen used wedding present money to commission sixteen colored drawings of London River: Westminster Bridge, Chelsea Reach, Cheyne Walk, the Isle of Dogs and the rest, by Alan Carr Linford, then only twenty-two. They were hung up the staircase at Clarence House, and are now mostly in Windsor Castle, which has since accumulated more Carr Linford commissionings, twenty-four of the castle itself, for instance, and several of those German family homes: Heiligenberg, Salem, Wolfsgarten, Darmstadt. These, and other pictures by living artists, Topolski among them, were paid for out of a special "pictures and books" account into which, with the Queen, he put money aside in the days before inflation made such a prospect laughable, at least for him. On his 1956–57 world tour in the royal yacht he took along Edward Seago, RWS, RBA, who painted for his supper, to put it like that, and afterward made presents of the delectable results. (Other results were many of the photographs later collected in *Birds from 'Britannia.'* Is photography an art? You could say so from these. He does his own dark-room work, including enlargements that sometimes go on exhibition for good causes.)

The Queen's Gallery was his idea. Since 1962, for a few shillings, or a few pence, decimalized, anyone caring to walk five minutes from Victoria Station can see the changing exhibitions of eye-soothing works hitherto reserved for the eyes of monarchs and their associates alone.

Though his office can tell at a glance where all the recent purchases are, from Balmoral to the Yacht, his own paintings are harder to trace. He's think this modest and proper. A lot have been given away. Some are at Wood Farm, Sandringham, the weekend cottage that cuts the cost of opening up the House; some at Windsor, in Prince Charles's rooms and in guest bedrooms, lots stacked unframed against the walls of the rumpus room there: paintings of flowers, the occasional still life, landscapes (sometimes of the familiar Norfolk flatlands, often of some remote scene that's caught his fancy on his world travels). Ask where he finds the time and it just stays a question mark; and you could hang another over the ninety or so albums, in the same room, containing his own indexes of his own photographs, with contact prints for reference.

He has an eye for a vista. At Sandringham he's thinned out presses of trees in a couple of places to make grassy punctuations, known to municipalese as picnic areas. The park's open to the public, so that's for them. More practically, he's concerned with improving the shooting by judicious cutting and planting over the rest of the estate. The economy there is delicate. What's grown gets sold, whether it's birds, beef, timber or fruit. ("We have a contract with Ribena," he said, waving from the Landrover toward fifty acres of black currants.) Prize cattle win prizes. When father, son and friends knock down a thousand pheasants they don't eat them, though guests get a brace to take away. Sandringham needs the money. There are over three hundred tenants' properties to be maintained, cottages to be built for the estate's pensioners. If Sandringham House never opened, the twenty thousand surrounding acres might break even, but as things are it's a struggle, and the Duke is the head struggler. With the supervision of the other estates, it's one load he's been able to take off the Queen's shoulders.

Changes at Windsor, inside and out, during the last fifteen years or so, have been a combined effort with the Queen, from decisions about paper and paint to the rearrangement of the pictures in the State Apartments. He'll go down with the superintendent of the castle into the picture store, where Van Dycks and Zuccarellis are propped incongruously with, say, a highly representational portrait of Kaiser Wilhelm II, take his jacket off and heave them around to find what he wants. He planned the layout, with brother-in-law Snowdon, for the display of the Old Master drawings. Again, the public is admitted (Windsor pays for itself, and something over for charity), so it's partly for your pleasure and mine. The same goes for his redesigning of the East Terrace gardens there—though this was for his own pleasure too: his study overlooks them.

"It was a singularly unattractive garden.[5] We tore up the previous pattern and made every kind of model, until we arrived at the present form, a kind of spoke system, with beds round the fountain." He wasn't mad on the fountain, either. Who wanted "a sort of huge black figure of a man strangling a snake," all among the English roses? He worked out something of his own, the lotus-leaf design now familiar to summer visitors. In the face of dubious official squawks he proposed it as a temporary replacement, had it knocked up in Roman cement and bronze-painted. It was there for three years. "And when they found there wasn't a riot of disapproval they eventually had it properly cast in bronze." (Yelp of triumphant laughter.)

He gets on with artists. It isn't just that their skills fascinate him; their honesty and directness strike an answering chord. No

---

[5] Back in 1925, Queen Mary complained that it was "quite lamentable," but nothing was done, chiefly because of a sharp difference of opinion between the Privy Purse and the Office of Works about who should pay. They were still wrangling in 1938, when an estimate looked pretty reasonable, by present standards, at £157. 1s 5d, and the Office of Works was offering £46. 10s as a starter. Then the war hung it up. Prince Philip finally moved in and got results in 1957.

fundungus, which is his word for meaningless trappings. Being a
bit larger than life is no bar, either. Craggy old Uffa Fox (if boat-
designing isn't an art, name one) is probably the best-known non-
conforming friend, a prince on the water being irresistible to
cameramen—if he sinks you've got the shot of the year. (Dining
one night on *Britannia*, where not only a menu but a program of
the accompanying music is provided for guests, Uffa said, "What
would happen if we asked them to play something that isn't down
here?" Philip was delighted. No one in those well-behaved circles
had ever thought of such a thing. "Let's try," he said. Uffa sent
out a note to the Royal Marines Band asking for a bit of Massenet.
The steward was back at once, saying that it would be the next
item. Philip was more delighted than ever. It had opened up a
delicious crack in procedure. And the Marines, even in this unexpected quarter, had done it again, which was pleasing for their
Captain General.)

Other friends get less into the news: painter Feliks Topolski, say,
whose slashing ferocious concepts, towering energy and scorn for
the art of the auction rooms could hardly fail to appeal. His usual
stationery is brown wrapping paper, headed with some dim linocut
of a Topolski work, and the sprawling hand is ever announcing,
"Just off to Milan," or, "When I'm back from Warsaw." The
world's larger walls are filled with his creations. The Coronation
murals in the palace cover 382 square feet.

The area comes into it because that's how a fee was arrived at.
The paintings were Prince Philip's idea, to be paid for out of his
own pocket, which was deeper then. But when a brown paper
letter came in,[6] suggesting with endearing vagueness a price of
three to four thousand pounds, the Duke's financial advisers con-

---

[6] There were to be many of these, beginning "Dear Philip" and continuing with
happy informality. He wanted to superintend the installations at the time of the
French state visit in the spring of 1960. "I hope I shan't inconvenience General
de Gaulle too much."

sidered themselves alerted. They asked around. The view of the Fine Arts Department of the Arts Council, relying on square measure and the fees paid Topolski for his 1951 Festival of Britain murals, was that £1528 would be about it. (Someone had by now quoted £875 just to frame them. Top people get asked top prices. On a palace challenge they came down to £595. A man eventually did the job for £120.)

On the strength of the Arts Council figure of £1528 the royal patron sent down a memo. "Offer him £2000." Topolski agreed happily and immediately—or as soon as he was back from Delhi, Tokyo, or wherever he happened to be.

Paid with thanks, and no hard feelings.

So few, in fact, that the office became thoughtful, some five years later, on learning that another commission was going Topolski's way. If it was a commission. No one seemed clear. Arrangements by word of mouth are one of his staff's administrative headaches. But the work suddenly seemed to be in process, and hadn't got far when a proposal came from the Ministry of Works for a portrait to go in the Council Chamber at the Ministry of Defence. They suggested some suitable artists of impeccable conformity. It was the Government's duty, they added, "to encourage the production of works by artists of the highest calibre." This got a marginal note: "Unctious [*sic*] rot." The civil servant as connoisseur was no more up his street than Topolski's. And a memo to the office: "I would very much like Topolski to be considered."

The sittings yielded an equestrian portrait twelve feet tall, part likeness, part caricature, powerful, enormous, in swirling plumes and a stiff breeze, with a faint high-nosed resemblance to the Duke of Wellington. The Ministry saw it, disapproved, and said so.

The subject had his own doubts, frankly. It was hauled out to Windsor, nevertheless, on some curiously loose sale-or-return basis, and was still there, a giant question mark, in January 1967, when James Orr sent up a note with much between the lines: "The Lord Chamberlain's Office are asking what you would like done with the latest Topolski painting of you on a horse, which is at the moment in the Grand Entrance at Windsor. Jim." His Royal Highness replied tersely, "What's biting them? It's to stay there pro tem, or until he does some more work on it. P." (When last seen it was down in the picture store, with the Van Dycks, Zuccarellis and Kaiser Bill.)

In the meantime, the whole question had been forced to the surface again by a request to borrow it for an exhibition. Whose was it to lend? Topolski hadn't yet been paid (not that he was worrying). Was it still his? Or was it the Duke's, who'd commissioned it? If he had. All was misty. Chance arrangements at the Queen's Birthday Parade—where, of all occasions, the portrait first seemed to have come up—defy contractual interpretation. The sitter thought he was under no obligation to buy. The artist, but with undimmed amiability, thought he probably was. The question of the price, like much else, remained hazy.

Time went by, and nothing settled. Feliks roared around the world, from time to time flinging off parcel-paper letters full of exuberant chat about people and places. One of them, saying that he could fit in some repainting before going to Poland, was the first news some had had that he didn't consider it finished. The Admiral's protective antennae were already in a state of some quiver over the whole affair, and he sent this upstairs with a spidery note: "Look out." Sympathetic vibrations were even set up in the adjoining Household, where the Queen's assistant private secretary, Sir Martin Charteris, a man of gentle wisdom, took a well-qualified consultant out to Windsor on an appreciation and costing expedition, and reported that something around £500 or £750 might be about it. Passing up these findings, the Admiral was stern. Economically it wasn't even thinkable. "A few days ago

your credit balance stood at the magnificent figure of 15s 2d. . . ."
Times were getting tougher for a patron of the arts.

There was an agreeably dramatic conclusion. Charteris recalled
that the price of the famous Leonardo cartoon bought by the Royal
Academy had been settled by an expert tribunal. Why not the
same solution? "On that occasion the answer was £750,000. Let's
hope our three wise men don't set their sights so high." They
didn't. Not quite. One independent assessor thought it might
fetch "in certain quarters" about £1000. Another grudgingly put
it at £500. The third couldn't visit Windsor until some time later.
The suspense was stimulating. Artist and sitter exchanged gleeful
notes: "This becomes thrilling and risky," wrote the one. The
other "simply can't begin to imagine what the findings will be!"

The last of the wise men, a fellow portrait painter of eminence,
found the thing "brilliant," and had no idea what price to put on
it. But *Fiddler on the Roof* was the talk of the town just then, and
its hit song (which Topol was singing) inspired him to a punning
postscript: "*If I were a rich man,* I should hope that Mr. Topolski
would accept 5000 guineas for this picture."

Even in a PS, the figure was there. With the other two it made
disastrous arithmetic, and there was a pause at the palace end before
negotiations were resumed. "Dear Feliks . . . The sad fact is
that I simply can't afford the £2166 which is the average of the
assessors' estimates. . . ." The reply was swift and characteristic,
proposing a simple way out: "If you care for the picture, I should
like best to give it to you." Did the advisers blush, even though
their motherly concern had been plumb in the line of duty?

Touched, and striving after a form, the patron proposed a solution of his own. If, he wrote, the 5000 guinea man had instead
gone along with the £1000 man, the average would be "roughly
£834." How about that? The soul of amenability, Topolski
accepted like a bird—and flew off, no doubt, to Lisbon, China,
Tel Aviv.

But they never got a portrait of Prince Philip in the Council Chamber at the Ministry of Defence.

The man who popped the pun into the postscript was Edward Halliday, RP, RBA, ARCA, and he still isn't sure how big it went. He's painted five portraits of Prince Philip, and more than one of the Queen and the Queen Mother. During one sitting, when HRH affected to be busy with speech notes, it turned out that he was actually doing a drawing of Halliday, who wishes he'd grabbed it. Recently, painting Prince Charles in his sitting room at the palace, he saw one of his own works on the wall, a conversation piece done at Clarence House when the two older children were small. "It's my favorite picture," said Charles, which wasn't mere diplomacy, because he didn't know who'd painted it. Halliday had the satisfaction of putting it in the background to the portrait, a bit of fun that doesn't come every painter's way.

Perhaps one of his most significant moves was to bring about the meeting with designer Gordon Russell, which first drew Philip into the world of industrial design. Halliday was painting the Gordonstoun portrait, and mentioned that Russell was organizing an exhibition called "Design at Work." This was in the shoddy times of 1948. Apart from the products of the ordnance factories, the consumer hadn't had anything of quality through his hands for years. Philip, alive to the link between beauty and function that few could miss after half a lifetime in ships, went with Halliday to the Arts Club for lunch—the kind of informal jaunt that was easier then than it would be now—surprised a few members with his outspoken views on art and artists (but delighted them by having any, all the same), shot searching questions and became a humming champion in Russell's crusade for better things. He was soon to be giving time, help and advice. "Most important of all," says Russell, "he gave me his personal support publicly, at a time when

I was much harassed by sniping from outside." As with youth, Philip helped to hoist a shadowy cause into the daylight of general esteem, and backed Russell again when the Design Centre itself came up as an idea—another that had to prove itself through a barrage of sniggers. Now, after seventeen years, the Centre's seal on anything from carpets to coffeepots means that they do the job with grace. Let's risk it and say elegance. The Duke of Edinburgh's Prize for Elegant Design now comes annually. He chairs the panel of judges and makes the presentation.

It has a counterpart in Australia, which he let himself in for in February 1965 at a dinner in Sydney, by saying that if the Industrial Design Council of Australia would like to devise an award he'd put his name to it. At their end it probably sounded simpler than it was. When draft proposals turned up at the palace they were inevitably but thoughtfully shredded; he revised the nature and conditions of the award, hated the title, which came out in the draft as "His Royal Highness the Duke of Edinburgh Australian Design Award" (they'd have sweated blood working that one out), and changed it to the Prince Philip Prize for Australian Design. In their reference to highly qualified judges he knocked out the highly qualified. What else? The pattern was familiar. He's an inveterate corrector. Three years later he presented the first scroll in Melbourne. It wasn't a prize, because he'd decided that the winner should design his own, and it wasn't ready yet. Five days after the presentation he was ripping off a three-page letter (from Admiralty House, Singapore), with comprehensive recommendations for improving the next year's arrangements.

He once told the convocation of the Royal College of Art:

> Industrial design, or art in industry, is really a misnomer. The artist or designer may work in industry, but the stuff

he designs ends up in the home, in the streets, in the office and in the workshop. I'm sure that people like seeing and living with nice things. I don't believe that the critical faculty is automatically switched off on leaving an art gallery. After all, most people take their eyes with them to work, just as they do to the National Gallery or the bathroom. . . .

You're lucky if you own a picture painted by an RA, but most people have got to live with furniture, domestic objects, cars, shops, pubs, and everything else that surrounds us in our daily lives. It's inevitable that we should see more advertisements than old masters.

It was a fairish speech, one of many on the subject, and with neat bits. ("I realize I'm preaching to the converted, but I believe that it isn't a bad idea to give even the converted a bit of encouragement now and then.")

In another one, eight years later, as president of the Royal Society of Arts—you thought this was just another of those figurehead jobs?—he presented Russell, now Sir Gordon, with the Society's gold medal for services to industrial design. Russell, receiving it, made the point that the president himself was equally qualified.

"Who's giving this medal, you or me?" said the uncultured, polo-playing clot.

"The newly wed couple did not dress for dinner. The menu was vegetable soup, roast chicken and a sweet, followed by coffee and brandy. Today they will breakfast on bacon and eggs, preceded by a grapefruit cocktail."

Daily Mail, 1947

"A car-carrying raft is being added to the yacht's equipment so that the Duke can play commandos."

Sunday Express, 1956

"After one bad miss at polo he shouted, 'Oh! Damn it!' and the shout was so loud that it could be heard across the field."

Daily Express, 1957

"The Duke's stay at Gibraltar—only four hours' flying time from London—had been regarded by certain American newspapers as evidence of a Royal rift."

Manchester Guardian, 1957

". . . one of the most remarkable Royal love matches ever."

Daily Mirror, 1962

PHILIP RAPS PRESS AGAIN.	*Daily Express*, 1963
PRESS ANGERS DUKE.	*The Guardian*, 1969
STICK TO POLO, DUKE TOLD.	*The Times*, 1968
BLACK MARK, PRINCE PHILIP!	*Daily Mail*, 1964
PRINCE PHILIP STARTS STORM.	*Daily Mail*, 1967

"Prince Philip's appeal to British industry to 'take its finger out' was very damaging, a Wigan electrical engineer said this afternoon."

Evening Standard, 1961

'BELT UP' ADVICE TO THE DUKE.　　*The Times*, 1966

CAR CRIPPLES ACCUSE SILENT PHILIP.　　*The People*, 1970

RAMBLERS GIVE PHILIP A TELLING OFF. *Daily Sketch*, 1965

MPS SAY 'CENSURE PRINCE.'　　*Sunday Telegraph*, 1967

PHILIP PUTS WILSON ON SPOT.　　*Daily Express*, 1969

PHILIP IN EAST OF SUEZ ROW.　　*Daily Express*, 1968

'PRAVDA' REBUKES PRINCE.　　*Daily Mail*, 1969

"Such men are dangerous and must be stopped, and only continuing vigilance will ensure that the Duke keeps his nose out of politics and sticks to polo in his spare time."

Daily Worker, 1956

TOM JONES HITS BACK AT PHILIP.　　*Sunday Express*, 1969

"Prince Philip, easily clad in light corduroys, coloured sports shirt and loosely knotted tie, handled the jeep skilfully."

Daily Mail, 1947

SHOULD PHILIP DRIVE THE QUEEN?　　*Daily Express*, 1957

PRINCE PHILIP AND THE NEWSPAPERS. *Sunday Express*, 1957

"Prince Philip sprayed water from an electronic garden spray over two photographers when he visited Chelsea Flower Show yesterday."

Daily Mail (and others), 1959

PRINCE PHILIP CRITICISED.　　*Sunday Telegraph*, 1964

Arts and Crafts

PRINCE PHILIP CRITICISED.   *Daily Telegraph*, 1961

PHILIP, THE PEOPLE'S CHOICE FOR PRESIDENT.
                              Daily Mirror, 1969

No comment, really, except to say that it's been going on for about a quarter of a century now. And, in passing, that the story about spraying the photographers is the archetypal (and for some reason the most indestructible) myth. The man taking Prince Philip around said, with misplaced roguishness, "If you press this button you'll soak those cameramen." "Not likely," said HRH. So the man pressed it.

Nor did he pelt reporters with nuts at the monkey-house enclosure on Gibraltar. He did say, when he saw them perched in the holes in the rock face, "Which are the monkeys?" And apologized afterward.

In the News

*"As so often happens, I discovered that it would
have been better to keep my trap shut."*

A favorite request by interviewers is for a breakdown of his typical
working day. He tries to be patient, though the effort sometimes
shows. He's been asked so often, and there's no answer. A year
is the nearest to a pattern, and then only because of implacably
recurring fixtures, mostly with the Queen. On other days he can
be doing anything, and anywhere. "February and March are
usually good times for foreign visits. There's nothing much going
on here, and in any case the weather's usually better abroad."
Well, that's frank. But the visits are work. At Program Meetings
he'll cast around for compensations, whose existence he never pretends to disguise. Fiftieth anniversary of the Royal Australian
Air Force? "We could make it a visit to, oh, somewhere like
Thailand. Suppose we went to New Guinea? I mean, you fly

down to Fiji, ending up, say, at the Galapagos, and then take the yacht to Acapulco and fly back from there. And the yacht could come back through the Canal." Interesting, if it came off (it will have done by this time) but hardly typical. Or there's a projected State visit to Turkey. The British Columbia Centennial Celebrations? In that case, we could . . .

His last time but one in British Columbia had been in autumn 1969. Canada east–west, Ottawa to Vancouver, a dogleg south into the States and east again: Wyoming, Iowa, Washington, New York. Home by Greenland and the rim of the ice cap. By the time he got back, that time, clangers as well as autumn leaves had fallen, and more to come in an overcrowded week that was at least typical in one way, as a reminder of his rich opportunities for putting his foot in it and, by inference, his dexterity, in the main, at keeping it out.

It's worth a look.

The Canada trip took about three weeks, its chief object to nourish the Canadian end of the Award Scheme, though in fact there were only a dozen or so direct Award occasions. There were other things to be fitted in. Visits to service units and installations, to observatories, schools, universities (an honorary D.Sc. from the University of Victoria), a planetarium, the proposed site for an Olympics village, assorted displays, from Girl Nautical Cadets and the Boys Brigade to flying sharks and marlins (Vancouver) and those old moon rock samples (Ottawa). He lunched or dined with soldiers, sailors, airmen, the Canadian Council of Christians and Jews, the Rotarians, the US Pilgrims, the English-Speaking Union and President Nixon, to name a few. Met premiers, ambassadors, governors, called on nine eminent mayors, shook the hands of lesser functionaries by the roomful.

Not counting a Second Lesson, read in Christ Church Cathedral, Ottawa, there were eight speeches, eight press conferences, two TV interviews. He glided off ninety-three times by car, took up and put down the Andover twenty-five times and piloted it for most of the sixty-odd hours in the air. Twelve meals taken in flight. Intermittent helicoptering. Finally roosted at RAF Benson in the early hours of Saturday morning, November 8, well behind schedule after a refueling diversion from Goose Bay, Labrador, to Stephenville, Newfoundland. It had been a long, dark haul. That evening viewers saw him, as crisp as usual, in the royal box at the Albert Hall, for the British Legion Festival of Remembrance. Sunday morning, which was wet, a wreath to be laid at the Cenotaph, where Biafra demonstrators scuffled with police on the sidelines. Dress, Admiral of the Fleet. Lunch and change. Colonel of the Welsh Guards, for the Regimental Memorial Service in the Guards Chapel, 3 P.M. Read the Lesson. Afterward take the salute on Horse Guards Parade.

True, the details are looked after. No teasing decisions about costume. (Memo from the office to valet Joe Pearce: "Lt.-Cmdr. Pike telephoned to say that the First Sea Lord will not be wearing gloves at the Cenotaph.") Someone takes care of the flowers. (Memo to the office from the Lord Chamberlain: "May I remind you that His Royal Highness's wreath should be no more than 24 inches in diameter, without any folding stand, and that this should be laid flat, and should be sent to the Home Office on Saturday, 8th November.")

So to the Monday, which had a late start, for him. Nothing until 11 A.M., with a meeting of the Council of St. George's House at Windsor (but he was in London, and had to get there). Still, there'd been the papers to read. The BBC had put out, the night before, the *Meet the Press* interview, recorded in Washington the previous Wednesday for American television, and the front pages exploded as one over his references to the rocky royal budget. . . . A move to smaller premises, might have to give up polo, the

Queen in the red. . . . Though some papers plunged into the well-squeezed but inexhaustibly juicy topic of the monarchy's house-keeping, and a few sympathized with a family batting along on an income fixed eighteen years before, there were those who predictably hung their fun on the "indiscretions" of Philip.[1] The *Daily Mirror* printed his name bigger than its own, and gave up so much of the page to indignant headlines that there was hardly room to start the story. They were all questions, and wanted to know why he should make these startling revelations to the Americans instead of the British, and if the Queen was privy to his intentions . . . or, better still, because you could get political dabblings into it, did the Government get advance warning of what he was going to say? (This gave a Labour MP a great idea for a question in the House: "Did Ministers know in advance about Prince Philip's comments?") As he wouldn't have made them if they hadn't been invited, they might as well have asked whether the Government had been briefed on what questions the CBS interviewers had up their sleeves.

But at least, since the program had been viewed by the British millions, reports couldn't give the impression, as so often, that he'd suddenly sprung up on a wayward impulse and volunteered a wild statement. It was known, for once, that he'd been in the hot seat, handling tricky material without (naturally) those word-weaving evasions of the politician in the same fix. In the middle of the uproar a lady from Bushey Heath wrote to the editor of *The Times:* "Sir: The Duke is a joy. Some of those American questions were stinkers." That, with the dockers' move to buy him a polo pony, and a motion of congratulation tabled by three Liberal MPs, was about all the joy he got. By this time the American

[1] Routine news items tend to call him Prince or Duke, and save the Christian name for when there's a pother on. It's then a showbiz category, where fame and familiarity hold hands. "Philip says 'Thanks but No' to Dockers"—*Daily Mail*, a few days later, with "Gary's Night Out with Julie" in the next column.

questions covered a second interview, on NBC's *Today Show*, when Miss Barbara Walters had shot the highly charged word abdication at him. The story broke in the London evenings of the Monday, and next day everything blew up on the new tack like a battery of Whakarewarewa geysers. Bill Heseltine's telephones were warm to the touch. "No Abdication Says Palace." You'd have thought that it had been virtually on, but called off at the eleventh hour. To the British reader, of course, abdication means the shocking business of Edward VIII, anyway, and not a sensible, graceful and constitutional surrender of the Throne, in due time, to the Heir.

All he'd said, in any case, was that as far as he knew any abdication talk was only a rumor, and its disadvantages might outweigh its advantages. " 'Abdication' Pros and Cons," said the *Evening Standard*. It was on the streets as he made his way to the London Palladium for the Royal Command Variety Performance on the Monday evening. White tie and tails, a cheerful grin, handshakes for Mr. Bernard Delfont, Sir Lew Grade, Ginger Rogers, Cilla Black, Herb Alpert, Frankie Howerd, Danny La Rue, Des O'Connor, Harry Secombe and Mr. Tom Jones. A kind word to all. To Mr. Jones, it was reported, "What do you gargle with, pebbles?" You have to find something for everyone on these larks, and if this was what he found, not perhaps ideal, the manner tempered the matter and no offense taken. The artist later recalled the encounter as "very friendly," and was therefore surprised to hear that the next day, lunching with the Smaller Businesses Association, the Duke had talked about his hideous singing. In fact he hadn't. Only about his choice of hideous songs. And even that was only as a glancing illustration of a point—itself not the nub of the discussion—about modern society's unequal prizes. Is there anyone who hasn't said the same, these days, with pop stars in clover, and coal being mined for peanuts?

But we're still on the Monday. The Variety Performance had

"It's only a matter of a short time of bird-watching and photography before the question of survival of species begins to dawn on the mind." Tower Island, in the Galapagos, 1964.
(Photograph by Aubrey Buxton)

But there are fields of nature study nearer home than the Pacific. Spring, 1969, a beer and an apple on Hilbre Island, off England's northwest coast.
(Photograph by Eric Hosking)

"I have lots of uniforms." But this one is the property of the Guild of Air Pilots and Navigators, kept for the use of the Grand Master.
(Smiths Industries, Ltd.)

Painter. "I don't claim any exceptional interest or knowledge or ability. It's strictly average."
(B.B.C.-I.T.V. Consortium)

Flying a BEA Trident.
(*BEA*)

May 4, 1953. "Wings" day. The five stars are his insignia as Marshal of the Royal Air Force.
(*London News Agency*)

Polo at Cowdray Park. "It's no good being fit for something else, you have to be fit for riding and you have to be fit for polo-playing. Then you have to get accustomed to the ponies, and get them to play for you, because they need as much practice as you do. So if you're going to play it well, there isn't any time to play anything else."
(*Keystone Press Agency*)

With the Queen in the Music Room. Buckingham Palace. There are formal photographic sessions from time to time. (Lord Snowdon–*Camera Press*)

And, less formal, almost all the time. Coming ashore from the Royal Barge. (*Crown Copyright reserved*)

1966. A bamboo barge in Jamaica. Princess Anne had been with him to the Commonwealth Games at Kingston. Prince Charles later joined them from school in Australia, via Mexico, and all flew home to Aberdeen, for Balmoral. *(Reginald Davis)*

With Andrew and Edward. "We've always made a point of trying to be at home and available to the children during the holidays. Then we enter a period of term, which is term for them, and, so to speak, term for us." *(Reginald Davis)*

Bonfire at Sandringham. "I suppose inevitably most people would prefer
not to be working, and taking it easy in the country."
(*Council of Photographic News Agencies*)

1968. State Visit to Brazil. After a Remembrance Sunday service in Rio de
Janeiro.
(*Reginald Davis*)

1969. A conference in Ottawa. "I've been lectured to by all the experts in a great many fields, and inevitably something has to stick." (*Photograph by George E. O. Lilley*)

topped off a busy day. A meeting, a lunch, a new probation hostel opened, three hours at that impressive Management Centre. Home at seven. Leave for the Palladium, 7:55.

If he found his evening out less than transporting, he wasn't alone. When the recording was televised someone wrote to the *Daily Mail:*

> Twinkle, twinkle, TV star,
> How did you get up so far?
> If this is the best that can be seen,
> No wonder they sang God Save the Queen.

Never mind the meter, it spoke for many. Later in the week he received an unsolicited note of condolence, tying the experience neatly in with the Monarchy-in-the-Red headlines: "Having seen on TV the Royal Variety Show I am only too pleased to vote for an increase in your allowance. If you and your Beloved Queen could endure that and still smile, you deserve a good rise."

But the Monarchy-in-the-Red story was already losing ground to the Philip-and-the-Abdication story, and both were soon to be outstripped by the Philip-Insults-Jones story. And even that couldn't win, in the end, against the undefeatable Philip-Attacks-Pressman story. Nothing's ever going to beat that one, ruling out a third world war.

At the fateful luncheon of the Smaller Businesses Association no pressmen were supposed, or at least expected, to be present. And they wouldn't have been, if the Prince hadn't already been building up, during the North American trip, to one of his news-value peaks. It wasn't only the rich stuff on television. There'd been a great little titbit from Calgary, Alberta, cattle city at the foot of the Rockies, where he said, "Not another one?" when they handed him the ceremonial cowboy hat. Later, in Vancouver, reporters wanted the insulting conduct explained. He apologized.

He hadn't meant to be rude, but he'd collected several hats on previous visits (the first in 1952): "Once given the key to the city, you don't go on getting keys to the city." The practical view. But civic hearts are tender, and half an hour after the Vancouver touch-down he'd wounded another lot, by forgetting what to call the new annex he was opening to their City Hall. "I declare this thing open—whatever it is." Another apology. Speaking without a prepared draft was "skating on very thin ice, and I go through occasionally." ("Philip's Thin Ice," said the home headlines.)[2]

Preparing drafts had been hard to fit in. The annex was his last job on that Tuesday, except for an after-dinner speech to come at the Hotel Vancouver (the Canadian Council of Christians and Jews, and no corns trampled: at any rate there was nothing from the agencies about Philip in Race Bombshell). He'd already done an after-lunch speech at the Empress Hotel, Victoria, to the combined Men's and Women's Canadian Clubs. Before that, a school visit with Award Scheme displays, and a tour of the Maritime Museum; after it, the degree ceremony at the University, a graceful word, academic handshakes, tea and an airport dash for the flight to Vancouver; take-off, put-down, smiles for the photographers (these are always amateur as well as professional: "Wave, Philip!" they cry), off to the City Hall, call on the mayor, and so to the grand opening of the new—of this—er—(Thinks: "Aren't I speaking at some dinner or something tonight?").

The day before had been easier. No flights, only one speech. Still, the comings and goings on his program sheet were timed at 0945, 1000, 1030, 1055, 1110, 1210, 1240, 1400, 1445, 1615, 1715, 1745, 1800, 1915 and 2000—for dinner at Government House.

But the communicators were alerted. Even before the hat and

---

[2] The annex is now known by everybody in it as the East Thing. Opening it wasn't quite the ceremony the home papers suggested. "It was raining," HRH says, "and I wanted to get on with it: especially as the total audience was about fifteen passing shoppers under umbrellas."

the annex he'd given signs of going critical, newswise. He'd told a press conference in Ottawa, asking about the future of the monarchy in Canada: "If at any stage people feel it has no further part to play, then for goodness' sake let's end the thing on amicable terms without having a row about it." If he hadn't gone on to explain that monarchies exist for the people and not for the monarchs with that carelessly quotable "We don't come here for our health," it might have got no more play than the same answer to the same question two years earlier in Australia, when pulse rates remained normal. It's the verbal flourish that gets them, and a smoother man wouldn't use it. This one plunged the home papers into a frenzy of inquisition, led by the *Mail*'s week-long symposium on "Do We Need the Queen?" billed as "a rivetting [*sic*] series" answering "the unexpected question Prince Philip prompted in Canada." They'd missed the point—which wasn't the function of the monarchy in Britain but in far-flung dominions whose new generation was feeling its own feet and thinking of standing on them. (The *Mail* verdict, with a sprinkling of dissenters, was that we did need the Queen, even though in a last burst of heart-searching by polled citizens she came second to her husband among "The Royals We Would Most Like to Meet.")

By the time Prince Philip brought the Andover into RAF Benson, the stage was well set. To the royal finances, the "abdication," the hat and the annex had been added a couple more deplorable items. He'd spoken in Toronto about "dressing up the Christmas broadcast and calling it 'The Queen Show.' "[3] Practically lese-majesty, and look who from. It was only a passing

---

[3] The dropping of the Queen's broadcast had recently been announced, exciting much interest and more theorizing. As he had explained on *Meet the Press*, it was only being given a miss for that year (1969), which had already seen the release of the Royal Family film, and the televising of the Prince of Wales's elaborately ceremonial investiture at Caernarvon. You could plug things too much. Besides, it gave time to think of a different way of doing it for Christmas 1970.

remark, but made to a journalist who thought he had the authority to quote it, and did. Then came the disgraceful non-event at La Guardia, New York, when he was to talk to the press and walked out without uttering. Who did he think he was? Hardly anyone troubled to explain that the conference site had been chosen by idiots, in the open, with warming-up Boeings blotting out all hope of audible speech. The correspondents weren't to blame, but what with one thing and another he wasn't feeling too affable toward the newspapers in general by the time he got home. It would be something of a relief to be able to talk freely to the Smaller Businessmen.

What happened there was really no one's fault. He'd been asked to speak at the lunch, but had said he'd rather not, he'd like "an informal discussion, and to ask some questions." Whether he was told that a Press Association man would be there, and forgot, or by some rare oversight wasn't told at all, is hard to come at. Either way, it wouldn't have mattered so much if the PA man had been Ronald Gomer-Jones. As the agency's Court reporter for twenty years (known among fellow members of the Savage Club as "Jones the Palace"), he would have been spotted, and the Duke would have realized that he was back in the gold-fish bowl. It was quite a small company. But Jones the Palace had to cover an investiture that morning, and thought he couldn't make Belgrave Square in time. So two other reporters were sent, Leonard Moxon and John Shaw. Moxon had the lunch and most of the discussion, and the Duke assumed that this taker of notes, whose face he didn't know, was taking them for his hosts as a private record. It wasn't until Moxon discreetly slipped out to get something on the telephone in time for the evening papers, and Shaw took his place, that the guest of honor woke up to things. "Who are you?" Shaw told him. It wasn't a success. The Duke expressed himself, and a few seconds later the light went out in the phone booth in the vestibule and the astonished Moxon found he had company.

"I hope you're not reporting what I've been saying. It was a completely informal discussion, and I didn't know the press were there. It's chaps like you who get me into trouble." There's some doubt that chaps was the actual word, but they'd been well within their rights, and armed with palace press cards. They later got an apology.

It turned out to be apology week. Miss Walters apologized to the Duke for landing him with a hot one on the *Today Show*. The Smaller Businesses Association apologized to him for the mess-up at the lunch. The Duke apologized to Tom Jones.[4] Heseltine apologized to the Duke, not only for the mess-up at the lunch, but for another over the Tom Jones apology. This Prince Philip had drafted as a personal letter. "Dear Mr. Jones," it began, "I've no doubt whatever that some malicious fellow will take delight in spreading a story that I said something unkind about you the other day. . . ." The tone was sincerely regretful that feelings might have been hurt. It went down for typing. The palace press office assumed it had gone off and said so to clamoring inquirers. Tough luck, because it hadn't. Prince Philip and the Admiral had held it back for a bit of a think, which caused Jones renewed surprise on the following day, when he read about the royal apology that he hadn't had. Tricky. Ought the letter now to go? It was decided yes, but in the third person and over the Admiral's signature. The substance wasn't changed much.

By now the pro and con Tom Jones correspondence was flooding in. The pro and con "abdication" flow had been nothing by comparison. Both sides were nasty. Stuffed shirts from Cheltenham applauded the Duke nauseatingly for saying what he hadn't in fact said, and were about evenly balanced by the abuse from the opposing camp. Seventeen schoolgirls from Warwickshire put their names to a sheet of well-rounded invective. Another writer

---

[4] They've since met, and straightened everything out.

began bluntly, "I don't know who's got the biggest head in this country, you or Lester Piggott." Obvious nuts apart, all received civil replies.

Both Miss Walters and the Smaller Businessmen were assured that they were to feel in no way responsible for what had happened in their respective trouble spots. To Miss Walters, a personal note:

> It was very kind of you to write such a nice letter. Please don't worry about it. The early reports were based on hearsay, and as soon as people saw and heard the question they realised there was no sensation. I rather suspect that life is so busy that journalists only have time to discover the subject of a discussion, without reading what was actually said.

The week went on. From Belgrave Square, his next stop on the Tuesday was at the Design Centre, Haymarket, where he selected the winner of the 1970 Duke of Edinburgh's Prize for Elegant Design, and inspected and opened an exhibition of telecommunications to mark the GPO's metamorphosis into a public corporation. (In the morning he'd been down the Mile End Road to visit London University's Queen Mary College to see its new inventions laboratory.) He left at half-past six, and at half-past seven, black tie, was at Grosvenor House for a boxing evening, the playing fields to reap the proceeds; or, rather, some of them, because a pro-Arab parliamentary element had spotted that a share of the takings was earmarked for the Jewish National Fund; and the paper *Free Palestine* had demanded that he should cancel the engagement, which would be "an open affront to the whole Arab world."

This unwelcome political drama had blown up earlier, and he'd been taking decisions on it, among other things, while in Canada. On the suggestion of cancellation to avoid anti-Arab taintings, he wrote that it would merely lay him open "to the equal and opposite charge of being anti-Jewish." (The office sent him out a draft of their letter embodying this, but using the word anti-Semite, which he queried: "I seem to think Arabs are Semites too." They are.)

It went off all right in the end, but pickets of the Palestine Solidarity Campaign were investing Grosvenor House, and he was persuaded, with imagine what reluctance, to go in by the back door. He made a speech.

Wednesday started at ten. Interview at the palace with Rear-Admiral Sir Ian McGeoch to talk about the Royal Naval Sailing Association. At 10:30, interview with Mr. Nicholas Clarke, proprietor of Nick's Diner and related restaurants and a man with energetic ideas for raising the standard of British eating. They appealed: something might even be done at the palace; he was wafted on to the Master of the Household. At 11:45, the offices of the Diamond Trading Company in the City, followed by lunch and gifts: a copy of *The Central Selling Organisation and the Rough Diamond Industry*, which anyone would be glad to have, and, even gladder, a paperweight with an embedded diamond as a chaser. At 2:30, with the Queen, to Lesney Products, of Hackney Wick, three times winners of the Queen's Award to Industry. (It's interesting—he got one of the most enthusiastic receptions of his life from the people there, partly because they knew he was having a bad time, partly because here was *the* man, who'd been doing all the things he was supposed, now almost by national tradition, to do.) At 5:55, to the Royal Society of Arts, Adelphi, to present his Presidential Awards for Design Management. Take the Chair, open the proceedings, hear a symposium of speeches by representatives of the five winning bodies. Sum up with something worth saying about each, and about industrial design in general. ("There are no details, literally from letter headings to the screws you put in a door, too humble to be treated by sensible design standards.")

Dine there.

Thursday, still going strong. Major-General Girling at ten, director of Electrical and Mechanical Engineering, Army, to pay his respects on assuming the directorship. At 10:30 the curtains are closed in the Chinese Dining Room for two films about the Duke of Edinburgh's Award, and opened again for a meeting of the Award trustees, and a farewell presentation to Lord Hunt (of Everest), who's been running it since it started in 1956.

So to a quiet lunch. Well, three family, one equerry, eight guests—editor, architect, don, impresario, motor tycoon, broadcaster, MP, test pilot—and all away in time for that long radio interview for the BBC's listeners in India. 4:30, Sir Solly Zuckerman, with some required information about the state of Atlantic salmon fishing; and then probably an hour for a look at the desk before climbing into field marshal's mess kit and making the annual dinner of the Honourable Artillery Company by 7:15. He had declined to speak, leaving the star billing to King Olav of Norway, so it could more or less count as a night off. As the whole of the next day was going on an Army unit in Hampshire (chopper from Chelsea Barracks, 10:30, back at six) it was probably just as well.

That was the Friday. Somewhere he got in a bit of correspondence that day: to Guyana, on the danger of the marine turtle's becoming extinct; to the British Ambassador in Iceland, asking about a hydroelectric scheme. It was Prince Charles's twenty-first birthday, and he wasn't the only one, some may think, who deserved a party. Then there'd be the weekend papers to look forward to.

To church at Sandringham. "Quick!" says the Queen's equerry, bundling me into the last of the cars. They shoot off as the doors close, full belt for worship, spraying the sand-colored soup of the Norfolk roads over their glossy flanks. We arrive as the church clock begins to strike eleven.

It's one of the occasions when royalty carries money. You can't delegate when the sidesman comes around for the collection. Prince Philip, unfortunately, seems to have lost the pound he was provided with. Awkward, as the bag comes bobbing toward the front pew. There's some pocket-patting before he turns around and says, "Anyone got any cash?" Better organized, for once, I'm happy to come across with a loan of two 50p heptagons. Not only that it's a rare experience to finance a member of the Family, but the coins were among others he had a hand in designing as one of the Mint's advisers. (Not the shape, only the pictures. He'd worried about the sexlessness of Britannia. Couldn't they have "a body in the right proportions, that fills the robes"? And, on the obverse, "putting '70' in front of 'Elizabeth' looks ridiculous: all those initials are better behind the Queen's head, and it also keeps the lettering that much further away from the face.") Long before, in 1952, he'd helped to settle the look of the money for the new reign, the first to carry his wife's likeness. He didn't think some of the early likenesses very like, claiming to speak from closer observation than most.

The loan was refunded before lunch, when Princess Anne, noticing, voiced what sounded like an old grievance, that she'd had to find her own pound note, which was her last. So he refunded that too.

Rate for the Job

"There's no question of we just get a lump sum, and
we can do what we like with it."

<hr>

❈❈❈

His passport number is 1, which seems about right, as the Queen doesn't have one. Occupation, Prince of the Royal House.

Equally right, if a surprise, is that its back pages, while the currency restrictions were at their toughest, carried a note of those miserable £50 allocations just like everyone else's. "We don't get away with anything," says Leslie Treby,[1] who's run the clerical side of his office for more than twenty years. Still, together with the Admiral, he's wrenched the occasional concession. Four years ago the Treasury agreed that the laundry bills should be regarded as necessary expenditure: until then, if the Duke wanted to avoid the crumpled look at State banquets, the washing and ironing came

<hr>

[1] MVO, MBE, BEM.

out of his own pocket.[2] But there's really only one pocket. His income—curiously known to the Treasury as an "annuity"—goes into it. £40,000. It's recognized for tax purposes that about two-thirds of it is spent on doing the job: no allowable expenses, because he gets the money to work with and expenses is what most of it's for. Out of the rest, after tax and surtax, comes everything else.

His cat-among-the-pigeons remark about the state of the monarchy's housekeeping was simply a statement of fact. He's more concerned about the Queen's money troubles than his own, and has been taking things up, as you might expect, with the Chancellor of the Exchequer. His own approach is that you don't worry about money until there isn't any, and then only because you need it to do the job. No question of tucking the stuff away as a reassurance, in moments of gloom, that you're a man of substance—and, today, no possibility—the books for the last year or two show him well on the debit side.

It's his treasurer[3] and office who worry. Not that he's a loose spender. He's had his Alvis convertible since 1961, which should shake the change-every-other-year boys. Admittedly the yacht *Bloodhound*, recently got rid of as part of the essential cut-down, cost £11,000, but that was in 1962, nearing the end of the palmy days. He seldom got more than four days' sailing a year out of her; the rest of the time she was lent to clubs, acquiring prestige in competitions just by royal association.

"How does he earn his £40,000 a year plus perks?" asked the *Daily Mirror* at the time of those American TV disclosures. Also:

---

[2] Program Meeting jokelet, finding that a lunch at the palace clashes with an invitation from the British Launderers Research Association: "We shall have to scrub the laundry."

[3] Now Lord Rupert Nevill, part-time successor to the Admiral, and an old friend.

"Does he really have to go abroad to make bad jokes about being down on his uppers?" It wasn't a joke, so good or bad doesn't come into it. But there's a joke of sorts in his great financial paradox. The more he does, the more he pays: for staff, office fixtures and fittings, clothes, travel, presents, tips. (He does the tipping for all who go around with him. Naturally. "When we're in his party," said the Admiral, "we're only another sort of servant.")

It's the staff that causes the biggest crunch. That £40,000 sounds all right. But in 1969 the salaries swallowed £20,600 of it. And another thing. An item for household accommodation, which looks surprising among his official outgoings, means the accommodation he has to find for his Household. They're lodged, with the valets and others, in handy flats around St. James's Street—five minutes' walk to the palace, and no unthinkable hold-up in times of transport chaos. He pays their rent and rates; also telephones, because in theory he may want them at any time, and it can be argued that they mightn't be subscribers if he didn't; fair's fair.

Besides paying for the maintenance and running costs of his own car, he feels he should also chip in with something toward the official limousines in the Royal Mews. He uses them for work and he's paid to do the work and therefore finds the upkeep of two cars, the pay of two chauffeurs, and another £160 to keep them in uniforms, so the total chip-in here is now topping the £2000 a year mark.

Inflation apart, as he's made more and more work for himself he's shelled out in proportion. In 1953, before he really started pushing out the boundaries of his separate, post-Accession career, the staff salary bill was a mere £6000 or so. There were savings, which is just as well, because it's from them, now running out like bathwater, that the yearly deficits of the seventies are being made good. Even so, a lot of those dwindling reserves are out of reach for any ordinary use, in what are known as the Edinburgh Trusts: under the deeds, they can be used only for good works, to meet the ever-rolling stream of charitable demands. Everyone imagines there must be money to burn. University clubs, for instance, inspired to mount expeditions in the vacation—dig up the Inca ruins, canoe down the Zambesi—think of him as the first and readiest touch, and there's often a faint coolness in the letter of thanks when he comes up with only a hundred pounds. The only infusions the trusts get these days are from such odd items as television fees. He often doesn't get any, but if he does, that's where they go. There was once a personal windfall, for his contribution to the film about the Galapagos. After tax it went on polo ponies. Otherwise, the "annuity" is the sole source.

The trusts were his own idea. Though he isn't much interested in money, it wouldn't be like him not to run a finger down the accounts and stop here and there with an inquiring stab. Finding that the invested savings were yielding only a net £250 a year or so, hardly enough to paddle undergraduate canoers along the Manchester Ship Canal, he saw that to start the trusts and scrub around some of the tax would make a lot more sense. It means that for private purposes the money's gone for good. But at least when the appeals come in he needn't plead that the cupboard's bare. He'd hate that, having a generous streak; and the chances are that the alms hunters wouldn't believe it anyway. ("How nice it must be," once mused the *Sunday Express*, "not to have to worry about a sordid trifle like money.")

Putting aside bed and board, the perks aren't many, either official or personal. The official ones can often kick back, as with loyal but sometimes unwanted gifts sent by admirers overseas, which tend to incur customs duty and airport charges. Livestock can be worse. A present of falcons—nowhere to keep, no time to fly—had to be fostered out on a friend. It seemed only polite to meet the friend's out-of-pocket expenses. ("Falconer Prince," said the headlines, when the news seeped out.)

There's one useful perk. If it lasts. His postal and telephone services are free, lumped in with the Queen's. The two offices run up something like £50,000 worth in a year. The Duke's share is by far the smaller, in spite of all those good luck telegrams to the dinners he can't attend. But now that the Post Office is a public corporation, this may change. When the mails were Her Majesty's she could hardly be sent a bill. Now, it could be different. Both the Keeper of the Privy Purse and the Duke's treasurer are praying the blow won't fall. If it did, there wouldn't be much they could do to balance the books—and the imbalance, it's worth remembering, isn't the result of any "banqueting and display of wealth," against which the letter from Camden Town cautioned George VI so sternly at the time of the wedding, but of higher costs all around, and higher salaries for everyone but these particular employers. The palace pays selective employment tax. No government department does that.

Even as things are, not all communications are on the house. If his relations come to stay, and fancy a long-distance call to others in Germany, perhaps, or Greece, the cost is winkled out and he's charged with it. During the *Bloodhound* days, the Navy insisted that her position should be reported once a day (twice if the owner was aboard); it could only be done through ordinary ship-to-shore services, and wasn't cheap, so the office proposed to reverse the charges into the Admiralty. Agreement was generously prompt.

It isn't always so. There was a long battle with the Ministry of Works over who should pay for the office's new electric filing system, which revolves like a chicken-basting machine and throws up desired information at the touch of a button. (Or, frankly, sometimes doesn't.) Whitehall is a dogged foe, and fights by the book. In this case, the book had been written long ago. It said that filing meant cabinets, and cabinets meant carpentry; therefore as with desks, chairs, hatstands and other objects made in olden times with hammer and saw, they were supposed to come out of the £40,000. The office argued that they ranked with type-writers, photo-copiers and the like (which kindly come free from Her Majesty's stationery office, no one knows why, and it would be silly to ask). The office, itself pretty dogged in these matters, won the day. Or half won it. The Ministry agreed to lash out for the chicken-baster, providing that it was half the size needed. The other half of the records must be microfilmed, and the cost got out of the stationery office. It all took three years.

At the last count, the two systems between them packed in some 70,000 references. They need continual updating. A lot of them are people who tend to change their rank, their status, the letters after their name, to move, to marry, to die. Foreign visits, particularly, mean heavy checking before the event. Are the notabilities of Houston or Brunei, Reykjavik or Lima, still the same? Stands the first secretary of our embassy in Ankara where he did? You have to watch it in South America, where perhaps this year's president wasn't even there at last year's reception, and last year's president may not be anywhere. There's the matter of speeches. Your professional traveling lecturer, like the old time music-hall artist, can stick to the same old stuff by doing it in different places. With a traveling prince, the places keep coming around again. Audiences who attended the English-Speaking Union dinner in Ottawa last time will probably attend it again this time. Old jokes and stale arguments won't do. Press a button for the script and think of something fresh.

There are all those gifts to be given. The wallets, leather-framed photographs, cuff links. The links are prized and welcomed, and so they should be at about £20 a pair, but you need to know who's had them already. Handing over another lot looks like careless-ness. Any hint of perfunctoriness won't do here.

Overseas presents, if they're given in what the Treasury regards as the course of duty, don't now have to come out of the donor's pay. If they did, he couldn't do it. The 1956–57 world tour, what with one thing and another, dented his resources to the tune of £8000.

The Treasury should have been grateful to get all that spread of goodwill for nothing. It was a conception on the grand scale, pinned originally to his opening of the 1956 Olympic Games at Melbourne. He got out the maps and charts, casting around for ways of fattening things up. "It soon became apparent," he wrote later, "that there were a good many island communities and outposts in the Indian Ocean, the South Pacific, the Antarctic and the Atlantic, which cannot be visited by air, and are too remote and small to get into the usual tours [the Queen's State visits]. Although it meant being away from home for three months, including Christmas and the New Year, I decided to try to arrange the journey out to Australia and back in the Royal Yacht *Britannia*."

In the event, he had to fly out to Mombasa and join *Britannia* there, but most of those far sprinklings of the Commonwealth saw him, as the Queen's representative, and for once felt not forgotten. Deep in the Antarctic he gave a party on board for the lonely men of the survey base on otherwise uninhabited Deception Island, off the tip of the Graham Land Peninsular, and ran a film for them. ("I showed them *Seven Brides for Seven Brothers*, but I'm not sure whether it was a good idea, or whether it was perhaps slightly misjudged.") He enjoyed himself—even on the 3800 miles of open sea to Graham Land from the Chatham Islands in the Roaring Forties—but it wasn't all *dolce far niente* even in warmer waters. The ship's bulletin for the day on Tristan da Cunha makes that plain, though its style reflects the cheerfulness that went along with the chores:

> Tristan da Cunha was a most impressive sight when we
> anchored at 0930 this morning. For a brief moment the
> 7,000-foot peak above the sheer cliffs appeared through a

break in the almost permanent cloud that surmounts this very inaccessible island.

It was bright with a fresh breeze and immediately the long boats of the fishermen put off and sailed out to us, bringing with them the Administrator, Mr. Forsyth-Thompson, and his wife, and the Chief of the island, Mr. Willie Repetto.

The Duke of Edinburgh, dressed as an Admiral of the Fleet and accompanied by the Chief, boarded one of the long boats and at the Chief's invitation took the helm and sailed the long boat ashore. On the beach he was greeted with the cheers of the fishermen while the women-folk of the island added theirs from the cliff top.

Behind the beach stood the canning factory for the island's main industry—crawfish—which His Royal Highness inspected on the way to the settlement. An amusing spectacle was the transporting of the instruments of the Royal Marine band by ox-wagons from the beach. After climbing a cliff-side track Prince Philip arrived at a beautifully decorated archway of welcome, where he was greeted by Dr. and Mrs. Gooch, Mr. Stapleford, the agricultural adviser, and his wife, and Mr. Harding, the schoolmaster, and his wife. Donkeys, usually a familiar feature of the island, were absent, having been driven to the other side of the island lest they should eat the arch of welcome.

His Royal Highness was conducted by the Chief and the Administrator to a succession of croft-like thatched cottages where he saw groups of the women colourfully dressed in their best clothes carding and spinning wool. It was in one of these cottages that Prince Philip received a special welcome from Martha Repetto, the head-woman of Tristan. Next door he was shown an exhibition of the crafts of the island. This included amongst samples of island knitted clothing, models of boats and marbles made from eyes of dried bluefish. There should have been six of these, but the Chief's cat had swallowed two of them the night before.

Before going to the Library for a reception of the islanders, Prince Philip visited the church, where he was shown an ensign given by H.M.S. *Magpie* during her last visit a year ago. After lunch at the Administrator's house, Prince Philip saw the school, and then walked to the site of the new hall. The whole community was assembled there for the laying of the commemorative stone. Fallen in in front of the dais was a guard of honour of Brownies, Girl Guides and Sea Scouts, and after the Administrator and the Chief had delivered speeches of loyalty to the Queen and of welcome, His Royal Highness laid the stone and presented to the islanders a battery-powered record player with amplifiers. His Royal Highness accepted from the Chief several beautiful and representative presents from the island. He left to see the Store, a miniature agricultural show, the hospital and then a football match between the island and the ship's company of *Britannia*. The game was played on what can only be called a rugged pitch which gave a distinct advantage to the side playing downhill, so long as they were able to pull up before the cliff edge. The islanders, dressed in long white trousers tucked into football socks, looked like a team of Morris dancers, and displayed an agile knowledge of the tricky terrain. The enthusiastic crowd gave vent to such cries of "Keep it on the island" and "Mind the precipice." The game, which gave great amusement to all, ended most satisfactorily at 2–2.

In the School Hall Prince Philip and his party joined in the island dancing, and the music was provided by the Royal Marine band and the local accordion band alternately. This ended a particularly colourful and unusual day and His

Royal Highness was given an enthusiastic farewell before entering the long boat for *Britannia*.

The bulletins were intended to keep the newspapers back home in touch with what was going on, and Michael Parker remembers a mild resentment, by the touring party, at the small coverage they got. It took the journey's end to make the news. Parker's resignation, well supported by the fatuous tattle in the American press about the royal marriage heading for the rocks, got all the coverage anyone could want, though not of the ideal kind. Disappointing. After all that good work. And the bills still to come in.

But at least someone had the kind thought of celebrating the traveler's return by giving him lunch at the Mansion House. His speech was a run-down of the 40,000-mile journey. There were no topical references, though the papers were still having a ball. ("He is a man without a real job," explained *The People* the Sunday before, under the headline "Prince Philip and the Rumours.") If the speech didn't consciously set out to show that he'd been working, no one hearing it could have imagined otherwise. But he didn't rub it in, and made it clear that he'd had some laughs. Was full of praise for Australia and the Australians ("They are rightly proud of their achievements, and we ought to be too"), and for the spirit of the young Englishmen marooned on those Antarctic bases, grateful for all the welcomes he'd been given, excited to have met Fletcher Christian's grandson—on Norfolk Island, where the *Bounty* mutineers had been settled from Pitcairn a hundred years before. But he was chiefly full of the scattered British communities he'd resolved from the first to visit:

> For most of my life, to be away four months from home meant nothing at all. In fact, it would have been more surprising if I had spent four months consecutively at home. This time, for obvious reasons, it meant much more to me.

But I believe there are things for which it is worth while making some personal sacrifice, and I believe that the British Commonwealth is one of those things.

Nothing about how it had punished his pocket. He probably felt it was cheap at the price.

His only other expedition on anything near this scale was in 1959, and the Government's idea. He was in any case off to represent the British Association at two mammoth scientific assemblies in Delhi and Karachi, and afterward on to Bermuda for its 350 anniversary celebrations as a Crown colony. They felt it would be useful if he took in some fragments of Commonwealth missed the time before. The office said he was flattered to be asked, but couldn't afford to go. The Treasury blew the moths out of its purse, and offered to pay. He went. It was a great breakthrough. Until then, the £40,000 was supposed to cover engagements abroad as well as at home.

It still doesn't mean that he gets away with anything. The Foreign and Commonwealth Office approve the program, and get the bills. Any departures for personal frolics, and he gets them. If he likes to give presents not directly in the line of duty, that's his headache. After polo in Mexico in the spring of 1970,[4] fifteen pairs of cuff links went winging off, at £21.10s a pair (one of the designs submitted by Asprey's was quoted at £48.17s 6d). That Variety Club tour of America and Canada set him back £365 for marks of esteem. He now and then shows his gratitude to his inner circle, personal staff, Queen's Flight air crew, equerries, police officers, valets. After Australia, 1968, for his third Commonwealth Study Conference, £300 worth of cuff links were specially designed by guess who, with a coroneted kangaroo on one side and

_____

[4] Not a jaunt on its own, but wedged in between the official Cape Kennedy visit and the visit to Australia with the Queen.

the conference badge on the other. If a girl goes along from the office, taking her corner of it with her, it usually means a bracelet, which comes a bit more expensive. It doesn't tot up to a major drain, but the busier the life the bigger the bounty. There are good years and bad: 1969–70 went through with only £540 on presents—though the trusts were screwed for some £1500 for donations, cups, trophies. (It's still his own money.) There used to be Christmas presents for those who serve him exclusively, but it got a bit out of hand. Now there's a party at the Café Royal: it's for all comers, including grooms, chauffeurs and the maid who cleans his room. Compared with Christmas boxes it probably comes out on the economical side at £120 or so, but neither the Treasury nor the trusts is going to cough that one up.

The polo, it can't be denied, costs a bomb. His one real extravagance, and keenest enjoyment. We can grudge it, if we like (it's any of our business?), but there are men who spend more on motorcars. Again, there are good and bad years. The factor is pony wastage. (Prince Charles also buys ponies, but then he's a lot richer than his father.) It isn't only the animals and equipment—he's a great stick-buster on the field of play—but, for instance, the grooms. They may sound as if they come from the Mews, but they don't. He pays, houses and clothes them.[5] There are vets' fees, horse medicines, feed and stabling. No wonder the cry of "Bloody animal!" rings out sometimes over Windsor Great Park. (Times are more permissive since an "Oh, damn it" was thought worth reporting.) Well, no, that isn't why. And the anger is almost always with himself. Handing over the abused creature afterward he'll say, "Went rather well today?" He's a good

---

[5] By contrast, he has to buy all his own uniforms, and it's a formidable wardrobe. However, he's graciously allowed to treat one-third of his civilian tailor's bill as an official expense.

player. Out of the four hundred or so in the country, experts put him in the first eight. As it's polo that keeps him fit for the daily round, perhaps the office should think about working on HM Inspector to get it made deductible. In less exposed circles your really bright tax adviser gets away with feebler propositions than that.

It's the cost of the polo that inhibits his office from pressing for a rise. Pleas of poverty wouldn't go well with this handsome economy to hand, though a few comparative figures, say for a man who runs an ocean-going yacht, might help. When Victoria sought a bit extra for Albert, and got it, she took the line that he couldn't even afford to keep a pack of hounds, which no gentleman should be without. Those were the days. The office's only hope, from a crudely practical standpoint, is that as he gallops into his sixth decade he'll begin to think of giving the game up. They shouldn't rely on it.

He's less gadget-minded than the stories suggest. Gadgets for gadgets' sake strike him as absurd. He has tape recorders, who hasn't. A couple of pocket ones are used for notes on the spot, transcribed daily into a sheet of reminders, people to thank, better ways of doing things. There's little recreational gadgetry. The only recent toy, acquired in 1970, is a stone polisher, lapidary machine or tumbling barrel, as the makers variously describe them. On his first show of interest he was offered an all-electric affair at £230; when they lowered their sights to a do-it-yourself version at £35, he wrote, "This looks just the job."

The photography costs a bit. But he's had his Swedish Hasselblad camera a long time, the pocket Minox longer, and resists, on the whole, the inexhaustible accessory temptations known to all photographers. There's shooting and fishing (no big-game hunting), and he has to find, though for some reason it may be assumed otherwise, his own licenses, also rods, guns, cartridges, though there's not much chance of lashing out on new guns these days. He spends money, not much, on canvases, paints, brushes, buys his own books, magazines and newspapers—though what could be easier, yet more impossible, than to let the publishers know that he would be pleased to accept them as a gift? You could say the same for guns, cameras and motorcars. And for the services of doctors, dentists, oculists, physiotherapists (that wrist is expensive). It would never do.

"I can't help feeling surprised," he began a speech at a Chartered Insurance Institute dinner, "that you have asked me to propose this toast. As far as I know, my life has never been insured."

It still isn't. No point. Ordinary heads of families, worried in the night, like to think that if they pile up on the M1, or their airplane falls out of the sky, wives and families are provided for. In his case they're provided for anyway. Oddly, yet understandably, he feels deprived over this. Or did, at first. Unnatural, not having to worry about your nearest and dearest because they'll be taken care of by the State. But he's accepted it now. Just another irritating example of being treated as a special case.

The office, at any rate, has no hurt feelings. A fat life premium thumping out once a year would add to its troubles. The Admiral, before he went, got out a simple but painful inflation graph. It showed that the £40,000 would have to be roughly doubled by 1975 to make both ends meet. That looks about right, as it's been halved, in real values, since 1952.

Or, of course, there's always the alternative of saving more money by doing less work.

First Person Singular

I started all this under a handicap. I admired him already. It will be all too apparent that this hasn't changed much. When I told an old friend of his that I should have to find some warts, if the whole thing wasn't to look like a slap-up public relations job, his answer was that when I found them they'd probably turn out to be only pimples. Disappointing. I sought his own help on that. He wrote, "I have a—I hope—reasonable appreciation of my weaknesses and faults, and I quite see the need for them to be put in, if only to give some kind of roundness to the 'character.' If you haven't discovered enough already I'm quite prepared to suggest a few!" We neither of us had any real luck. I was later driven to put a PS on a letter to him: "Please send long list blemishes, blunders, idiocies, inadequacies, backslidings and assorted deficiencies." If it wasn't meant, or treated, seriously, it shows the problem I had. That it wasn't solved doesn't worry me too much now, and is in any case well taken care of elsewhere. An eminent and caustic broadcaster once described him as a buffoon. I can only speak as I find.

What I chiefly found was an invincible honesty, about himself and everything else. It can be disquieting. He sent back some early chapters, with copious corrections of fact, in a wrapper marked, "Proverbs, 28:23." I hastened to my Old Testament: "He that rebuketh a man, afterwards shall find more favour than he that flattereth with the tongue."

And great kindness.

At our first meeting I asked him if he wanted to see the stuff. He said, "Well, it's up to you. I mean, whatever's helpful to you. I can certainly look through it if you'd like me to. If not, obviously not. Either you can use me as it suits you, you can say, 'Look, I'm stuck, what do I do next?,' or, 'I've written this bit, do you think it's lousy?'—I mean, if you like working that way. On the other hand, if you want to work like an artist with a shroud over your head, that's up to you."

"I can come and see you, Sir, if I'm in trouble?"

"Oh, yes. Oh, lord, yes."

"There are bound to be things in it that'll make you mad."

"No, no, I shouldn't think so. I shouldn't worry about that."

In fact, a few things did make him a bit mad in that first draft, though less so, perhaps, than this chapter will. They were chiefly inaccuracies and misjudgments. The last had hurt his feelings— a lot easier to do than you'd think—which horrified me, and I wrote and said so, and got four pages of comfort by return of post.

I expected, and found, that those who knew him well would yield, under interrogation, nothing but golden opinions. What surprised me (when you think of some of those headlines) was that people who didn't know him at all, in the personal sense, played the same unhelpful old record.

One of his gifts is to keep laughter and deep seriousness going in double harness. He dashed off a late note about this last chapter—before it was written. "You might ask whether all this rushing about is to any purpose. Am I just doing it to make it look as if I'm earning my keep, or has it any national value?" He expanded, with two foolscap pages about the monarchy, our lack of a written constitution, our theory of democratic government, the changing role of the hereditary Head of State. "I think you might like to discuss the changes in 'style' and 'function' since the last reign, and what—if any—influence I have had on them." We no longer had Presentation Parties, Courts, State Balls, Levées, yet many of the great ceremonies (the Opening of Parliament, the Birthday Parade) remained the same. How far did this give the impression that nothing had changed inside? What of the Commonwealth, now that the political links had gone? Had his own traveling any point? Did greater personal knowledge of the Sovereign mean less mystery?

"Sir," I could only reply . . . there were others better equipped to examine these questions, and in other books. For me, and for this book, their significance was that he was asking them.

I thought of something he'd written, in the same field but a different key, to Uffa Fox. Uffa had suggested, after the last Opening of Parliament, that the Sword of State, which had nearly overwhelmed Lord Mountbatten (and Viscount Montgomery the time before) was too heavy to be held upright throughout the Queen's speech, and should be lowered to an at-ease position. This, said Prince Philip, might prove "a tricky evolution," as it rested in a halter around the bearer's neck, and would have to be unshipped and shipped again. He went on: "Incidentally, the 'Sword' walks beside the 'Cap of Maintenance,' which is carried on a stick. I'm not sure what could be done with that while standing at ease. Come to think of it, only the English would think of carrying a hat on a stick at a ceremony of State."

I have other flashes.

In a pub in Sussex just after the 1970 State visit to New Zealand and Australia, I heard an Australian voice at the bar mention his name. "Melbourne, it was, the week before I came home, and it was bloody great, it was marvelous. Well, I'll tell you, he actually spoke to a friend of my mother's. Well, she was a neighbor, and she was in the crowd, and Phillup spoke to her, this neighbor of mother's, and it was, well, I'll tell you, it was . . . *wooooo!*" The vocabulary failing, he shot both arms into the air, like a man saving two goals.

Buckingham Palace, a car for Heathrow waiting at the King's Door. He comes down the stairs, laughing, with Prince Charles, Prince Andrew and Prince Edward. He peers at Charles's tie and scratches at a stain on it, while Edward rolls head over heels down the last few red-carpeted steps. They all call him "Pappa," and all kiss him good-bye.

Late for that canteen breakfast at Sondrestrom, I got into a terrible mess eating an orange. I should have known better, everyone else being finished and free to watch the fun. He was opposite, and enjoyed it most. "You want another plate"—skimming one across. "Have a spoon. Try a knife. Why not put it in the glass?" Even as a butt, you enjoy his enjoyment. That night, after dinner at Government House, Ottawa, an equerry moved discreetly about the drawing room taking breakfast orders. When he got to me, HRH looked up very straight-faced from the next group. "He just likes an orange."

I once asked if he missed the simple amenities of ordinary life. Walking in the park, say.

"It's like saying don't you miss going to the moon. I mean, I just haven't the opportunity of going to the moon. You can say, do I miss being in the Navy. Well, I'm not in the Navy. It's all hypothetical. Do I miss caviar, because I haven't got it today? You can't answer that question. You can't go through life desperately wanting to be somebody else, wanting to do something else all the time."

An American in the airplane out of Mexico City asked me, in the friendly American way, what I'd been doing there. I dropped the name gladly. "Sure," he said. "I saw him in Chicago once. We were on some kind of bridge, and he waved up from the car, and my wife said, 'He could put his shoes under my bed any time.' Get that. My own wife."

Driving to Balmoral in the Landrover he was stopped by a man with a puncture, who didn't notice who was behind the sunglasses, said that he'd passed an AA service post a mile down the road, and how about his fellow motorist nipping back and organizing some assistance. Philip U-turned and nipped back, presently reappearing with a passing shout that help was on the way. (The patrolman, who knew his president's number plates, broke the news, but it took the man with the flat tire a day or two to draft his letter of thanks.)

At a Program Meeting, discussing an engagement to be undertaken jointly with the Queen: "Well, all I know is that the Queen told me this morning that it lasts four hours, and recommended me not to go."

Michael Parker, 1970:

"With the job itself, starting from the very beginning, when there was nothing at all, he had to build it up brick by brick. Apart from the King [George VI], I was surprised, to be perfectly honest, that he didn't get a great deal of help—that there wasn't a collection of great men in the land who had suggestions to make. He had to think it out alone. I know that his prime object, from the word go, was to be of service, and to help the Queen. Nothing's ever changed that, and nothing's stopped it, and he pitched into it with a vigor that was absolutely staggering. I don't think he's let up. I've watched it over the years, and he still keeps up this incredible pace, and I've actually said to him from time to time, 'Hey, what about it? It's time you eased up somewhat.' And, you know, he grins a bit, and he says, 'Well, what would I do? Sit around and knit?' There's never been a word of complaint, about his work, or his life. And I only hope that with his fiftieth birthday coming up next year, the United Kingdom shows its gratitude for what he's done . . . for the constant flogging up hill and down dale and around the world, and in and out of film premieres ad nauseam, and making hundreds and hundreds of speeches, and never really stopping. Because they're the most extraordinarily lucky country to have him."

I asked him one of those terrible old questions.

Q: What are your proudest achievements, something you
        would like to be remembered for?

HRH: I doubt whether I've achieved anything likely to be re-
        membered.

Well, all right. You can't argue. But he isn't finished yet.
Anyway, some people get remembered just for being the people
they are.

Some Books

Alexandra of Yugoslavia, HM Queen. *Prince Philip, a Family Portrait.* Hodder & Stoughton, 1959.

Andrew of Greece, HRH Prince. *Towards Disaster.* John Murray, 1930.

Battiscombe, Georgina. *Queen Alexandra.* Constable, 1969.

Channon, Henry. *Chips* (Diaries). Weidenfeld & Nicolson, 1967.

Christopher of Greece, HRH Prince. *Memoirs.* Right Book Club, 1938.

Cookridge, E. H. *From Battenberg to Mountbatten.* Arthur Barker, 1966.

Cordet, Hélène. *Born Bewildered.* Peter Davies, 1961.

Duncan, Andrew. *The Reality of Monarchy.* Heinemann, 1970.

Gordon, Caryl R. *Wings for a Prince.* Published privately, 1969.

Hatch, Alden. *The Mountbattens.* W. H. Allen, 1966.

Heckstall-Smith, Hugh. *Doubtful Schoolmaster.* Peter Davies, 1962.

Hollis, Leslie. *The Captain General.* Herbert Jenkins, 1961.

Hourmouzios, S. L. *The Royal House of Greece.* Information Department of the Prime Minister's Office, Athens, 1967.

King, Stella. *Princess Marina.* Cassell, 1969.

Laird, Dorothy. *How the Queen Reigns.* Hodder & Stoughton, 1959.

Lee, Arthur S. Gould. *The Royal House of Greece.* Ward Lock, 1948.

Massie, Robert K. *Nicholas and Alexandra.* Gollancz, 1968.

Moran, Lord. *Winston Churchill, The Struggle for Survival.* Constable, 1966.

Morrah, Dermot. *The Royal Family.* Odhams, 1950.

Nicholas of Greece, HRH Prince. *My Fifty Years.* Hutchinson.

Nickolls, L. A. *Royal Cavalcade.* Macdonald, 1949.

Nicolson, Harold. *King George the Fifth.* Constable, 1952.

Philip, HRH Prince. *Selected Speeches.* Oxford University Press, 1957.

Philip, HRH Prince. *Prince Philip Speaks.* Collins, 1960.

Philip, HRH Prince. *Birds from 'Britannia.'* Longman, 1962.

Philip, HRH Prince, and Fisher, James. *Wildlife Crisis.* Hamish Hamilton, 1970.

Russell, Gordon. *Designer's Trade.* Allen & Unwin, 1968.

Shew, Betty Spencer. *Royal Wedding.* Macdonald, 1947.

Stewart, I. McD. G. *The Struggle for Crete.* Oxford University Press, 1966.

Sutherland, Douglas, and Purdy, Anthony. *The Royal Homes and Gardens.* Leslie Frewin, 1966.

Thomson, Basil. *The Allied Secret Service in Greece.* Hutchinson, 1931.

Tisdall, E. E. P. *Royal Destiny.* Stanley Paul, 1955.

Wainwright, David. *Youth in Action.* Hutchinson, 1966.

Worsley, T. C. *Flannelled Fool.* Alan Ross, 1967.

Wulff, Louis. *Elizabeth and Philip.* Sampson Low, 1947.

Index